DIAMOND DOLLARS

"*Diamond Dollars* provides an insightful look at the business of baseball—at the free agent market, teams' scouting and player development systems, and how clubs market their brands. The book mixes Vince's business acumen as a top executive at a Fortune 50 company with his passion for the national pastime."
    —*Mark Attanasio*
    Chairman and Principal Owner, Milwaukee Brewers

"Vince Gennaro shows a profound understanding of the economics of a team's baseball decisions. His analyses of a team's win-revenue relationship, the player development system, and player valuation make for a remarkably innovative examination of the baseball front office model that's just as informative for a baseball executive as for a fan."
    —*Chris Antonetti*
    General Manager, Cleveland Indians

"*Diamond Dollars* offers up exciting and stimulating new ideas about the business of baseball. It provides a set of metrics for decisions that have typically been a 'gut feeling' for many organizations. I think teams should make this required reading for everyone in their organizations."
    —*Jim Beattie*
    former General Manager, Baltimore Orioles and
    Montreal Expos

"Vince Gennaro has written the best book I've read on the business of baseball. It serves as both a "how-to manual" for baseball owners and a tour guide for fans who scratch their heads at the things their teams do. It should find plenty of readers in both camps."
    —*Dave Studenmund, Editor, The Hardball Times Annual*

Diamond Dollars
The Economics of
Winning in Baseball

Vince Gennaro

Diamond Analytics
Purchase, New York

TABLE OF CONTENTS

Acknowledgements

I owe a debt of gratitude to many for their help with this book. At the top of the list are special thanks to some unique websites that make detailed baseball data available, some of which exist out of the pure passion of their founders. Retrosheet, The Baseball Cube, Cot's Baseball Contracts and Baseball-Reference are multi-source websites that integrate data and information that make possible the analyses that form the foundation of this book. I also rely on the innovative statistics developed by the top-flight analysts and writers at Baseball Prospectus and The Hardball Times, and utilize these stats for the basis of new metrics throughout my analyses.

I'd like to thank reviewers at various stages of the manuscript, primarily Dave Studenmund and Jim Beattie, for their insightful challenging comments and suggestions, all of which made this a better book. I also appreciate the opportunity to utilize longtime friends Steven Brown, Stephen J. K. Walters, as well as the Westchester Baseball Group as a sounding board for some of my ideas and concepts. The Society for American Baseball Research (SABR) continues to be a stimulating forum for the exchange of ideas and has served as a laboratory for the incubation of some of my concepts and analysis.

I am most grateful to Jim Walsh, the founder of Maple Street Press, who has become a true partner in this endeavor. When Jim contacted me to urge me to consider this book I initially resisted. As I better understood his new company's focus on producing innovative sports publications for the thinking fan, I promptly reversed my position and engaged in one of the most enjoyable projects of my career.

I deeply appreciate the support of my family. My wife Karen, and my daughter Danielle, have been both helpful and supportive. A special thanks to Luz Hernandez for her loyal support.

Foreword

I've always believed that building a Major League roster is part science and part art. Until about 10 years ago, most teams used more art than science. The artistry is in scouting, and amateur and pro scouts were the backbone of any successful organization.

Scouts use a subjective eye to evaluate players in an attempt to place them in an objective system. Players are ranked according to their five tools—arm strength, running speed, defensive ability, hitting for average, and hitting for power. Until 30 years ago, the only tool a scout had, other than his experience and his trained eye, was a stopwatch. Since the advent of radar guns, even scouts have added some science as they can now objectively measure arm strength, a significant advancement when scouting pitchers.

In recent years, the front offices of baseball teams have undergone a change. Statistical analysis has grown in acceptance and many teams now employ it in their player evaluations. Because of the exorbitant amounts of money invested by owners, it is no longer the norm to have baseball operations run by former scouts, players, coaches, or baseball-lifers that started out as an intern in the mailroom.

Teams are now hiring lawyers, MBAs, and young executives that bring innovative ideas from the business side of the game into the baseball operations office. They want a system they can rely on without years of personal baseball experience, one that, when combined with good scouting, produces better results, namely a winning team at a reasonable cost.

Expanding the role of statistical analysis to the business side of baseball, *Diamond Dollars* utilizes this information to the delight of fans and owners alike. You will see how Vince Gennaro has combined the insight of a seasoned business executive with some innovative statistical and economic analysis and brought it to bear on the business side of the game. Teams have intuitively recognized the relationship of wins to revenue, but Gennaro quantifies this critical relationship. He then reveals how this is only the beginning of understanding how a player's specific value is derived for different teams, under different circumstances.

Diamond Dollars quantifies why the Yankees and not the Royals sign players to huge contracts. If the Yankees win the division, get into the playoffs and perhaps win the World Series, the Yankee fans will pay back this salary for years to come through the sales of tickets, beer, hotdogs (or sushi if you like), cable TV subscriptions, merchandise and sponsorships to the degree that at the present time a team like Kansas City could not realize. Although the Detroit Tigers lost in the World Series this year, they could measure the considerable financial carry-over of a deep run into the 2006 postseason to 2007 and beyond, attributable to this one year of success. *Diamond Dollars* underscores how vital it is for every team to understand the relationship between revenue and winning, getting into the playoffs and maybe even winning the World Series. As you will see, this relation- ship varies for each organization but can adjust over time as a result of better teams or even cultivating the team brand.

In addition, Gennaro can evaluate and measure the efficiency of a team's scouting and player development systems in turning out valuable major league players. *Diamond Dollars* will illustrate why good roster management for most teams demands that a certain part of a major league 25-man roster include young, inexpensive, productive players that contribute to the win total for a team. Gennaro even shows how to measure the effect that the strength of a team's brand, fan loyalty and an individual player's popularity, concepts separate from baseball stats, can have on the bottom line of a team.

Any owner of a baseball team should make this required reading for all of his employees. As the general manager of a Major League team using the approach outlined in this book, my neck would feel more comfortable whenever I placed it on the line. *Diamond Dollars* would help me to present a more compelling argument to reassure the owner that a player I want is worth the money.

As you read the pages ahead, you will be given the structure to ask the right questions about baseball decisions, and the metrics to help you find a way to make the answers more meaningful. No longer are we relegated to guessing what the impact of spending money on scouting, player development or free agents means to the bottom line. *Diamond Dollars* will give you an in-depth look into the investment decisions and the business framework of baseball as it should be managed. Much as a scout evaluates his young prospect using the five-tool yardstick, Vince Gennaro will present you with the five tools of baseball team evaluations. After reading it, ask yourself, "how does my team measure up?"

Jim Beattie, former General Manager, Baltimore Orioles and Montreal Expos
February 2007

Preface to the 2013 Edition

The baseball world has continued to evolve since *Diamond Dollars* was first released in March of 2007. Certainly the dollars have gotten larger. When *Diamond Dollars* was first published, only 13 players had signed contracts valued at over $100 million. As I write this in the winter between the 2013 and 2014 seasons, we expect the total will triple by opening day. The opening day payrolls of the top five spenders in 2007 totaled $676 million. For 2013 the top five totaled $910 million—an increase of 35%. The New York Yankees built a spanking new ballpark that has served to increase their ticket revenues by more than the total local revenues of about one-third of MLB teams. Skyrocketing local television rights deals, some of which are intertwined with team ownership stakes in regional sports networks, have given local revenues a shot of adrenaline for a handful of clubs. For the Dodgers the mere prospect of a future TV deal propelled the price of the franchise to over $2 billion, more than double the sale price of the Cubs, only three years earlier.

There have been on-field changes as well. Instant replay has grown from entertaining TV viewers to assisting umpires adjudicate safe-out calls. Data has invaded MLB dugouts, helping teams routinely position three infielders on one side of the second base bag. Big Data has taken hold in front offices, allowing savvy teams to diagnose a pitcher's repertoire down to the angle of break on his slider, or his favorite three-pitch sequences. From a fan perspective, we can watch a game from our home on two screens—the regular telecast on TV and a secondary, data-oriented, perspective of the game on our iPad, in real-time. To some, it makes going to the ballpark an ordeal. I'm still waiting for the app that puts peanut shells on the floor of my family room and fills the air with the smell of ballpark hot dogs.

Despite the scope and scale of changes in baseball, many of the concepts laid out in *Diamond Dollars* have withstood the test of time. I've had the opportunity to consult with teams using their proprietary financial data to model, test, and validate many of the concepts laid out in this book. One such concept is the fundamental relationship between winning and revenues, more specifically the assertion that not all wins are valued equally. Wins that have a greater impact on the probability of reaching the postseason are more valuable than wins that have little material effect on whether or not a team qualifies for a postseason appearance. Another related concept is the carry forward impact of reaching the postseason. One playoff appearance—the gift that keeps on giving—can generate incremental revenues for up to five years, although the positive benefits wither as time passes. The win-curve, a phrase first discussed in this book, has become a staple of the baseball analysts' vernacular.

Another important concept that has become commonly used on various baseball analytics websites is the definition of a player's asset value (also known as "surplus value"). I define it as the difference between the actual cost of a player's performance versus the market value of his performance. Much of the content in *Diamond Dollars* draws on the tools I used in my business career to support decisions I was facing, and adapts them to the business of baseball. While the magnitude of the dollars referenced in many of the chapters has evolved, many of the principles discussed in this book still prevail in today's world.

In general, baseball analytics has continued to gain momentum in the recent years. There has been growth in analytics-oriented websites and the mainstream media has become more analysis-friendly. The choice of Felix Hernandez for the Cy Young Award in 2010, despite a 13-12 record is a tribute to the acceptance that wins and losses are hardly within the control of the pitcher and that a true evaluation involves digging deeper into more meaningful measures of performance. Zealots for deeper insights like Brian Kenny, Joe Posnanski, and Nate Silver have elevated the profile of thoughtful, often rigorous analysis to gain new answers to old questions.

I'm often asked, "have we learned everything we can from statistical analysis in baseball? Can it still be a competitive edge for teams?" We are miles from mining all of the insights analytics offers to us. One reason is the continuing advances in technology in both the areas of data capture and processing data. For the better part of a century we drew on *outcomes* of the batter-pitcher match up—from box scores and play-by-play accounts—as our primary source of data and the object of our analysis. The data set available to analysts has grown fifty-fold over the last decade. We have morphed from focusing on only the resolution of the batter-pitcher match up (i.e., strikeout, double, HR, etc.), to what happens *during* the plate appearance, which I call *process* measures.

We now capture data via sophisticated cameras and doppler radar that details a pitcher's release point, the angle and amount of break on his slider, and the precise location of the pitch as it crosses the plate. When a hitter makes contact, we now know the vertical and horizontal launch angles of the ball, as well as its initial speed off the bat. This data allows us to learn orders of magnitude more about a player's talent level, his dollar value to his team, the effect of the ballpark on a player's performance, and dozens of other questions that are relevant to team decision makers.

Coupling the revolution in data capture, which allows us to gather twenty or so metrics for each of the 700,000+ pitches thrown over a major league season, with innovative processing technologies, allows us to interpret and display the multi-dimensional world of baseball data in ways we hadn't imagined just a decade ago.

We've even evolved to a point where baseball analysts have our own annual conference. The SABR Analytics Conference, which I co-founded along with SABR's Executive Director Marc Appleman, brings 500+ baseball analysts together with virtually all the MLB teams and baseball media to discuss the current state of baseball analysis, data, technology and innovation. Each March in Phoenix when the event concludes, I realize we are closer to the beginning than the end of baseball analytics. In American history terms, Bill James was our Christopher Columbus. Perhaps in the next few years we will cross the Mississippi River.

Vince Gennaro
December 2013

Preface to the 2007 Edition

Except for anniversaries or birthdays of loved ones, remembering dates from years past is generally of little value. For some reason, in addition to the important ones, I've always had a series of dates stuck in my head—like May 17, 1957. As a five-year-old, I walked through the concourse and up the ramp, until a sea of green grass appeared. It was more vivid than any green I had ever seen. The rest of the evening was a blur. Fortunately we have Retrosheet (*www.retrosheet.org*) to fill in the details. The Tigers' Billy Hoeft bested the Yankees' Johnny Kucks. Kaline homered and Mantle singled, but the details are unimportant compared to my first look at Yankee Stadium from the inside. The seed of the ballpark's image had been incubating as I sat in front of a small black and white television watching as Mel Allen described the action and as I listened to Red Barber paint a picture with words on my crackling transistor radio. Even Barber's artistry did not prepare me for the stunning vision of grandeur in the Bronx.

It's easy for a five- or ten-year-old to be immersed in baseball, particularly growing up in the 1950s and 1960s in baseball's "holy land"—the New York area. Of course, I played too, day and night, but on April 26, 1970, I charged a slow grounder and tore my anterior cruciate ligament in a semipro game in front of a handful of big league scouts. My dream of playing professional baseball ended long before my eighth knee surgery and probably not even because of it. As the years pass, baseball's role in one's life changes. In my early 20s, the dilemma was getting tougher each year. How do I integrate baseball into my life but still make a life for myself? I chose to go to business school at The University of Chicago, partly because of my adoration of Milton Friedman and the school's reputation in economics, but the allure of Wrigley Field sealed the deal. Two years later it was a race to the wire to see if I would attend more finance lectures than Cubs' games. I'm embarrassed to say which won.

As I learned a few things about economics and business, it was impossible for me not to think of them in the context of baseball, so much so that I developed a model to quantify a player's dollar value to his team—vintage 1979. The *Sporting News* was intrigued enough to write about it. After reading about it, Nolan Ryan was intrigued enough to talk to his agent Dick Moss. On April 19, 1979, in his office in New York, Mr. Moss graciously told me that he was fascinated by the work and that it even made sense, but that no one in baseball was ready for it. Undaunted, I traveled to the Winter Meetings later that year to meet with executives from the Astros, Cardinals, and Braves, only to confirm Moss' instincts. So I did what any 27-year-old, aspiring baseball analyst with an MBA from The University of Chicago would do. I bought a women's pro basketball team and moved to St. Louis to run it. Ironically, the date the league folded, preceded by two of the longest years of my life, somehow escapes me.

In the mad scramble for self-respect that followed my foray into sports ownership, I relegated baseball down a notch into a three-way tie for "most important in my life," along with my family and my career. As a testimony to my new priorities, when I decided to join Pepsico, in a Dallas-based job, I gave very little consideration to Arlington Stadium. Over the nearly two decades and four cities with PepsiCo, I learned a lot about business and economics first hand. I got to build brands, namely Doritos', when we launched Cool Ranch' and brought in Jay Leno to do commercials, run a billion-dollar bottling business, and be president of a division. While baseball may have taken a back seat, it only drifted down one layer of consciousness, always lurking. I signed sponsorship deals with Major League Baseball (MLB) teams that helped build the businesses I was running and influenced Pepsi' to sign their MLB-wide sponsorship package.

On the family side, baseball became a centerpiece of my relationship with my now 20-year old, Derek Jeter–adoring daughter. And lucky for me (and her), baseball is the one sport my wife truly enjoys, and not even my obsession could cause her to lose interest. While I found the time to watch games in 26 ballparks over the years, my perspective on baseball became shaped by my business experience, including my direct dealings with baseball insiders. I began studying the game from a variety of angles with a much broader perspective than I had as a grad student in Chicago. I watched closely as baseball went through dramatic change over the years, including revenue sharing, $100 million player contracts, and luxury suites that situate fans closer than the pitcher to home plate.

With change comes complexity. In the 1940s and 1950s, general managers such as Frank Lane and his contemporaries ran ball clubs on instinct and intuition. When baseball was a mom and pop business (the 1918 New York Yankees grossed the equivalent of $700 per day), one could get by with that approach. Today teams are multidivisional conglomerates, with media properties, real estate interests, and even other pro sports teams intertwined like the wires in a phone company switching station. Today when a team prepares to negotiate with a free agent, they ask themselves, "How much money will we get back if the player performs the way we expect?" It's not a simple question. If the team wins five more games next year, how many more tickets will they sell, what will happen to their broadcast ratings, or rights fees, and do they have any "pricing upside?" If the team makes the playoffs, how much will revenues rise and for how many years? If they own their own regional sports network, what will happen to advertising revenues, distribution fees, or the asset value of the network? What about revenue sharing and the valuation of the franchise itself? These are the questions a baseball team needs to address every time it considers a free agent signing or other investment-related decisions. Instinct and intuition are enviable qualities that every management team in any business needs to be successful, but they no longer carry the day.

Much of this book is about how the different parts of a baseball team, its revenue streams, its cost drivers, and its on-field performance, are inextricably connected. It's about providing tools to go with the intuition and instincts. Not every decision will, or should be, a slave to the numbers. Sometimes a team makes a player acquisition or a marketing decision because they consciously "investment spend" or because it's the right thing to do to build the fan base or give back to the community. But even those decisions deserve the scrutiny of a decision process that any well-run, hundred-million-dollar business would utilize. Any fan should be interested in the analyses and conclusions talked about in this book, as it may help explain how your team is thinking, or not thinking, about the scouting and player development or the international free agent market.

Amidst all the change, fortunately, some things stay the same. Through all its turmoil, upheaval, and booming expansion, much of baseball is the same as it was 50 years ago. Today's ballparks bear a striking resemblance to the parks of the 1950s, save for the gourmet burgers and frozen margaritas. Even though the grass will never be greener than it was my first time at the Stadium, I enjoy the ballpark as much today as I did then. I've watched the Brewers play the Rockies in an exhibition game in Arizona, and I've been to the Super Bowl. Maybe I'll see you at the Yankee game on May 17, 2007, at "The Cell" in Chicago. I'll be there. I'm pretty good with dates and never forget an anniversary.

Vince Gennaro

January 2007

1 | The Major League Baseball Business Model

The business of baseball is in the throes of major change. A flood of competing entertainment options, from a wave of new, consumer-friendly movie theaters, to the proliferation of video games, coupled with new media and the Internet, have forever complicated the business landscape of America's game. Potential adversity from new-found competition is often a call to arms, and Major League Baseball (MLB) is rising to the occasion. MLB has capitalized on new revenue streams made possible by the Internet, a steady flow of new stadiums, and the emergence of team-owned regional sports networks. Major League Baseball Advance Media (MLBAM), the division of MLB that houses *MLB.com* and provides subscriptions to broadcasts, highlights, and other streaming content to fans worldwide, will generate $260 million in revenue in 2006. A nascent division that began in 2000, MLBAM is expected to ride a phenomenal growth wave to produce a $1 billion annual revenue stream by 2011.[1] A wave of 24 new ballparks, from U.S. Cellular in Chicago (1991), to new ballparks for the Twins, Nationals, Mets, Yankees, A's, and possibly the Marlins, by 2011, have generated hundreds of millions of dollars in new ticket, luxury suite, and concession revenues. The cost for a family of four now averages over $170 to attend a big league ball game.[2] A hot dog and a Pepsi˚ have been replaced by gourmet barbeque ribs and a frozen margarita, at three times the price.

Team-owned regional sports networks, such as YES (Yankee Entertainment and Sports) and NESN (New England Sports Network), have become vogue in the past five years. Bold teams with a vision and a substantial fan base view them as ideal vehicles for financial growth. They allow teams to deliver telecasts of games directly to viewers, while creating additional "content" about the team, its players, and its history, in order to "build the brand" in the mind of consumers. Through mostly high-definition telecasts of 125 games, extensive pre- and postgame and batting practice shows, and features such as "Yankeeography" and "Kids on Deck," the YES Network has created near round-the-clock propaganda, filling fans' heads with everything Yankee. YES has even capitalized on the reality television craze with its own "Ultimate Road Trip," which chronicles four fans' 162-game coast-to-coast journey, presumably for Yankee fans to watch other Yankee fans watch the Yankees. The bottom line is that the YES Network generated baseball-related revenues of over $200 million in 2006, exceeding the total estimated revenue of all but six MLB teams.[3]

The huge size of baseball as a business has triggered changes in the way teams manage their balance sheets, income statements, and cash flows. Under the old management model, an MLB team might have made multimillion-dollar decisions based primarily on instincts and intuition. Despite being replete with statistics measuring everything that happens on the field, there were few metrics to measure the success of business processes, the return on capital from the signing of a high draft pick or free agent, or the price elasticity of a proposed ticket price increase. Baseball teams operated more like a Hollywood director filming a movie, as an artistic endeavor, largely on feel and instinct based on decades of experience in the game. A new generation of owners who have come from "traditional" business are bringing some of their success formula to bear on their baseball business. They evaluate the efficiency of drafting college players versus their high school counterparts, who often take longer to mature into big league contributors. The new breed of owners has an interest in fielding consumer research to learn about the psyches of their fans, or use metrics to monitor processes that will bring quality improvements to their product. The new management model can be characterized as bringing a more systematic approach to running the baseball team as a business, which does not translate into any less focus on winning. In fact, a more systematic, analytical approach is likely to eliminate wasteful spending, create clear priorities, and allow a team to focus more productive dollars on the goal of winning.

Much of this book lays out new analytical approaches and tools that can help baseball make the transition to the new management model. We'll create a framework designed to provide an answer to some important, but previously unanswerable, questions:

- What is the financial payoff to the Angels from improving from an 89-win to a 95-win team?

- How much is Derek Jeter's performance worth to the Yankees, and how much additional value does he generate for the brand with his aura and charisma?

- With one of baseball's most productive farm systems, what is the Twins' cost per marginal win of drafting and developing their own players?

- Why are players like Prince Fielder and Hanley Ramirez among a team's prized possessions, and what is their asset value?

- If a team that was prolific at developing home-grown players, such as the Braves or A's, wanted to swap prospects in exchange for proven major leaguers, what is the exchange rate of tomorrow's wins for today's wins?

- What is the dollar value of turning over the roster by trading a player nearing free agency to free up a roster spot for an inexpensive talented rookie?

- What is the dollar value of the St. Louis Cardinals' fan loyalty to their team and brand?

These are the kinds of questions we'll delve into in this book and the types of analyses we'll engage in, but first we'll set the foundation for the way the business of baseball is structured and operates.

Baseball's Idiosyncrasies

Baseball, as a sport, has unique nuances that elicit a reverence and passion among fans. The absence of a game clock means there is no stalling in baseball. The game is built around 27 outs, without regard for time. The diamond is brilliantly designed to create countless close plays at first base that seem to beg for instant replay to validate the umpire's out-safe call. The asymmetry and unique footprint of each ballpark gives true meaning to home field advantage. Baseball, as a business, also has quirks and idiosyncrasies that make it drastically different from the manufacturing company or retail chain down the street. While Wal-Mart employees can be quite engaging, they are not highly visible public personalities whose every move is chronicled by the daily newspapers like the lives of major league ballplayers. The equivalent of a $150-million annual revenue company, an MLB team is high profile, with a much stronger identity within the community than most other businesses of comparable size.

As it relates to the sports world, the business of baseball operates within a unique framework. Unlike the NFL, whose business model revolves around national broadcast agreements, the revenues that fuel MLB teams are predominantly generated by each team within their local market. The NFL generates over $2.5 billion in annual broadcast revenue from DIRECTV, Fox, CBS, and ESPN.[4] In all, about 80% of the NFL's estimated $5 billion in revenue is shared among the league's 32 teams.[5] In contrast, despite similar total revenues of about $5 billion, only about 25% of MLB revenues are shared. About $1 billion of these shared revenues come from MLB's national TV contracts combined with the fast-growing revenue stream from MLBAM. Another $300+ million changes hands as a result of a revenue sharing program detailed in the 2002 Collective Bargaining Agreement (CBA). Hence, revenues generated by each MLB team at the local level will ultimately decide a team's economic success or failure.

Consistent with its local revenue model, baseball's heritage is local. The game began to grow in popularity more than a century ago as a game of the people. As a grassroots sport, towns, schools, factories, and companies had baseball teams, and much of small-town America's summer social calendar revolved around the team and its games. Baseball's emergence predated the communication and media culture brought about by television. The notion of a team affinity based on geography was a natural result of the way in which the games began and took hold. Conversely, professional football was more of an outgrowth of the popularity of college football. Also, the immense popularity of the NFL is an outgrowth of television, which has provided it with a national setting and launched it as a national sport. Even today the popularity of any Super Bowl game has less to do with the size of the market of the games' competitors and more to do with the engaging story around the teams and their players.[6] On the other hand, a World Series between two small-market teams is generally a broadcast dud, even if there are superstars or strong human interest stories.[7]

Despite baseball's local orientation and Darwinian-style local revenue model, MLB teams compete in a national labor market to staff their player rosters. Once a player reaches six years of Major League service time, he is free to peddle himself to any team. This means the small-market Kansas City Royals must battle the financially mighty New York Yankees to win a prized free agent's services. What if the Royals were in a position to challenge the American League royalty for a pennant but were one player away from glory? Could they bid toe-to-toe with Steinbrenner's Bronx Bombers? A pennant-contending, 95-win Royals team would likely draw about 2.5 million fans per year, compared to a Yankee pennant-winning team, which will draw 4 million fans.[8] The average ticket to a Royals game in 2006 was under $14, while the Yankees averaged over $28.[9] Just comparing home attendance receipts, this translates into a $77-million revenue advantage, $112 million to $35 million, for the Yankees over the Royals. The gap widens dramatically when the revenues from concessions, parking, luxury suites, corporate sponsorship, the YES Network, and Yankee logo merchandise are added.[10]

The net result is that a successful Yankee team will generate over $360 million in local revenue, while a pennant-winning Royals club will be fortunate to bring in $72 million.[11] Adding $40 million from MLB's central fund, distributed evenly to all teams, takes the revenue scorecard favoring the Yankees to $400 million versus $112 million. Even if baseball's revenue sharing and luxury tax take $100 million from the Yankees and redistribute $30 million to Kansas City, as it did in 2005, that would still leave the Yankees with a $158-million total net revenue advantage, $300 million to $142 million (see Figure 1.1). (The *actual* revenue gap between the two teams is much greater, as the Royals have averaged about 60 wins over the past three seasons, translating to estimated total net revenues of about $80 million, versus the hypothetical 95-win team that generates $142 million.)

Comparative Economics NYY vs. KCR
Hypothetical 95-Win Seasons

	NYY*	KCR*
Estimate of Gate Receipts	$ 112	$ 35
All other Local Revenues**	248	37
Total Local Revenue	$ 360	$ 72
+ MLB National Revenues	40	40
+/- Revenue Sharing***	(100)	30
Total Revenue	$ 300	$ 142

* Dollars in millions
** Includes Yankees' share of YES Network revenues attributable to on-field performance
*** Revenue sharing includes luxury tax payments

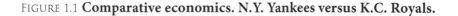

FIGURE 1.1 **Comparative economics. N.Y. Yankees versus K.C. Royals.**

If we think of a team's revenue stream as the cornerstone of its resource base, it would seem that New York is capable of outbidding Kansas City for any free agent, leaving the Royals to pick from players the Yankees and their wealthy peers are willing to bypass. This example of the revenue disparity between MLB teams with significant resource bases and their less fortunate counterparts speaks to the importance of scouting and player development. While the Yankees seem to supplement their free-agent acquisitions with an occasional home-grown player, most teams attempt to build their roster from the opposite perspective. They supplement the fruits of their scouting and player development systems with a well-timed free agent (or two) to elevate the club into a postseason contender.

Following the 2001 season, MLB released unaudited financial data for each team and the consolidated totals for all teams combined. While the data probably raise more questions than they answer about the definitions of specific line items and the esoteric accounting rules behind them, it at least provides a broad understanding of how an MLB team sources its revenue. At the time, about 20% of all MLB team revenues were national revenues, distributed evenly to each team. (The percentage has probably grown closer to 30% for 2006, as the five-year-old data precede the enormous success of *MLB.com* and include national broadcast contracts that are out of date.) The data also shed light on the mix of the remaining 80% of team revenues—local revenues. On average, nearly half of a team's local revenues are from regular season gate receipts, which accrue entirely to the home team. Local broadcast agreements totaled approximately 20%, although these data predated the emergence of regional sports networks such as the YES Network (Yankees) and NESN (Red Sox), which would lead to a higher mix of broadcast revenues. Three percent of local revenues, *across all teams,* are attributable to revenues generated by appearing in the postseason. (However, for the eight teams that *appeared* in the postseason, it represented 4.5% of their reported revenues, and for the World Series competitors, the Yankees and Diamondbacks, it represented about 9%.) The final revenue category released from the commissioner's office is termed "all other local operating revenue." This broad category includes concessions, parking, luxury suite revenues, in-park advertisements, and merchandise sales of items containing the team logo and accounts for the remaining 28% of all local revenues for MLB teams. While these are league-wide averages, with dramatic variability across teams, it does give us a picture of the landscape in which MLB teams operate (see Figure 1.2).

MLB team revenues are only half the financial equation. Publicly available information regarding MLB teams' operating expenses is limited, but

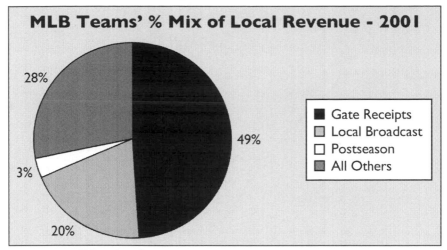

FIGURE 1.2 **MLB mix of revenue.**

the data released by the commissioner's office in 2001 provide some insight. Nonpayroll operating expenses averaged over $54 million per team, ranging from $35 million (Montreal) to $83 million (New York Yankees).[12] If we project increases of 5% per year in these costs, 2006 nonpayroll team operating expenses would average about $70 million per team, ranging from $45 million to $105 million. The estimated range of net revenues is $80 million for a last-place Kansas City team to $300 million for the Yankees.[13] If we compare the range of net revenues per team to the range of nonpayroll operating expenses, we can get a sense of the room left for player payroll. If the team with the lowest net revenue also had the lowest operating expenses, it would allow for about a $35-million payroll to break even, while the highest net revenue matched with the highest operating expenses would allow for a nearly $200-million payroll to break even (see Figure 1.3).

Even with the revenue sharing program from the 2002 CBA, which is designed to narrow the financial gap between the haves and the have-nots, any system that creates an affordable payroll range of $35 million to $200 million presents a challenging business environment for MLB clubs. If a team finds itself at the bottom end of the affordable payroll range, rather than go dollar-to-dollar with the big boys, it may need to take a different tact to compete. Building a strong player development system to feed the big league club with young, inexpensive talent is one tonic for a weak financial proposition. However, this approach is not a short-term fix, as it can take years to harvest the success of player development. Long before

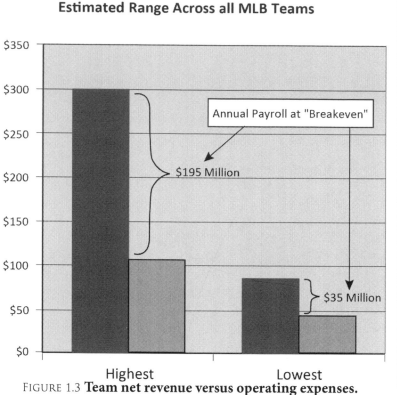

Figure 1.3: Net Revenues and Non-Payroll Expenses Estimated Range Across all MLB Teams

FIGURE 1.3 **Team net revenue versus operating expenses.**

the success or failure is declared, teams are tempted to shift their priorities elsewhere to try to get a more immediate payoff. A club always has the option of deficit spending, with payroll expenses elevated to a level that puts the club in the red for a period of time. However, there is little evidence that owners are willing to tolerate extensive losses indefinitely. To thrive over the long term, a team must have a financially viable proposition in which a team can be competitive without hemorrhaging cash. Gone are the days of the benevolent owner who runs the team as a public trust for the benefit of the city and the pleasure of its fans.

The harsh financial realities that confront MLB owners often cause them to turn to their state and local governments for support. Some owners exploit the notion that baseball is still viewed as a public good by many of its fans. In the same way one expects local government to fund and support bridges and tunnels to make it easier to navigate through town, some expect their city to provide economic support for a baseball team, for the entertainment and enjoyment of its citizens. Unlike bridges and tunnels, which are largely functional, baseball teams tend to engender an emotional relationship with the locals. This emotional relationship has implications for the business of baseball. It helps build the economic value of teams by providing a support base for public funding of stadiums. Without the emotional relationship between local citizens and their teams, one would not likely see the level of support for publicly funded stadiums we have witnessed over the past 15 years. Subsidies for teams in the form of public funding for stadiums have often gone far beyond the economic value to the city.[14] If prominent retailers such as Target or Kmart could stimulate a proportional level of public support, they would never need to spend their company's money to buy real estate and build another store, they would simply rely on public funds to shoulder the burden, the way some baseball teams are able to do.

Cities have bought into the mystique of supporting their local baseball teams (or luring a new one) to the tune of over $3 billion dollars of *public funding* for stadiums since 1991. However, the tide is turning. If we divide the decades of the 1990s and 2000s into three timeframes—stadiums opened in the 1990s, those debuting from 2000 to 2006, and the five new stadiums on the drawing boards expected to be opened by the end of the decade—we see a shift from public to private funding. For the nine stadiums that opened in the 1990s, 81% of the nearly $2 billion of estimated stadium costs were publicly funded. For the next nine stadiums, debuting between 2000 and 2006, public funding slipped to 55% of the $3 billion in construction and land-acquisition costs. Finally, six proposed stadiums, for the Yankees, Mets, Twins, Nationals, A's, and Marlins, scheduled to open by 2011, are expected to be 45% publicly funded.[15] As more studies show the lack of economic benefit to communities from new stadiums, and MLB attendance and revenues continue to grow, the public is asking owners to shoulder a larger proportion of their stadium costs. New stadiums have become an integral part of teams' economic success since the early 1990s, adding as much as $30 million annually to a team's revenues for the first few years after the stadium opens.[16]

THE TENSION BETWEEN WINNING AND FINANCIAL RETURNS

Every owner needs to believe there's a financial formula that will sustain his or her team, one that will allow it to compete while creating financial returns for the ownership group. The challenge for MLB ownership is managing the tension between winning and delivering financial returns. This involves a complex equation of balancing franchise value and cash flow with the team's win–loss record. Hundreds of millions of dollars of capital are at stake in the ownership of an MLB franchise, with investors expecting positive returns in the form of growth in asset value—the franchise—for eventual resale. Cash flow is also an important variable, as any owner wants the pursuit of winning to be self-funding, so as to avoid "capital calls"—additional investments to subsidize the team's operations. Winning is a key part of the equation for two reasons: it affects both the revenue and the cost side of the business, and it is the reason many MLB owners become owners. The allure of a pennant or World Championship can be powerful, especially for owners who have generally had great success in other businesses. They are accustomed to winning, and if they did not believe they could do it again in baseball, they would have put their investment dollars and energy elsewhere. Winning is partly driven by the desire for ego gratification from succeeding in a high-profile business, in view of millions of adoring fans, and partly an acknowledgement that winning can be a key contributor to superior financial returns.

In contrast to the individual owner, another type of MLB owner is the corporate entity, most of which are in media-related businesses, that views ownership of a baseball team as a synergistic investment destined to help build value in its other businesses. For example, if the team's owner is also a broadcast entity, the broadcast company may buy the team's broadcast rights at a below market rate and make a profit by selling advertising for the telecasts. The corporate owners *may* be a bit more bottom-line focused, but it is rare to find an ownership group that wants to win at any expense or, on the other extreme, wants to pad their bank account and says, "to hell with winning." Owners want a reasonable equity return for their efforts and believe they have the ability to manage the delicate balance of building a winning team without devastating the team's finances. They dream of some day winning a championship but are likely not prepared to risk their accumulated wealth to increase their chances.

An owner who was not prepared to operate with sustained losses was former Marlins' owner Wayne Huizenga. In 1997 he realized the dream of every owner when he assembled a World Championship team. He did not skimp his way to the top, as he did it with the seventh-highest payroll in MLB ($48 million). His dream turned into a nightmare when he realized that the revenue he hoped for did not materialize. In two years he "liquidated" the Marlins by ridding the club of a virtual All Star team: Moises Alou, Kevin Brown, Devon White, Gary Sheffield, Jeff Conine, Rob Nen,

Al Leiter, and Bobby Bonilla. The eight players' salaries represented nearly 70% of the 1997 Marlins payroll. By 1999 only two Marlins, Alex Fernandez and Cliff Floyd, had salaries *greater than $325,000,* and the total team payroll of $15 million ranked dead last in the league.[17]

Sometimes we fall into a dangerous trap of trying to characterize owners by their desire to win versus their desire for financial returns. Most observers would judge the Yankees' George Steinbrenner as being on the extreme "winning" end of the scale. In reality, during the recent decade of the Steinbrenner regime, the Yankees have harmonized winning and financial success better than any team in baseball. He has "monetized" the benefits of building a winner in more ways than any other team. While no one would doubt his sincere desire to win championships and his pride in Yankee pinstripes, it is probably as financially rewarding as it is ego satisfying. The sheer size of the New York market, coupled with Steinbrenner's business acumen, ensure that he wins at least as much in his pocketbook as he does in his heart.

Conversely the Florida Marlins' owner, Jeffrey Loria, might be perceived as an owner who cares only about money. After his 2003 World Championship season, the resulting attendance and financial gains were disappointing. After failing to gain local government approval for a new, publicly funded domed stadium, Loria scaled back his investment in team payroll to match (if not overcompensate) for the team's modest revenue prospects. To some, this will be read as a lack of interest in winning, while others could interpret it as fiscal responsibility.

The tradeoff between winning and financial returns is further complicated by the cost side of the ledger. While winning generates revenue, it costs money to field a winning team. Studies have shown a connection between payroll level and winning, but it is unclear which comes first.[18] There are many paths to building a winning team: a $200-million free-agent laden payroll for the 2005 Yankees or the predominantly home-grown $49-million World Champion Florida Marlins of 2003. Of course, luck, chance, and biomechanics also play a role. What if Kerry Wood and Mark Prior had never seen the disabled list or if Alex Gonzalez had cleanly fielded a routine ground ball in the sixth game of the 2003 National League Championship Series (NLCS)? Imagine the additional wins and potential pennants, or even a World Championship, on the *north side* of Chicago.

One framework to help analyze a team's tradeoff between winning and financial returns is to think in terms of the marginal revenue from winning versus the marginal cost of winning. Marginal revenue is an estimate of a team's incremental dollar revenue from each additional win. Fans tend to reward their winning ball club with more of their hard-earned paychecks in the form of attending more games, buying more team merchandise, and viewing more telecasts. The key question is, "just how many additional dollars will fans spend?" (In the next several chapters we will discuss in detail statistical estimates of the relationship between winning and revenues for various teams.) Also, not every win is created equal. Wins that place a team in contention for the postseason generate more revenue and, hence, are more valuable than wins that get a team to .500.

A team's marginal cost of winning is driven by two key factors: the strength of a team's scouting and player development system and the productivity of its free agents. A higher mix of young, inexpensive, Major League–capable talent on a team's roster results in a lower the marginal cost per win. The level of productivity a team gets from its free-agent signees—the players on the high end of the pay scale—will also determine its cost of winning. If a $5 million per year free-agent pitcher out-performs everyone's expectations, the high productivity (the player's win contribution per dollar spent) will help keep a lid on the marginal cost of winning.

The marginal cost of winning is an important consideration when a team contemplates a roster move, as it can vary when a team adds or subtracts players. For example, when the Yankees traded for the Phillies' Bobby Abreu in July of 2006, they might have used the following thought process. If the Yankees viewed themselves as a 94-win team without Abreu but had the opportunity to add a "6-win player" for $15 million in annual salary, their marginal cost per win would be $2.5 million over the 94 to 100-win portion of the curve. In the highly competitive American League East Division, improving from 94 to 100 wins might make the difference between going home in September and reaching the postseason. In the case of the mighty Yankees, the revenue from the six additional wins and the "insurance policy" to reach the playoffs, and its accompanying revenue stream, make them one of the few teams that could make the Abreu math work. (We will discuss the value of a win in detail in Chapter 3, Winning by the Numbers.) At any point in time the marginal cost of winning will depend on the price and productivity of a potential player acquisition. Each prospective deal a team considers will have its own unique economics, taking into consideration the players being traded, the difference in salaries, and the number of additional wins the transaction is expected to yield.

THE FIVE-TOOL FORMULA

Regardless of where an owner resides on our continuum or the shape of the marginal revenue–marginal cost curves, the executives running the business and baseball operations of an MLB team struggle daily with the balancing act of fielding a competitive, entertaining team and managing the club's finances. They know the formula—that blending winning and financial returns begins with a strong scouting and player development system. While there are no guarantees in baseball, a prolific farm system can trigger a virtuous cycle that gives any team an inside track on building and sustaining success. Here's how the formula works: an ample flow of homegrown talent creates personnel depth and a pool of low-priced, quality players to staff the Major League roster, laying the foundation for a quality team at a modest payroll. This strong foundation, in turn, enables the club to selectively cherry-pick the free-agent market to fill voids at a reasonable price, further strengthening the roster and leading to a cost-efficient competitive team. A competitive team generates stronger revenues, and if they can inch their way beyond contention into a playoff spot, they could realize significant revenue for the next several years. This cost-efficient contender should see improvement in cash flow, potentially funding a few more dollars to be spent opportunistically on the free-agent market. A winning team will contribute to stronger brand equity as fans embrace and identify with the team's success. A stronger brand, coupled with the increased revenues from winning will increase the value of the franchise. And they all lived happily ever after...

Although it sounds logical, and even simple, in the real world teams must overcome major obstacles—prospects that never fulfill their promise, free agents who don't live up to the hype, fans who fail to show up at the turnstiles, and a more than occasional Tommy John surgery. For some teams, the formula's math can vary, leading management to different points of emphasis. A team with a larger revenue base (the Yankees) may not need to be as cost-efficient with their payroll for this formula to work. A team in a smaller market that may have a lower revenue base (the Pirates) may need an even greater flow of young talent from the farm system to keep a lid on payroll. A team with an ambivalent fan base, whose revenues are less responsive to winning (the Braves), may warrant more focus on marketing to build the brand. There are even short-term ways to circumvent the formula. Being the beneficiary of a publicly funded stadium can substantially boost revenues for several years before the novelty wears off and revenues settle in at a sustainable level. The best-run teams will use this new-found cash to invest in winning, either in payroll or the longer-term approach of building a player development system, viewing it as a way to jump-start the formula.

While there will always be variations of the formula, as long fans continue to value winning and baseball maintains its current structure (an amateur player draft, six years of Major League service before a player can choose his employer, an openly competitive free-agent market, and a team's financial success driven by its local market), it will be difficult to make the formula obsolete. How does a team pursue the balance of winning and financial returns via the formula? What core competencies does a team need to develop and hone in order to be successful? The core competencies that are embedded in the formula are the management equivalent of baseball's five-tool player. Instead of hitting, hitting with power, running, throwing, and fielding, the management version of the five tools embodied in the formula means an approach that relies on developing deeper insights into to how the pieces of the formula interconnect, not just conceptually, but quantitatively. For each team this means understanding:

- The relationship between winning and revenues in the local market and using it as the foundation for building value in the franchise

- The true economic value of a player and how to use it in making personnel decisions

- The impact of a high-performing scouting and player development system and the know-how to create it

- The attitudes and preferences of the local fan and using these to shape a comprehensive brand-building plan for the franchise

- The discipline and metrics necessary to align and execute the critical elements of each of the steps

Much of this book focuses on building an analytical model around this formula. By quantifying many of the key elements (a team's win–revenue curve, the dollar value of its key players, the dollar value of drafting and successfully developing players, and the dollar value of the team as a brand), we move from a conceptual framework to seeing how teams implement a five-tool management approach. Teams operating under the new management model that are predisposed to an analytical approach might use all or parts of the five tools to manage complexity and create a blueprint for striking that ideal balance between winning and financial returns.

WINNING AND REVENUE

The first tool is *to understand the relationship between winning games and revenue*. Winning games generates revenue because fans demonstrate a willingness to reach into their wallets and reward a team for its on-field success. Fans pay for wins in the form of attending more games, watching more telecasts, buying more team merchandise, and bearing the burden of ticket price increases. Add to the formula the additional fans who are attracted to a winning team, and the revenue potential multiplies.

Quantifying the revenue impact of winning allows a team to create a financial scorecard for their on-field success and to measure the compatibility of winning and financial returns. The value of a win is affected by team-specific factors such as market size, ticket prices, the loyalty of a team's fans, and the stadium—both the quality of the asset and the ballpark experience—as well as the team's level of competitiveness. The revenue implication of improving a team from 88 to 93 wins and placing them in the thick of playoff contention is quite different than improving a team from 78 to 83 wins.

THE VALUE OF A PLAYER

Determining the value of a win also provides a framework for measuring the dollar value of any player—the primary asset of an MLB team—based on his playing performance and contribution to the team's wins. *The ability to place more than an intuitive value on a player* will help a team's general manager and owner make better-informed decisions about player acquisitions, including free-agent signings, as well as provide a ceiling for salary negotiations with players. While the player's performance and even his popularity and fan appeal are important factors, much of a player's true economic worth to his team is situational. The economic worth of a player to his team is dependent on the market in which he plays, the strength of the brand of his team, and the quality of the team (i.e., is it a playoff contender or second-division club). It may come as no surprise, based on the comparative financials reviewed earlier, that Alex Rodriguez is worth considerably more to the Yankees than he is to the Royals, even if both were 95-win, playoff bound teams. A less obvious conclusion is that he is worth dramatically more to a 95-win Yankee team than he is to an 85-win Yankee team.

A player's value can also be impacted by his consistency. Even if a team judges Edgar Renteria to be the on-field equivalent of Jimmy Rollins, should it matter that Jimmy Rollins has been remarkably consistent, while Renteria has been up and down? Does Rollins provide greater value to his team because he's less prone to injury or simply a more consistent shortstop? In the securities markets, performance variation is a form of risk, and higher risk generally commands a higher return. The baseball compensation translation of this principle would have Rollins being paid more (all other things being equal) than Renteria, even for the same *expected* performance level.

While much player valuation analysis focuses on a player's performance value to his team, there is another potential element of player value: a player's worth to *other teams*. The demand for a key player can be bolstered by a team's perception that the player represents the last piece of the puzzle—their ticket into the postseason. For teams in playoff contention, any player who may fill a key void can be worth considerably more than if he were to contribute to an 80-win team. Reaching the postseason carries an impressive financial windfall for teams. Since fans pay for winning in the form of increased ticket sales, a playoff appearance can generate a healthy revenue stream for several years. Understanding the way in which teams in playoff contention affect the secondary market for players, including the mid-season trade market, can help us quantify the trade value of players.

SCOUTING AND PLAYER DEVELOPMENT

The third tool is *building a best-in-class scouting and player development system*, the lifeblood of any organization, as it represents a team's captive pipeline of playing talent. Assembling superior playing talent is the primary enabler of winning games, but it also is the largest cost component of owning and running a big league ball club. Building a top-flight scouting and player development process lowers the financial costs of winning by tipping the roster toward lower-priced, home-grown talent, while less competent rival teams will be forced to fill more roster spots through competitive bidding in the free-agent market. The resource base and financial realities of most teams prevent them from being active in the free-agent market year after year. A store-bought team is an expensive proposition, and even the nearly limitless pockets of the Yankees require that they develop some home-grown talent to supplement their acquired stars. For the Kansas City Royals and Minnesota Twins the situation is different. To stay financially afloat, they need to grow *most* of their talent at home and benefit from a "salary discount" for the first six years of a player's Major League service. The typical salary level for a player's first three years of Major League service is the legislated minimum of $380,000 (in 2007). Even a player with four to six years of service, whose salary can be recalibrated through an arbitration process, will likely be performing at a discount to free-agent salaries. Despite this discount, even arbitration-eligible players are becoming cost prohibitive for some teams, raising their marginal cost of winning above their marginal revenue curve. Teams like the Reds and Marlins have responded to their costs and revenues being "upside down" by trading players like Austin Kearns and Josh Beckett for younger, more affordable talent.

Although no team can expect to corner the market on young talent, if a team builds a best-in-class competency in selecting and developing young players, they can "monetize" this advantage by using surplus talent as currency in trades with other teams. The Red Sox used four promising prospects, including "can't miss" shortstop Hanley Ramirez, to acquire Josh Beckett, Mike Lowell, and Guillermo Mota. (Mota was subsequently packaged with another "stud" prospect, Andy Marte, in a trade to Cleveland to acquire a starting center fielder for the Red Sox, Coco Crisp) The importance of developing players can be summed up by taking a top-line look at the draft track record of several teams during the 1990s. The teams that had the greatest number of draft picks who ultimately reached the big leagues were the perennially competitive St. Louis Cardinals and the winning machine known as the Atlanta Braves. At the other end of the spectrum were the Cubs and the Brewers, both of which suffered through weak drafts that no doubt contributed to lackluster on-field performance from the mid-1990s into the early 2000s. The new ownership in Milwaukee, along with general manager Doug Melvin, appears to be in the midst of a turnaround. They have placed a much higher priority on the draft and have shown some success in using it as the foundation to assemble a competitive, youth-oriented ball club.

BUILDING THE BRAND

The fourth tool is *building the brand*. Think of the Chicago Cubs or St. Louis Cardinals as a brand that has a certain amount of equity with its fans and corporate sponsors, which contributes to loyalty. Building the team brand improves the payoff from on-field success by expanding the team's fan base or by intensifying fans' loyalty. Effective brand marketing will help create an emotional bond between a team and its fans. This emotional connection with fans is a lynchpin to unlocking revenues in many areas, from ticket price increases, to merchandise sales, to improved television ratings. A high degree of brand loyalty translates into customer retention, even in the face of adversity. Few teams can anticipate on-field success year-after-year. Fans are more willing to maintain their support of the team if there is an emotional connection.

Even luxury suite sales and corporate sponsorships are impacted. Many corporate sponsors are not making purely financial media buys when they choose to affiliate themselves with an MLB team. Instead they are translating their feelings and emotional connection to the team into a perception of the value of a sponsorship agreement. Sponsors know that consumers are increasingly more difficult to reach as their attention is scattered. They see a sports team affiliation as one way to piggyback on the fans' focus and borrow some of the emotional connection and try to bring it to their brand.

THE NEW MANAGEMENT MODEL

The fifth tool is making a commitment to the *new management model* that draws on the volumes of information available today but relies on analytical templates to know which critical bits will ultimately be needed to make a go–no go decision regarding a draft choice, a free-agent signing, or an innovative ticket pricing plan. To some, it may be simple business, but it is becoming increasingly complex, and the magnitude of the dollar implications of most decisions begs for using tools to augment the judgments by savvy, experienced baseball people. It's often not about getting *more* information, but rather about *processing* the information you have in such a way that it adds to the team's insights. It also helps to manage the baseball business as a series of *processes* (the amateur scouting and draft process, the international scouting process, the player development process, etc.), with metrics in place that give the organization's leaders a dashboard, or high-level view of how each process is performing against its goals.

THE WIDENING REVENUE GAP

Ironically, the great success MLB has enjoyed over the past decade has placed great stress on its business model. As revenues have grown dramatically, the financially successful teams have widened the resource gap between themselves and the have-nots. This revenue disparity, coupled with the sheer magnitude of revenues (by 2010 the Yankees may be a half-billion-dollar annual revenue business), have mandated that teams manage the business differently than they did 20 years ago. Maximizing the revenue from new stadiums, building new revenue streams, and staying connected with fans through new media are no longer optional. Teams like the Yankees, with their overwhelmingly successful YES Network, and the

Red Sox, with their innovative ways to add in-stadium premium seating, are raising the bar. Teams that only pick the low-hanging fruit and do not fully capitalize on these opportunities will be left in the dust. Their revenue base is likely to fall far short of what it takes to field a competitive team.

The bulging revenue of the teams with the highest resource bases changes the dynamics of the free-agent market. When the Yankees and Red Sox build their brand and their fan connection through revenue-generating tactics, they also increase the marginal value of a win. This dynamic encourages the high-revenue clubs to bid even higher for the last piece of the puzzle in the free-agent market—the player who ensures that the team will reach the postseason. The Yankees and Red Sox revenue models practically *demand* that they reach the postseason year after year. These high-resource-base teams set the market for free agents. Even if the theoretical average of the prices each team would pay for a player stays the same, the free-agent market moves when the highest bidder perceives his marginal revenue from wins to increase. Low-resource-base teams have no choice but to excel on the other end of the pay scale, the farm system. More than ever before, the revenue gains at the top of the MLB food chain have raised the importance of player development at the lower end of the food chain. Teams like the Royals, Pirates, and Twins need to be better at selecting and developing talent just to survive.

As baseball revenues continue to grow and small-market teams, large-market teams, and the players' union jockey for a larger slice of the pie, the economics of baseball are more than ever before linked to what happens on the field. MLB is a finely tuned ecosystem that may be on the verge of falling out of balance. The revenue explosion of some teams may be baseball's global warming. To date, baseball's revenue sharing system has an affect comparable to increased gas prices. It has made people take notice of the issue but hardly solve the dilemma. Regardless of how MLB tweaks revenue sharing to address competitive balance issues, each team can take matters into its own hands by focusing on the formula. By developing and adhering to a plan that strengthens player development, builds the brand, understands the true value of a win and the value of its players, a team raises its chance of success.

Endnotes

1. Maury Brown, "MLBAM: The Stealth Money Machine," December 5, 2005, *www.hardballtimes.com*.

2. Data from the 2006 Fan Cost Index, published annually by Team Marketing Report (TMR), from their web site, *www.teammartketing.com/fci.cfm?page=fci_mlb2006.cfm*.

3. YES Network revenue estimates from AskMen.com, creative sports marketing. From publicly available information and statistical modeling, I have estimated the revenue of all MLB teams. This includes only YES revenues attributable to the Yankees; that is, it excludes NJ Nets telecast revenue. Based on these estimates, only six teams (Mets, Red Sox, Cubs, White Sox, Dodgers, and Giants) other than the Yankees will have total revenues in excess of $200 million in 2006.

4. Bill Saporito, "Inside Business, The American Money Machine," December 17, 2004, *www.Time.com*.

5. Ibid.

6. There is a negative correlation between national TV ratings for the Superbowl and the population of the participating teams from 2001 through 2006.

7. Excluding Boston's captivating "reversing the curse" World Series of 2004, there is a .93 correlation between national TV ratings for the World Series and the population of the participating teams from 2001 through 2005.

8. Projections of Kansas City Royals and New York Yankees attendance and revenues are based on regression analysis that estimates the relationship between a team's wins and its attendance and revenues.

9. Ticket prices are from the Team Marketing Report web site, *www.teammartketing.com/fci.cfm?page=fci_mlb2006.cfm*.

10. Estimated actual local revenues for the 56-win, 2005 Royals are less than $45 million.

11. These estimates are generated by the author's model, which estimates the relationship between winning and revenues for each team. The value of the YES Network's baseball-related revenues is imputed in the Yankees revenue estimate. These estimates will be discussed in greater detail in Chapter 2.

12. Operating expenses included in the unaudited financials released by MLB Commissioner's office on November 25, 2001.

13. Based on regression analyses to estimate the total local revenues at various win totals for each team.

14. Roger G. Noll and Andrew Zimbalist, "Sports, Jobs & Taxes: Are New Stadiums Worth the Cost?," *The Brookings Review*, 15 (No. 3, Summer 1997).

15. Data for stadium costs and public–private allocation is from *www.ballparks.com*.

16. See note 14.

17. Salary data from the USAToday.com salary database, *http://asp.usatoday.com/sports/baseball/salaries/teamdetail.aspx?team=20&year=1997*.

18. Andrew Zimbalist, *May the Best Team Win*, (Brookings Insititution, 2003), 43–46.

PART ONE

WIN-REVENUE RELATIONSHIP

It is no secret that fans "pay" for wins. The more a team realizes on-field success, the greater the fan interest and support, the higher the broadcast ratings, and the better support from sponsors—all of which lead to higher revenues. The key question is how much more? MLB teams are constantly faced with balancing the tension between winning and financial returns. In today's complex business environment, with high priced free agents and $100 million payrolls, it's not enough to know that winning breeds revenues. Teams need to have a handle on how much revenue they can expect as an 85-win team versus as a 90-win team.

Chapter 2, "The Power of Winning," speaks to all the ways in which winning can lead to revenue growth and why fans are motivated to devote more of their time and hand over more of their hard-earned cash to their favorite team when its win total improves, especially when it contends for a cherished playoff berth. We also discuss some of the underlying logic behind the "win-curve"—the quantitative relationship between a team's annual win total and their expected revenues.

Chapter 3, "Winning by the Numbers," reviews the results of the statistical analysis of the estimates of teams' win-curves, characterizing each team by the size of its revenue opportunity from winning. The discussion covers the various "layers" of revenue that comprise the win-curve: revenue from regular season wins, as well as the future revenues that are accrue to a team for reaching the postseason, or winning a World Series.

2 | The Power of Winning

According to a well-known cliché winning is contagious, but it can also be lucrative for a Major League Baseball team. In fact, winning is the foundation upon which a baseball team's financial success is built. Every other component of the revenue equation operates with a little more energy and efficiency when the pump is primed with a winning ball club. A winner breeds increased demand for tickets, with higher attendance leading to more concession, parking, and merchandise revenues. Fans are also willing to pay higher ticket prices because they see greater value in supporting a winning team. Since more eyeballs are attracted to a winning team's broadcasts, more advertising dollars can be demanded of sponsors and sometimes higher subscription fees from cable operators. When a team wins, it will be paid more from sponsors for in-stadium ads and signage, and branded beverage and food companies pay more for the rights to distribute and sell their products at games. In general, revenue growth is easier to come by when a ball club is winning.

What are the psychological underpinnings of winning, and why is it so important to fans that they will pay for it? A study by John Burger and Stephen Walters, economics professors at Loyola University in Maryland, identified two classes of fans: the "purists" and the "bandwagon fans." The latter become avid followers only when the team is winning and held in higher esteem in their city.[1] Other studies have shown that competitive athletic success triggers the brain to produce hormones that enhance our self-confidence, and although it may not be rational, fans respond to wins and losses as if they participated in the competition.[2] Add to these studies the notion of people's urge to be part of groups or social organizations, and we can piece together a theory of why winning has such a dramatic effect on fans. Possibly the purists, who have already declared their loyalty, dial up their intensity when the team is winning by indulging in the team's success: more games attended, more games watched, and so on. At the same time the bandwagon fans feel the intensity of those around them and strive to be part of an "esteemed" group: fans of a winning team. Whether the groundswell behind a winning team is a product of neuroscience or simply creates a more enjoyable social experience, the psychological effect appears palpable—so much so, that fans will *pay* for it in various forms, including with one of their most valuable commodities: time and money.

An alternate and potentially less ethereal explanation of this fan behavior is that winning is baseball's measure of product quality. If we define the product that an MLB team produces as a *competitive sporting event, played at the highest level of performance*, then product quality could be defined by a team's winning percentage. A 95-win team produces a higher quality product than a 75-win team. Certainly other factors enter into the total quality equation, such as the condition and location of the ballpark and the quality of its amenities, including the entertainment aspects of presenting a ball game to fans. However, team quality has a great bearing on consumer demand for ball games, much like product quality would for any consumer product.

Even a cursory look at raw data indicates the relationship between winning and attendance—proxies for product quality and revenue. Figure 2.1 is a simple scatter plot of the New York Mets attendance levels and wins over the past 40 years. The scatter plot visually displays the relationship between the two variables: wins (on the vertical axis) and attendance (on the horizontal axis). The correlation coefficient for Mets wins and attendance is .70, which can be interpreted as a strong relationship between winning and attendance. The correlation coefficient measures the strength of the relationship between two variables. If wins and attendance were perfectly correlated, meaning they moved in lock-step, the correlation coefficient would be 1.0. Conversely, if there was no discernible relationship, meaning the two variables were statistically unrelated, the coefficient would be 0.[3] The example of the Mets is typical across all of Major League Baseball. My analysis of all teams shows that even though the strength of the relationship varies from team-to-team, every team shows some positive relationship between winning and attendance.

On another level the New York market is an excellent laboratory in which to test the power of product quality—the relative quality of competing products in the same market. Higher product quality should lead

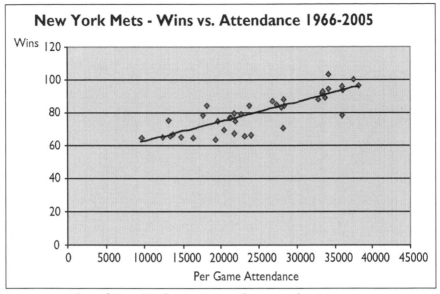

FIGURE 2.1 **Plot of New York Mets attendance and wins.**

to more sales in the form of greater attendance. The loyal purists might increase the number of games they attend, and the more fickle bandwagon fans may jump on board. Some of the bandwagon fans may even be "switchers," who owe no deep loyalty to the Yankees or Mets, but gravitate to the team with the highest-quality product. In 1969, in just their seventh season, the Mets won the World Series and forever shed their "new franchise halo" by becoming a full-fledged adult. From 1969 through 2005, the New York team with the most wins has led in attendance 31 of the 37 years (see Figure 2.2).[4] The Mets win total exceeded the Yankees in 13 of the 37 seasons and they outdrew the Bronx Bombers 14 times. (The year 2006 is excluded, as the teams had identical records.)

In a direct show of appreciation for winning, fans attend more games and spend more of their entertainment budget on tickets, concessions, parking, and souvenirs. Fans also show a willingness to pay higher ticket prices to watch a winning team versus a mediocre, noncompetitive team. In a practice that has become commonplace, teams attempt to monetize their winning by raising ticket prices following a winning season. Teams that win 85 games or more have raised ticket prices for the following season by an average of 13.4% versus 5.7% for teams who won 75 games or fewer.[5] There appears to be no unusual attendance responses to these ticket price changes, suggesting that fans found them rational and were willing

Figure 2.2: Yankees vs. Mets								
Attendance and Wins								
NYY minus NYM			NYY minus NYM			NYY minus NYM		
Year	Wins	Attn/game	Year	Wins	Attn/game	Year	Wins	Attn/game
1969	-20	-13671	1981	25	16761	1993	29	6713
1970	10	-19353	1982	14	8866	1994	21	9276
1971	-1	-14765	1983	23	8754	1995	11	5838
1972	-3	-14892	1984	-3	5127	1996	21	8180
1973	-2	-8174	1985	-1	-6584	1997	8	10051
1974	18	-5545	1986	-18	-6168	1998	26	8238
1975	1	-5264	1987	-3	-7487	1999	1	7214
1976	11	7181	1988	-15	-5476	2000	-7	4422
1977	36	12793	1989	-13	-9070	2001	13	7993
1978	34	16225	1990	-24	-8967	2002	28	7363
1979	26	22042	1991	-6	-5370	2003	35	14620
1980	36	17720	1992	4	-381	2004	30	17980
						2005	12	15562

Box = Years in which team with most wins did not have highest attendance

FIGURE 2.2 **Thirty-seven years of N.Y. Yankees and N.Y. Mets wins and attendance figures.**

to absorb the aggressive increases from the winning ball clubs and tolerate the more modest increases from losing teams.

In addition to the direct impact of higher attendance, teams act as "resellers" of fans devotion, packaging the increased attention in the form of viewer ratings for telecasts of games and charging advertisers higher rates for broadcast sponsorships as their message reaches more wallets. Analyzing broadcast ratings data for selected MLB teams indicates that ratings for a consistent 90- to 95-win team can be twice as high as the ratings if the same team is a 75-win club. The amount of revenue differential depends on the size of the market and the team's rights' fee arrangement with the broadcast network, but it is clear that the benefits of winning go well beyond game attendance.

WINNING PAYS DIVIDENDS WITH SPONSORS

Another way teams can monetize winning is through corporate sponsors who crave association with a winner. For example, sponsors are anxious to pay money to be "the official soft drink of the New York Yankees"—a designation that may help improve fans' perceptions of the soft drink brand. Beyond delivering a selling a message on a sign on the left field wall, sponsors can also enhance the image of their brand by affiliating with a winning team. This means on-field success yields higher demand by potential sponsors, translating into more sponsors and a higher price tag to join the winning team.

To realize the financial benefits of winning is the aspiration of every Major League ball club. The Cleveland Indians of the late 1990s are a perfect example of how winning can create economic value and build financial success. Admittedly the Tribe's winning was augmented by a new ballpark with charisma, but they also had the fallout from the work stoppage of 1994–1995 to overcome. The 1994 season ended in August, and the 1995 season resumed some four weeks late on April 25, leaving the baseball fan with a nasty hangover. Even after adjusting for the attendance and revenue effect of the strike and the short-term positive impact of Jacobs Field, winning meant dollars to the Indians. In 1993, as the bricks and mortar of Jacobs Field were being assembled, the Indians were signing their young, talented nucleus to long-term contracts in an effort to preempt their free agency in the near term. This was a bold move by then-GM John Hart, considering that the 1991 team lost 105 games, anchored by Carlos Baerga and Albert Belle. Kenny Lofton, the third member of the core, was brought in for the 1992 season to complete the foundation of the mid-1990s pennant-winning clubs.

I was fortunate to have a box seat to watch their great on-field and financial run, as I was leading Pepsico's soft drink bottling business for the Midwest, based in Cleveland. During the 1993 season Coca-Cola* was enjoying a 30-year reign as the exclusive soft drink of the Cleveland Indians, entitling them to in-stadium signage, promotional programs, and the exclusive availability of Coke products at Tribe games at the old Cleveland Municipal Stadium. With the hopes that the combination of a new ballpark in rejuvenated downtown Cleveland and a soon-to-be winning ball club would ratchet-up fan interest and attendance, the time seemed right for Pepsi to attempt to unseat Coke as the Indians' soft drink sponsor. My Pepsi team was able to wrestle the rights away from Coke for a reasonable $850,000 per year. While this rate was somewhat higher than the average

MLB team-beverage deal in the mid-1990s, it was justified by the expectations of increased attendance and fanfare from the unveiling of a new ballpark.

The 1994 Indians opened the season in the new Jacobs Field and quickly showed that they would be a force in the newly created American League Central Division. When the season ended abruptly as a result of the players' strike, the Indians were playing .584 baseball—projecting to 95 wins over 162 games. In the strike-shortened 1995 season the Indians were playing .698 baseball—projecting to 113 wins over a full season. As the Indians embarked on their first trip to the postseason (and ultimately the World Series) since 1954, fans were whipped into a frenzy. Tribe logos and banners permeated northeast Ohio, from schools to churches. It was common to see a school bus full of grade school girls and boys wearing Indians' hats and sweatshirts. The Indians not only captured the American League pennant, but also the affection of a city starved for a winner. By 1996 the winning was paying handsome dividends for the business known as the Cleveland Indians. The ball club was in a record-setting run of 455 consecutive home sellouts in the 43,000-seat Jacobs Field.

When faced with the renewal negotiations of Pepsi's multiyear soft drink sponsorship, the financial value of winning became crystal clear. With the conviction that their winning club would continue to sell out Jacobs Field and captivate the fans of northeast Ohio, the Indians' executive team approached me with their price for a new deal. At first glance, the price of $1.6 million per year, nearly double the price of the previous deal, seemed outrageous. After weeks of negotiating and getting little movement from the Indians, I was forced to find a creative way for Pepsi to extract value from the sponsorship or potentially lose out to Coke. Since all Indians games were sold out, and tickets were included in our sponsorship package, I had the idea to barter tickets to grocery chains in exchange for preferential treatment over Coke. I was able to create an incentive program for the local grocery store chains to improve the merchandising and pricing of Pepsi products in their stores: larger Pepsi displays in prime in-store locations, at lower sale prices. The price for this privileged treatment by our local grocery stores was tickets to Cleveland Indian games to be used in consumer giveaways and internal incentive programs for grocery store personnel. Pepsi had something that Coke could not beat—tickets to sold-out Indians games. By garnering a significant advantage over Coke on the battleground of the grocery store floor, I knew our revenues, market share, and profits would soar. Everybody won. The grocery stores attracted shoppers and created some in-store excitement with Indians tickets for sold-out games. Pepsi grew revenues, share, and profits, and the Indians monetized the value of winning by effectively using scarce, high-demand game tickets as currency. This particular example may be dependent on the rare situation of the winning ball club being in a perennial sell-out mode, but in the same way the Indians' front office leadership team captured value, any winning team could employ creative means to monetize the value of winning.

For example, following their World Championship in 2004, the Boston Red Sox had several innovative ideas to monetize the power of a winning image with their loyal fan base. They came up with the idea of selling sponsorships to their regular season series with the Yankees, as well as opening Red Sox Taverns and selling Red Sox lager throughout the New England area.[6] To the dismay of baseball's most ambitious brands, the plans were said to be rejected by Commissioner Selig and MLB.[7]

OWNERS AND FANS ON THE SAME PAGE

Winning is a powerful revenue generator that has the potential to align the objectives of both fans and owners. Fans thrive on winning and are willing to reach into their wallets and pay for it, while owners also improve their revenues and can enhance the value of their franchise through winning. If this is true, why do fans and owners sometimes appear at odds? Fans, who define winning by the number of W's in the standings, sometimes accuse owners of not wanting to win. Owners, who also like wins, as well as dollars in the bank account, sometimes question fans' willingness to reward a winning team.

In September of 2006 a group of nearly 1,000 dedicated but frustrated Orioles fans walked out during a game at Camden Yards in protest of the ninth consecutive losing season by their beloved ball club.[8] The disgruntled fans took aim at owner Peter Angelos and claimed he had made bad player personnel decisions. "We want someone in there that will spend the money to do the things that will bring the fans back," said Oriole protester Eric Hunter.[9] Another fan who took part in the demonstration, Raymond Burke, said, "This is all part of my kids having the experience that I had as a kid coming to the games—of experiencing the great teams and teams that meant something to the community." Angelos' retort was to claim that a "$100 to $110 million payroll" was necessary to compete in the tough American League East Division, and in order to spend at that level, he would need to raise ticket prices.[10] While this conflict reinforces the importance of winning to a team's fan base, it also highlights the tension between winning and financial returns.

Angelos' estimate of the payroll necessary to compete with the Yankees and the Red Sox brings into question his expectations of the productivity of the Orioles' farm system. If a farm system fails to generate at least a trickle of Major League regulars, the team will need to either dip into the pricey free-agent market or swap talent to try to build a winning club. If a team follows the predominantly external talent route, the teams *marginal cost of winning* can skyrocket, possibly even surpassing the team's *marginal revenue from winning*, leading to a deficit spending scenario. When the cost of wins is greater than the revenue generated by the wins, a fiscally responsible owner is apt to slam on the brakes. What sometimes appears to be a lack of willingness to spend on the part of the owner is really a failure of the farm system to produce the right mix of players for the Major League roster and reduce the *need* to spend lavishly to field a competitive team.

Another possible reason for an owner to put a halt to spending may be a lack of understanding of the marginal revenue from winning. Not knowing how much revenue an 80-win team is expected to generate as opposed to, say, an 88-win team, means a team may not have a good grasp on how much they can afford to spend for a win, which can lead to whip-saw actions by a ball club. Indulging in the free-agent market without concrete knowledge of the expected financial return could trigger a death spiral. The sequence goes as follows: the team signs a high-priced free agent, becomes disappointed when the team improves but the revenues fall far short of expectations, and then vows never to make the same mistake again. Abstaining from the free-agent market during the following off-season causes fans to complain about management's "lack of commitment" and return the favor by withholding their support of the team, which becomes evident at the box office.

Much of the pain may have been avoided if the team's front office and ownership had a more intimate understanding of the relationship between winning and revenues. The win–revenue relationship, or win-curve, as it is referred to throughout this book, can serve as a guide to setting budgets and provide a valuable perspective on player personnel and compensation decisions. Much like any business, it is difficult to operate with discipline without a clear understanding of the financial parameters of the business. Much like a company that manufactures its products and resells them to American consumers, it's important to have a handle on consumer demand and how it responds to the quality of your product.

Navigating the Broadcast Revenue Maze

In recent years there have been significant developments in the way some teams broadcast their games, dramatically altering MLB's financial landscape.[11] The traditional approach has been for teams to sell their broadcast rights to a regional Fox Sports affiliate (or their competitor) in exchange for a rights fee. These contracts are generally multiyear, for a fixed amount of dollars over the life of the agreement, with some bonus provisions for the team reaching the postseason or other on-field success. The broadcast company—we'll call it Fox Sports North (FSN)—pays a rights fee to the team and sells the advertising time on team telecasts to consumer marketers. FSN figures that if the team wins (e.g., reaches the postseason), there will be greater fan interest, leading to higher ratings and more viewers. As a result, they will be able sell advertising at higher rates and pass *some* of the increased revenue back to the team in the form of a bonus. FSN is not willing to give up the entire upside resulting from an exciting playoff chase, since they are bearing a financial risk with a fixed rights fee. If the team plunges into the cellar and no one watches their games, FSN is still on the hook to pay the team the fixed fee.[12]

The alternative broadcast arrangement that has been gaining in popularity over the last several years is the team-owned regional sports network (RSN). RSNs have rewritten the economic rules of the game by giving team ownership a more direct vehicle to monetize fan demand. Currently there are 11 RSNs in operation, including 12 MLB teams. The Orioles–Nationals and the Cubs–White Sox share an interest in a local RSN[13] (see Figure 2.3 for the list of RSNs).

Understanding how revenues flow through the RSN when a team's on-field performance varies is more complicated. Under this scenario, the RSN gets subscription fees from cable distributors and satellite providers to "buy" their channel and carry it on their delivery system. The RSN then sells advertising time on telecasts for a second revenue stream. While this may not sound much different than the way in which a Fox Sports affiliate would operate, the big difference is that the team owns all or a large portion of the RSN. As a result, this arrangement places teams in the broadcasting business, with an equity position in any value created in the broadcast entity.

To determine the impact of a team's on-field performance on broadcast revenues, we need to account for the ownership structure of the RSN. To the extent that the team (or team owners) has an ownership stake in the RSN, we can "impute" a share of the profits to the team, as if the team and

Figure 2.3: Regional Sports Networks

Network	Team Affiliation
New England Sports Network (NESN)	Red Sox
Mid-Atlantic Sports Network (MASN)	Orioles, Nationals
YES Network	Yankees
Rogers Sports Network	Blue Jays
Turner Broadcast Station (TBS)	Braves
Comcast SportsNet Philadelphia	Phillies
Comcast SportsNet Chicago	White Sox, Cubs
Royals Sports Television Network (RSTN)	Royals
SportsNet NY	Mets
Sportstime Ohio (STO)	Indians
WGN	Cubs

Source: Maury Brown, The Baseball Journals

FIGURE 2.3 **Regional sports networks.**

the RSN were two divisions of the same company. We'll call this "creating transparency" regarding the ownership structure of the RSN. For example, the Boston Red Sox have an 80% ownership stake in the New England Sports Network (NESN), their RSN. In addition to the rights fee NESN pays the Red Sox for the right to broadcast games, by imputing a portion of NESN's profitability to the Red Sox, we can better understand their underlying economic payoff for winning games. We could not accurately assess the Red Sox's true financial gains from improving the team if artificial partitions blocked the flow of this important revenue stream. In addition to their rights fees, which show up on the Red Sox's financial statements, we may need to add another $10 to $12 million for the Red Sox's share of NESN profits.[14] It is critical to include the full value of the broadcast relationship when measuring the value of a win. The Red Sox's share of NESN's profits could mean an extra half-million to a million dollars per win over key segments of the Red Sox win-curve.

Another way in which RSNs alter the win–revenue relationship is by creating asset value in a broadcast network. In addition to the revenue impact, the team maintains an equity stake in a network (either directly or indirectly) and bears the risk and reward of the valuation of the network as an asset for potential future resale. Depending on the size of the market and popularity of the team, the Fox Sports–type arrangement would net a team a steady revenue stream of anywhere from $5 million to $50 million in straight rights fees. With an RSN a team has a variable revenue flow that is more closely linked to their on-field performance and their popularity *and* an asset that can be worth anywhere from $100 million for the newest upstart RSNs to nearly $2 billion for mega-RSNs like the YES Network. This asset value rises and falls with broadcast ratings and advertising and distribution fees, which can be greatly affected by a team's wins and losses.

So, what is the downside of a team choosing to go the RSN route instead of selling the rights to a Fox Sports–type of affiliate? Why doesn't every team do this? If a team is in a small market, or its team lacks the popularity and ratings to achieve some critical mass level, they may not have enough clout to secure distribution agreements with cable operators for the subscription fees that ultimately make the math work for the team. If the Pittsburgh Pirates, coming off consecutive 67-win seasons, tried to charge a $1.50 per month subscription fee to carry a Pirates-owned sports network, cable operators might say, "No thanks." Even if cable operators went with the plan, but offered the channel only as a premium channel to its customers, how many Pirates fans would pay to see their games on television? If the distribution into households is too low, there would not be much appeal to advertisers, cutting into an important portion of the revenue stream of the RSN. It adds up to a lot of risk to bear for a small-market, historically weak-performing team. As a general rule of thumb, if it's a great challenge to sell tickets to games, it will be an even bigger challenge to sell your own RSN to cable operators and advertisers.

THE YES NETWORK: THE YANKEE JUGGERNAUT

At the other end of the spectrum is baseball's premier franchise. The New York Yankees have converted winning into economic gain like no other team in MLB and possibly American sports history. In a perfect storm-type scenario, they have parlayed their current on-field success, their unmatched legacy of winning, the nation's biggest market, and the heyday of baseball popularity into a financial machine that would make many CEOs salivate. What Steinbrenner has accomplished on the playing field (six World Championships, including four in the past decade) pales by comparison to the amount of financial value he has created. In five years, from the end of the 2001 season to today, he has revolutionized baseball's economics.

The Yankees' not so Secret Weapon - The YES Network	Millions
Subscription + Ad Revenue (8 Million local subscribers + 2.4 million outer market subscribers)	$ 275
less "rights fees" paid to NYY*	(60)
less other operating expenses	(105)
YES Estimated Operating Profit	110
YES Asset Value	$1,900
*Michael O'Keeffe and TJ Quinn, "Yanks Losing at Moneyball", NY Daily News, 12/7/05	

FIGURE 2.4 **The YES Network.**

In the fall of 2001, coming off a World Series loss to the Arizona Diamondbacks, the Yankees had appeared in five of the past six World Series, winning four times. The Yankees drew nearly 3.3 million in attendance in 2001 and had a broadcast contract with the Madison Square Garden Network that netted them an estimated $40 million or $50 million in broadcast rights fees. Adding gate receipts, broadcast rights fees, and other revenues from concessions, merchandise sales and corporate sponsorships, the Yankees' revenue base for 2001 is estimated at $200 million.[15] Fast forwarding ahead to the fall of 2006, the Yankees have reached the World Series only once in the past five years (a disappointing loss to the Florida Marlins) while having made unceremoniously premature playoff exits in the remaining years. Despite their recent playoff stumble that has Yankee fans missing the good ol' days of back-to-back-to-back World Championships, the Yankees revenue base has blasted off like a Cape Canaveral moon shot. (In a world where everything is relative, their recent playoff stumble would be the envy of at least 25 other MLB teams.)

At the centerpiece of their financial success is the birth and maturity of the YES Network, the crown jewel of all RSNs. While they were far from the first team to own a network, preceded by the Red Sox's NESN, among others, in true Yankee style they did it bigger and better than anyone else. Possibly their success should have been anticipated as they configured the perfect formula to launch their own network: the nations' most storied sports franchise, at the top of their game following a string of World Championships, in the largest media market in the world. Let's also not discount the way in which the economic structure of MLB played a role as an enabler. In a league without a salary cap, where local revenues rule the roost and revenue sharing is no more than a minor nuisance to the wealthiest of teams, the Yankees had every reason to believe they had it within their power to control their own destiny. The formula was simple—continue to escalate payroll to buy whatever talent needed to stay ultra-competitive and ensure the success of their network.

In a "before and after" that would blow away any television commercial guaranteed to trim five inches off your waistline, the Yankees converted a revenue stream of $40 million or $50 million of rights fees into $60 million of rights fees, plus $110 million in YES operating profit, and a share of an asset valued at about $1.9 billion according to Kagan Research analyst John Mansell[16] (see Figure 2.4).

Since Yankee Global Enterprises LLC owns both the New York Yankees and a stake in the YES Network, all of the dollars from YES that can be imputed to the baseball business will not necessarily show up on the Yankees' profit and loss statements. Because the YES Network also gains revenues when the Yankees win and their broadcasts are in greater demand, let's break down the wall between the two and treat the revenues "transparently," giving the Yankees credit for increased broadcast revenues. Under this approach, the Yankees that generated about $200 million in 2001 brought in an estimated $400 million in 2006, a doubling of revenue in just five years. On top of the $200 million increase in revenue, adding in the asset value created in the form of the YES Network, and a $300 million estimate by Forbes' in the appreciation of the value of the team, the Yankees have created more than *2 billion dollars in value since 2001.*

While the Yankees annual payroll has increased by nearly $100 million over the same time frame and revenue sharing combined with luxury tax payments routinely top $100 million per year, the Yankees are arguably much better off today than in 2001, largely owing to the YES Network. The same can be said for Yankee fans who have day and night Yankee content at their fingertips. Even on nongame days, the YES Network is filled with player features, highlights of historic games, or even replays of the previous night's game. A network with a dedicated focus on one team has also brought innovation to viewers. In July of 2006, YES and DIRECTV announced the first-ever interactive content as a part of Yankee telecasts. In addition to extra statistics and access to other data, viewers will be treated to views from extra cameras. The "Bonus Cam" will be part of a split screen format isolating stars such as Derek Jeter or whomever else the game situation may bring into focus. The timing couldn't be better. As the Yankees ready themselves for their new smaller stadium scheduled to open in 2009, fans' access to tickets will no doubt be more curtailed. The new features on YES and DIRECTV create a premium viewing experience—a halfway mark between a traditional broadcast and live viewing—that allows fans to exert more control over what they watch, possibly softening the blow of not being able to afford or find a ticket to the game.

THE WIN–REVENUE RELATIONSHIP

The results of the statistical analysis—primarily multiple regression analysis—applied to revenue estimates of each MLB team generated several conclusions that were consistent across all teams (for a more detailed discussion of the methodology used in this analysis see the sidebar, Measuring the Impact of Winning on Revenues).

Winning Has a Definitive and Measurable Impact on a Team's Revenue

For all teams, there was a positive and statistically significant relationship between winning and revenue over a meaningful range—typically 70 to 105 wins.[17] The slope of the relationship differs by ball club, suggesting that some teams' fans are more responsive than others to improvements in the team's on-field performance.

At the Extremes, Regular Season Wins Have Little Impact on Revenue

While winning is an important revenue driver, at the extremes, a win or a loss means far less. For teams that win fewer than 70 regular season games, fans (and hence revenues) are not sensitive to changes in wins. For all practical purposes, a 63-win season is the financial equivalent to a 67-win season. The revenue a team generates when winning 70 or fewer games in a season is considered baseline revenue. From year-to-year, baseline revenue would typically vary based only on price changes (i.e., ticket price increases, new broadcast contracts, etc.), but over the long-term certain factors can cause baseline revenues to shift, as will be discussed later. Conversely, above 98 wins, there is a reduced impact on revenues.[18] Since a team has virtually secured a spot in the playoffs at that point, additional wins tend to add little to the local fans' enthusiasm. Any gains seem to be offset by the fact that the team is likely to play "meaningless" home games in September, long after they have clinched their playoff berth and are resting their starters to ready them for the postseason. These are not desirable games to attend, as fans' interest is already turned to the postseason. A statistical study by three University of Wisconsin–La Crosse economics pro-

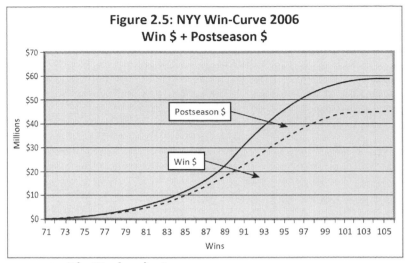

FIGURE 2.5 **The Yankees' win-curve.**

fessors supports this conclusion. They found attendance to be maximized when the home team has a 60% probability of winning, which translates into a 97- or 98-win season.[19]

The Win–Revenue Relationship Is Nonlinear

The win–revenue relationship (for shorthand we'll call this the win-curve) generally follows the same approximate shape for all teams, although the slope of the curve varies from team to team. Generally, each win from the 71st to the 90th has an increasing value. From the 91st to the 98th, win revenues increase, but at a gradually declining rate. From the 99th through 105th win, the marginal value drops precipitously until it essentially reaches zero at 106 wins. Figure 2.5 shows my estimates of the win-curve for the New York Yankees. Both regular season wins and the value of the postseason are reflected in the chart. (Note that the revenue scale on the y axis does not reflect the gross revenue, but rather Yankee revenue estimates net of MLB's revenue-sharing tax.[20])

The win-curve is nonlinear on two counts. First, fans are sensitive to a change in regular season wins, as it reflects the level of a team's competitiveness. From Figure 2.5 we can see as the Yankees approach playoff contention, fan interest escalates dramatically as they become a more appealing entertainment event. One plausible explanation is the bandwagon effect discussed earlier. When a team is in playoff contention, it attracts new fans, while existing fans increase their attendance frequency. Perhaps the Yankee example is even more intuitive in reverse. Given the high level of expectations in Yankeeland, if the team plays only .500 baseball, there is a significant backlash by Yankee fans, and attendance, fan support, and revenues would drop precipitously.

Another factor causing the win-curve to be nonlinear is the second layer of revenue: the postseason effect. Since the postseason effect is defined as (the probability of reaching the postseason) × (the value of the postseason revenue stream), it tends to increase until the team's win level ensures playoff participation. At 85 wins, a team has a 10% chance of reaching the postseason, but at 95 wins, the probability rises to 93%. These probabilities are reflected in the second layer of revenue: the expected value of the revenue stream resulting from the postseason.

WINNING CREATES REVENUE ON MULTIPLE LEVELS

A team can create four layers of value by winning. The first layer is the attendance and revenue changes in response to regular season wins (Win $). An 85-win team generates more revenue than a 75-win team and so on. A second layer is the revenue stream that results from a postseason appearance (PS $). Once a team reaches the playoffs, it can count on an additional revenue stream over the next four to five years. A third layer is the revenue boost a team realizes if it has the good fortune of winning the World Series (WS $). On top of the postseason revenue stream, there is yet another "kicker" if a team wins it all. Much like the postseason revenue stream, it accrues over subsequent years. Finally, the analysis indicates that revenues can rise or fall owing to chronic winning or losing. If a team has three successive years of more than 90 wins, or fewer than 75 wins, they are branded by their fans as chronic winners or chronic losers. As a result, the baseline revenues of a team, revenues that in the short term are not generally vulnerable to winning or losing, will actually shift upward for a chronic winner or downward for a chronic loser. Graphically, the multiple layers of value created by winning are shown in Figure 2.6. (Note: Accretion to the baseline from chronic winning and the erosion to the baseline from chronic losing (A/E $) only occur after three consecutive years of less than 75-win or greater than 90-win performance.)

Figure 2.6 captures the complex relationship between winning and revenues for a Major League Baseball team. The specific values and slopes along these curves can vary dramatically from team to team based on market size, the strength of the team as a consumer brand, local sports and entertainment competition, the legacy and history of the franchise in the market, ticket pricing, and accessibility to broadcasts, among other factors.

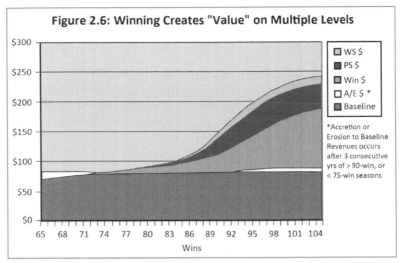

FIGURE 2.6 **Winning creates value on multiple levels.**

THE REVENUE-SHARING TAX HAS A DRAMATIC IMPACT ON MARGINAL REVENUE

The 2002 Collective Bargaining Agreement (CBA) stipulates that a portion of a team's revenues is taxed by MLB. In turn, these revenues are redistributed disproportionately to low-revenue teams in an attempt to improve competitive balance by transferring cash from the haves to the have-nots. One implication for the win curve is that revenue sharing tax weakens the connection between winning and revenues. Since the marginal tax on revenue is between 39 and 47%, each win is worth only 53 to 61% of the actual revenue it generates (from 2002 to 2006).[21] The remainder (the tax) is paid into MLB and redistributed on the basis of a team's revenues—the low revenue teams being the payees, while the high revenue teams are the payers—not based on wins. Potentially the biggest impact of revenue sharing is to depress players' salaries by reducing a team's marginal revenue from winning and thereby lowering the value of the player who contributes to those wins.

In the recently signed CBA covering the 2007 to 2011 seasons, revenue sharing has been adjusted via a complex formula that ultimately should create greater incentive for teams to grow their own revenues, as the marginal tax rate will be reduced. The teams on the receiving end of the revenue-sharing payments that formerly paid a 47% marginal tax should now pay a tax of slightly less than 31%. The high-revenue teams, which formerly paid about 39%, should now pay slightly more than 31% of their marginal revenue.[22]

HIGHLIGHTS OF WIN-CURVE

One of the results of the win-curve estimates effort is a segmentation of teams based on the severity of fans' responsiveness to changes in winning percentage. Examining only regular season wins (excluding the impact of postseason or world championship), there are four segments of fan responsiveness. The least responsive segment—the flattest win-curve—consists of teams who seem to gain very little economically from winning. The three teams that fall into this segment are the Chicago Cubs, the Atlanta Braves, and the Baltimore Orioles.[23] This lace of response may indicate a high degree of fan loyalty and strong branding by the team or, in the case of the Cubs, a legacy of middle-of-the-road performance and low fan expectations. In a 2001 study of Cubs' fans' loyalty, Dennis N. Bristow and Richard J. Sebastian of St. Cloud State University concluded that certain brands develop or acquire "social images" with which consumers may identify and become emotionally attached.[24] They also concluded that loyalty is based on a combination of a team's performance and fans' expectations.[25]

On the other extreme, the "win or die" category, which has the steepest win-curve, belongs to the Yankees. The curve (reflected in the marginal Win $ portion of Figure 2.5) indicates a sharp change in attendance, and hence revenues, resulting from changes in wins. This can be attributed to the Yankee fans' high expectations of their team and the lack of tolerance

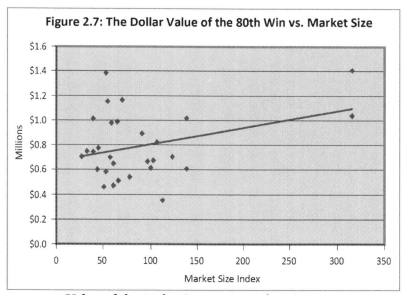

FIGURE 2.7 **Value of the 80th win versus market size.**

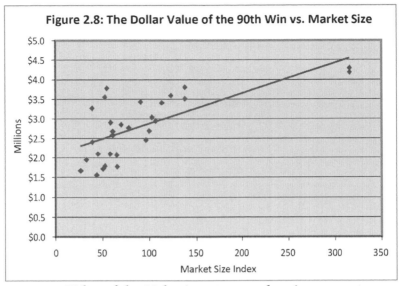

FIGURE 2.8 **Value of the 90th win versus market size.**

for mediocrity. It may also reflect the local competition in New York and the switching that occurs between Yankees and Mets fans. The second-steepest category—in which fans seem to demand winning and then aggressively respond to it—is composed of the Angels, the Red Sox, and the Blue Jays. These teams tend to enjoy a large "bang for the buck" when it comes to improving the team but also pay a steep price on the downside when the team fades from contention. The remaining teams fit into the broad category of "average" fan responsiveness to changes in winning percentage over the regular season.

This analysis sheds light on the important question of the relationship between market size and the marginal revenue curve. To what degree does the size of the market dictate marginal revenue and therefore give a large-market team an economic advantage in competing for top-tier free agents? The best way to shed light on this question is to compare the models' estimates of value of a win across teams. Since the value of a win changes as each team moves up and down the win-curve, we will use win levels—the 80-win level and the 90-win level—to compare the relationship to market size. At the 80-win level the scatter plot and trend line (Figure 2.7) show a modest relationship, with a correlation coefficient of .35.

When we view the scatter plot of the 90th win relative to market size (Figure 2.8), we see a stronger positive correlation with a correlation coefficient of .70. This suggests that the economics for a mediocre, noncompetitive team are not greatly influenced by market size. The large market–small market differential has a greater impact on the economics of playoff-caliber teams. It may also mean that the inclusion of the postseason bounty—the revenue stream that is apt to materialize when the team achieves postseason status—tips the scale in favor of the large-market clubs. In a later chapter we will more thoroughly compare the relative importance of market size, playing performance, and the team's location on the win-curve.

Winning is an important variable in the economic equation for an MLB team. It can have a dramatic impact on a team's bottom line and franchise value. The degree of impact depends on the market, the brand strength of the team, its degree of competitiveness, and the ability of management to harvest the fruits of building a winner. In the next chapter we will discuss in more detail how specific teams' revenues fluctuate with their on-field success and the role that the postseason, and its hefty bounty, plays in the revenue equation.

Endnotes

1. John D. Burger and Stephen J. K. Walters, "Market Size, Pay, and Performance," *Journal of Sports Economics* (May 2003). This study related a team's revenues to changes in a team's competitive status, concluding that larger markets tend to breed greater increases in attendance when a team is in contention.
2. Young H. Lee and Trenton G. Smith, "Why are Americans Addicted to Baseball? An Empirical Analysis of Fandom in Korea and the U.S.," *Western Economic Association Working Paper Series* WP2006-5 May 16, 2006.
3. If there was a strong negative relationship, in which the two variables varied inversely (as one variable rises, the other declines), then the correlation coefficient would be near −1.0
4. A more accurate calculation may be to define wins as the average of current plus previous years' wins. Using this blended win total, the highest-win team also enjoyed higher attendance in 32 of 37 years.
5. Analyzed data for ticket price increases from 1997 through 2001, using data from Team Marketing Report (TMR), Annual Survey of Ticket Prices.
6. Seth Mnookin, *Feeding the Monster: How Money, Smarts, and Nerve Took a Team top the Top* (Simon and Schuster, 2006), 315.
7. Ibid., 315.
8. David Ginsburg, "Oriole Protesters Walk Out on Team," *USA Today*, September 21, 2006, *http://www.usatoday.com/sports/baseball/al/orioles/2006-09-21-demonstration_x.htm*.
9. Ibid.
10. Ibid.
11. Broadcast revenue estimates are based on 2001 published team data but the numbers have been updated to reflect more current publicly available information.
12. As a result of this arrangement, I have built an estimate of a team's broadcast rights fees

into their baseline revenues. When creating the models to estimate the relationship between winning and revenues, I include an assumption that broadcast revenues can increase by only 5% (for teams in smaller markets) to 15% (for teams in larger markets) over the range of the win curve to account for a potential performance bonus.

13. From Maury Brown, *The Baseball Journals*, February 24, 2006*www.maurybrown. com/?p=48...* Recently, the Kansas City Royals announced they will disband their RSN in favor of a broadcast contract with Fox Sports Midwest, beginning in 2008. From Jeffrey Flanagan, "Fox Sports Midwest gets Royals TV deal," *The Kansas City Star,* December 6, 2006.

14. NESN profitability from Thomas Boswell, "Angelos May Have Won, but the Nationals Can't Lose," *The Washington Post,* April 1, 2005, *http://www.washingtonpost.com/ac2/wp-dyn/A17271-2005Mar31?language=printer.*

15. Based on the 2001 unaudited financial data released by the MLB Commissioner's office. Excludes the $16 million in revenue that the Yankees earned from their postseason, including their World Series appearance (*http://www.businessofbaseball.com/data/2001financials. xls*).

16. From Tom Stienert-Threlkeld, "Steinbrenner May Get New Partners in YES," *Multichannel Newswire,* August 21, 2006, *http://www.multichannel.com/index.asp?layout=articlePrint&articleid=CA6363941.*

17. Statistically significant at the 95% level for all teams and at the 99% level for 27 teams.

18. After 105 wins, there is no positive impact on revenues.

19. Glenn Knowles, Keith Sherony, and Mike Haupert, "The Demand for Major League Baseball: A Test of the Uncertainty of Outcome Hypothesis," *The American Economist* (Fall, 1992): 77. Although teams often perform better at home, a .600 winning percentage for the entire season is between 97 and 98 wins.

20. Gross revenues would be approximately 64% higher than the scale, as the revenues in the chart include the deduction for the approximately 39% revenue-sharing tax rate for the Yankees for 2005.

21. Andrew Zimbalist, *May the Best Team Win* (The Brookings Institution), 103

22. An excellent article by *Baseball Prospectus* author Neil deMause gives an early preview of the potential implications on revenue sharing of the 2007 CBA (*http://baseballprospectus. com/article.php?articleid=5680*).

23. This part of the segmentation does not include classification of expansion teams (Florida, Colorado, Tampa Bay, and Arizona) because of their limited history.

24. Dennis N. Bristow and Richard J. Sebastian, "Holy Cow! Wait 'til Next Year! A Closer Look at Brand Loyalty of Chicago Cubs Baseball Fans," *Journal of Consumer Marketing*, 18(No. 3) (2001): 259.

25. Ibid., 266.

Measuring the Impact of Winning on Revenues

My research and analysis indicates that there is a definitive and measurable relationship between winning ball games and a team's revenues. While the impact of winning is not always instantaneous, particularly in the case of the carryover effect of reaching the postseason, there are techniques to estimate the impact. The first step in quantifying the effect of winning on revenue for each team is to measure the impact on annual home attendance. I employed multiple regression analysis, with annual per-game home attendance as the dependent variable, to estimate the relationship between winning and attendance for 29 teams, excluding the Washington Nationals owing to a lack of historical data. Where available, I used 30 or more years of annual data, while in expansion markets I used every year of a team's existence. After experimenting with various definitions of "wins," a 50–50 weighting of previous and current year wins was used to define a team's win total. With the goal of isolating the relationship between winning and attendance, I had to adjust for other factors that might affect attendance. In addition to a team's wins, the independent variables used to explain the variation in annual per-game attendance included a new-stadium effect, work stoppages, a "new franchise halo," an expansion team's experiences in its first several years in existence, and a time-trend variable to capture the general growth of the industry over the time frame. Using this general framework, I estimated customized models for each team individually to capture the unique relationship each team maintains with its fans. Once the winning–attendance relationship is quantified, several additional steps are necessary to convert these estimates into revenues dollars. The first and more straightforward step is converting attendance into attendance revenue. My approach was to use Team Marketing Report's (TMR) average ticket price data, which is included in their annual Fan Cost Index survey. TMR calculates the average ticket price by using a weighted average of the price of tickets and the number of seats at each price point. For games that are not sellouts, it is possible that the actual annual ticket revenue would differ from the estimates based on the actual mix of tickets sold. While this is not a precise measure of actual ticket revenue, it is a reasonable estimate, using publicly available data, for both per game and annual ticket revenue. The second and more complicated translation is the estimate of non-ticket revenues, and how they respond as a team's win total varies.

$\longrightarrow$

The major local revenue categories include broadcast revenues, advertising and sponsorships revenues, food and beverage concessions, parking, and merchandise sales. For analytical purposes, revenues are divided into three categories: attendance, broadcast, and all other revenue. While the win–attendance relationship was estimated through regression analysis, an alternative algorithm was developed to estimate the relationship between winning and the two remaining local revenue categories: broadcast and all other. In developing the revenue estimates for the win-curve, a team's broadcast revenues from the traditional arms-length arrangements with networks are treated differently from those emanating from RSNs. In the former case the rights fee is included in the baseline revenues—the revenues a team would generate even if they won only 70 games in a season. The only incremental broadcast revenues for these teams as they increased their win total would be a 5 to 15% kicker, reflecting a postseason broadcast bonus, depending on the size of the market. In cases where teams had RSNs, I attempted to model the relationship between wins and ratings and reflect the resulting revenues in the win-curve estimates. Team revenue derived from sources other than attendance and broadcasts were taken form the 2001 database of team revenues published by the commissioner's office. I established a simple ratio between those revenues and attendance revenues. The ratio is generally held constant over the win-curve; if attendance revenue increases by 10%, then "all other" revenue increases by 10%. For all revenue categories, updated estimates were based on publicly available information to capture changes in broadcast contracts and other team agreements. The remaining major revenue component is "national revenue," flowing equally to all teams from sources such as national television contracts and MLBAM, which includes *MLB.com*. National revenues are *excluded* from the win–revenue analysis, as they are independent of any individual team's on-field performance. To estimate the postseason revenue stream, I began by estimating a "reasonable" number of full-season equivalent (FSE) tickets that might be sold in the immediate off-season in the wake of a team's appearance in the postseason. This estimate is based on several factors, including the teams' current season ticket base in cases where that information was available. The increased ticket sales assumptions were combined with an expected ticket price increase to estimate an attendance revenue impact. I then coupled this incremental ticket revenue with commensurate increases in "all other" revenue and potential increases in broadcast revenues to reach a first year (following the appearance

→

in the postseason) revenue impact. Finally, I made an assumption about the level of attrition over a four-year period, created a revenue estimate for each of four years following a postseason appearance, and calculated the net present value (NPV) of the revenue stream. For the additional kicker of winning a World Championship, I followed a similar process but assumed that only 12.5% of the NPV of the revenue stream should be counted as "value." Based on the logic that every postseason entrant has a one-in-eight chance of becoming a World Champion, I did not want to overvalue the accomplishment by assuming the full revenue value, since a considerable amount of luck is involved. I combined the NPV of the postseason revenue stream with 12.5% of the World Championship NPV, for a total NPV opportunity that a team would realize once it reached the postseason. To integrate this value into the win-curve, I estimated the probability of a team reaching the postseason at each win total and multiplied that percentage by the total opportunity. For example, let's assume a team would realize an estimated stream of revenues with an NPV of $30 million from reaching the postseason. Since the estimated probability of reaching the postseason with 92 wins is 77% and the probability at 93 wins is 84%, incorporated in the "value of the 93rd win" for our hypothetical team is 7% × $30 million, or $2.1 million. (This $2.1 million reflects the postseason and World Championship combined value but does not include the win dollars—the amount of attendance, broadcast, and all other revenue a team would earn in the current season by being a 93- rather than 92-win team.)

3 | Winning by the Numbers

For an MLB team, it pays to win, but in the local market-driven structure of MLB the spoils of victory can range from pennies to millions of dollars. The rewards for winning vary based on three key variables: an economic system driven by the size and fan loyalty of a team's local market; the team's level of competitiveness, defined by its regular season record; and the team's windfall of revenues from reaching the postseason. The win-curve is an attempt to quantify the implicit contract each team has with its fans, season ticket holders, and sponsors. At various levels of competitiveness—conveniently measured by annual win totals—fans will spend varying amounts of time and money to support their favorite ball club. The more successful the team, the greater the fan and sponsor support, and hence the higher the revenue totals.

To sort out these effects for each team, we can turn to the regression analyses to estimate the win-curve for each team. By analyzing historical data that capture fan behavior, we can ultimately assign an estimated dollar value for each win.[1] More specifically, the model estimates the change in a team's revenues at various levels of regular season wins. For example, the Houston Astros are expected to generate $1.2 million more as an 81-win team than as an 80-win team. That's equivalent to saying the value of the Houston Astro's 81st win is $1.2 million. At the extremes the Pittsburgh Pirates' 71st win generates about $300,000 in incremental revenue, compared to the $4.2 million that accrues to the Yankees for their 90th win. Later we will discuss the Yankees in more detail, but first let's examine the differences across markets and teams. Since the win-curves are not linear—meaning all wins are not valued the same—and the slope of the curve varies by team, an apples-to-apples comparison looks at the changes in teams' revenues at the same point on the win-curve. Figure 3.1 shows the value of the 81st win—the marginal or incremental value of the last win for a team that plays .500 winning percentage baseball for a season. Alternatively, we can think of the value of the 81st win as the difference in revenue for the team if it won 81 rather than 80 games for the season.

Figure 3.1: The Dollar Value of the 81st Win

Highest Value		Middle Value		Lowest Value	
Team	$ Value	Team	$ Value	Team	$ Value
NYM	1.4	CHC	1.0	ARZ	0.7
ATL	1.2	CLE	1.0	KCR	0.7
SFG	1.2	PHL	0.9	DET	0.7
HOU	1.2	Average	0.9	SDP	0.6
SEA	1.2	TOR	0.9	BAL	0.6
BOS	1.2	LAD	0.8	MIN	0.6
NYY	1.1	MLW	0.8	OAK	0.6
LAA	1.1	TBD	0.8	TEX	0.5
CWS	1.0	COL	0.7	CIN	0.5
STL	1.0	FLA	0.7	PIT	0.5

$ Value in Millions, based on 2006 win-curve.

FIGURE 3.1 **The value of the 81st win.**

When evaluating a team's marginal revenue at the 81st win level, the value is nearly entirely related to fans' immediate response to regular season wins. Since the probability of an 81-win team reaching the playoffs is 2%, only a small portion of the playoff revenue stream is included in the 81st win calculation. By contrast, if we look at the value of the 90th win (Figure 3.2), we incorporate more of the value of the postseason revenue stream, as well as capture the fans' response to a highly competitive winning ball club. Some teams' rankings change considerably when comparing the two different points on the win-curve. The Mets, Mariners, Giants, Yankees, Red Sox, White Sox, and Cardinals remain in the top one-third of

Figure 3.2: The Dollar Value of the 90th Win

Highest Value		Middle Value		Lowest Value	
Team	$ Value	Team	$ Value	Team	$ Value
NYY	4.3	BAL	3.0	COL	2.4
NYM	4.2	TOR	2.9	TBD	2.1
CHC	3.8	CLE	2.9	FLA	2.1
SEA	3.8	HOU	2.9	ATL	2.1
LAD	3.6	Average	2.8	MIL	2.0
CWS	3.5	TEX	2.8	OAK	1.8
SFG	3.5	LAA	2.7	CIN	1.8
PHL	3.4	ARZ	2.7	PIT	1.7
STL	3.3	SDP	2.6	KCR	1.7
BOS	3.0	DET	2.5	MIN	1.6

$ Value in Millions, based on 2006 win-curve.

FIGURE 3.2 **The value of the 90th win.**

revenue for all teams for both win levels. However, the Braves move from 2nd-highest at 81 wins, to 23rd at 90 wins, possibly reflecting Braves fans' weak response to their team appearing in the postseason and their relative apathy to a competitive team.

It's also interesting to evaluate the revenue change over five-win increments. For example, if we look at the marginal revenue when a team moves from the 86- to 91-win level, it sheds light on a team's economics in a playoff contention mode. Alternatively, we can think of the marginal revenue from the 78- to 83-win level as the economics of teams' quest for respectability. The marginal revenue totals in the latter case are more clustered than the marginal revenue for teams in playoff contention. To measure the dispersion of the value of wins for each category, we can look at the standard deviation across all teams. The standard deviation of the respectability category is $1.2 million, as opposed to $3.2 million for the playoff contention category. This difference may suggest that as a team moves up its win-curve to become a playoff contender, the rich get richer and the poor get poorer. The implication is that weaker-revenue teams can effectively compete with the "big boys," as measured by the value of a win, when both have noncontending status. However, when teams strive to reach that 90+ win zone in their quest for a playoff spot, it becomes more difficult for the economically challenged teams to compete for players with the high-revenue or high-fan-loyalty teams.

Included in the 86- to 91-win playoff contention marginal revenue estimate for all teams is a portion of an anticipated revenue stream that would accrue to the team for reaching the playoffs. The economically advantaged teams typically expect a higher postseason revenue stream, further separating them from their weaker-revenue counterparts and making it difficult for the disadvantaged teams to justify competing for players in the free-agent market.

A team's location on the win-curve—their absolute level of wins—has a dramatic impact on the value of a win. To understand the power of the win-curve location, you only have to look as far as the marginal revenue of a Twins team in playoff contention. A five-win improvement for financially challenged Minnesota, from 86 wins to 91 wins, would yield $6.8 million in incremental revenue. When comparing this revenue estimate with teams who are striving for respectability (the 78- to 83-win category), their marginal revenue is greater than all teams, except the Mets. The location on the win-curve is so important that it often trumps market size as the key driver of a team's marginal revenue opportunity (see Figure 3.3).

Figure 3.3: "Respectability" vs. Playoff Contention
$ Value of 5 wins—78 to 83 vs. 86 to 91

Team	78-83	86-91	Team	78-83	86-91	Team	78-83	86-91
CHC	4.8	15.9	OAK	3.0	7.7	SDP	3.3	10.8
NYM	7.1	18.0	STL	5.1	13.9	ARZ	3.6	11.3
LAD	3.8	15.1	PHL	4.5	14.5	BAL	3.1	12.3
BOS	5.8	13.3	HOU	5.9	12.5	NYY	5.6	18.4
LAA	5.2	11.8	SEA	5.8	16.1	CIN	2.6	7.5
CLE	5.0	12.5	MIL	3.8	8.5	COL	3.7	10.2
TOR	4.3	12.5	TEX	2.7	11.4	PIT	2.3	7.3
CWS	5.2	14.9	MIN	3.0	6.8	TBD	3.9	9.1
SFG	6.2	15.2	DET	3.4	10.4	FLA	3.5	9.0
ATL	6.1	9.6	Avg.	4.2	11.7	KCR	3.6	7.4

$ Value in Millions, based on 2006 win-curve.

FIGURE 3.3 **Five-win increments. The quest for respectability versus playoff contention.**

Differences in Teams' Win-Curves

The slope of the win-curve can vary across teams, reflecting the degree of fan responsiveness to changes in wins. Comparing the Yankees to the Braves illustrates two extreme examples. Yankee fans maintain high expectations regarding their team's competitiveness and expect the Yankees to win and reward them accordingly. To think about this in the reverse, or negative, we could say that if the Yankees don't contend for the postseason, attendance and fan support would drop precipitously, as the team would fall far short of fan expectations. The result is a steep win-curve. Conversely, the Braves have a long-standing, loyal fan base, which seems to be unfazed by their consistent success, leading to a flat win-curve. A comparison of the two win-curves shows that the Braves generate more marginal revenue until 89 wins, when the two lines cross and the Yankees leave the Braves in the dust from a marginal revenue standpoint. Moving from the 89- to 99-win level on the win-curve, the Yankees generate nearly $16 million more in marginal revenue than the Braves (see Figure 3.4).

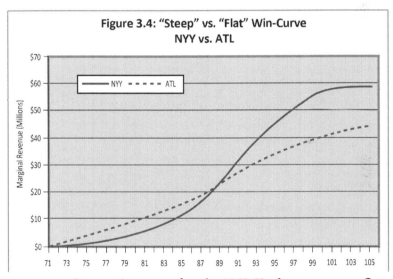

FIGURE 3.4 **Steep win curve for the N.Y. Yankees versus a flat win-curve for the Atlanta Braves.**

The Braves' difficulty in filling the stadium for postseason games may be an indicator that fans aren't as responsive to changes in the winning percentage. Since win-curves shift over time, it may take their recent fall from the National League East Division Championship perch before fans fully appreciate what they had for the past 15 years. Once the taste of success is no longer fresh in the mouths of Braves fans, they may once again crave it and be more willing to support a contending ball club. Another possible explanation for the Braves flat win-curve centers on their lack of World Championships. Generally, reaching the playoffs carries significant weight with fans because it represents a one-in-eight lottery ticket on a World Championship. With 14 consecutive playoff appearances, the Braves could only muster one World Championship in five trips to the Fall Classic, despite winning 100+ games more than six times. Perhaps the inability to convert a powerful winning machine with a formidable pitching staff into more than one World Series winner has left Braves fans jaded and cynical about trips to the playoffs.

Win-curves are estimates of a team's win–revenue relationship at one point in time, but several factors can influence the way the curves evolve over time. If a team's brand marketing efforts are successful in establishing a deeper connection with its fans, the bottom portion of the win-curve (the 70- to 80-win range) may flatten as increased fan loyalty cushions the revenue declines as a team falls from contention. Another factor that can affect a team's win-curve is competition from other sports. During the mid-1990s Cleveland temporarily lost its NFL team after it relocated to Baltimore. When pro football returned to Cleveland, the Indians' win-curve shifted. The new Cleveland Browns were another season ticket alternative for local fans and another major pro sports team on which companies could choose to spend their advertising and sponsorship dollars. The win-curve shifted in such a way that the Indians would need to perform at a higher level on the field to reach the same level of revenues.

One team that continues to be an enigma is the Chicago Cubs. On the one hand, the Cubs' revenue impact from changes in *regular season wins* is in the middle of the pack. Despite their large market, the high degree of loyalty from Cubs fans and the allure of Wrigley Field insulate their revenues in years when the team fails to contend, while stadium capacity limits their upside in contending years. When looking only at "win dollars," the portion of their win-curve that estimates revenue from the regular season and not the playoffs, the Cubs have a relatively flat win-curve. However, when the Cubs reach the postseason, their fans are expected to reward them handsomely. A postseason appearance will generate about $39 million in revenue for the Cubs over the following four to five years. When including "postseason dollars" in the calculation, the Cubs win-curve steepens considerably, implying that their large, loyal fan base will reach deep into their pockets to reward a playoff appearance.

On the surface this may appear to conflict with the already high attendance levels at Wrigley Field, even without producing a contender. If we think of the model's estimates as some form of demand curve, then it is incumbent on the team's management to find a way to monetize that demand in the face of limited capacity. The Cubs situation seems very similar to where the Red Sox were prior to 2003: a very popular team drawing near-capacity crowds, with the hopes of winning but no assurance of how to reap the financial benefits from winning. The Red Sox became very creative with new seating: Green Monster seats, right-field roof deck, the EMC Club, the Pavilion Club, and Pavilion Box seats, offering a unique vantage point to view a game. This enabled the Red Sox to significantly increase their average ticket price by building value for fans at the high end of the ticket-price spectrum. As the team won its first World Series in 86 years, these new seats, along with NESN, their team-owned regional broadcast network, became the key vehicles to monetize the demand from winning.

Think of the win-curve as a promissory note from fans to their favorite team that reads, "We the fans pledge certain amounts of our time, money, and attention to our favorite team, corresponding to various levels of on-field performance." It is still incumbent on the team to place themselves in a position to collect on the promissory note, with available seating capacity, strategic ticket pricing, a lucrative broadcast arrangement, and other creative sources of revenue. The Cubs may need to take a page from the Red Sox playbook in order to capture the demand that is reflected as opportunity on their win-curve.

THE FOUR LAYERS OF REVENUE IN THE WIN-CURVE

The win-curve is considerably more complex than simply measuring how many more fans attend games when a team wins 90 games compared to 80 games. Any estimate of the win–revenue relationship needs to capture the *multiple revenue streams* (attendance, local broadcast, concessions, local sponsorships, etc.), as well as *multiple layers of revenue* (win dollars, postseason dollars, World Series dollars). Before we discuss the fourth layer of the win-curve in greater detail—the erosion or accretion to baseline revenues—here is a short summary to define and clarify win dollars, postseason dollars, and World Championship dollars (see the sidebar in Chapter 2, Measuring the Win–Revenue Relationship, for a more detailed discussion of the methodology used to develop the win-curve):

- *Win dollars* represent the change in attendance, broadcast, concession, and other local revenues, based on the team's regular season win total. This represents the classic win–revenue relationship with the most direct and immediate payout. The win dollars are based not only on current year wins, but also on previous year wins. Season ticket sales and renewals and even a portion of individual and group ticket sales are greatly influenced by *last year's wins* and the off-season activity, which often influence fan expectations. By defining wins as a combination of current year and previous year, the win-curve attempts to capture this important lagged affect.

- *Postseason dollars* represent the probability of reaching the postseason, multiplied by the postseason revenue opportunity—the incremental revenue stream that is expected to accrue to the team from reaching the postseason. Although teams receive some net revenue from playing postseason games, particularly since their incremental player compensation is virtually zero, most of the financial benefit occurs over the next four to five years. Unlike *win dollars*, which are measurable in the current year, *postseason dollars* are largely forecasted revenues for future years, based on reaching the postseason in the current year. This includes future attendance increases driven by new season ticket subscriptions, higher broadcast ratings, additional sponsorship demand, and merchandise sales and other revenues that are stimulated by the increased popularity of a playoff-bound team.

- *World Championship dollars* are defined as the *additional* kicker to revenues if a team goes beyond just reaching the playoffs and wins the World Series. The Chicago White Sox experienced this following their 2005 Championship. In the months preceding the 2006 season, their season ticket sales increased beyond all expectations. Fans jumped on the bandwagon and basked in the glory of the World Series victory and purchased guaranteed access to future postseason games. This potential revenue stream is factored into the valuation of a win by adding 12.5% of the estimated value of winning the World Series to the *postseason dollar* estimate. The 12.5% reflects a one in eight chance that a playoff-bound team will win the World Series.[2]

The last layer of revenue impacting a team's win–revenue relationship is a longer-term effect we'll call the *erosion or accretion to baseline revenues.* It is the cumulative, long-term effect of successive winning or losing seasons and its impact on a team's baseline revenues—the revenues a team can expect if it wins 70 or fewer games. The model's estimate of baseline revenues are based on a team's current and recent past history of wins.

These revenues are not guaranteed in perpetuity to a team for simply showing up and taking the field. If a team wins 58, 56, and 62 games for three consecutive years, as the Kansas City Royals did for 2004 through 2006, baseline revenues will begin to erode. Fans are apt to become disgusted with the team and its lack of competitiveness, triggering an overall decline in fan interest and the value of the team as a brand. Baseline revenues will consequently decline. Conversely, if a team performs like the Yankees from 2001 to 2006 (see Figure 3.5), the opposite affect will occur. Baseline revenues will increase as fan expectations rise and the brand further cements its image as a winner in the minds of fans. The revenue base at the hypothetical 70-win level will increase. So the win-curve estimate of the marginal revenue a team gets from, say, 95 wins is tacked on top of the new, higher base of revenues. Think of it as more of an upward shift of the win-curve in the case of accretion (Yankees)—baseline revenues rise—or a downward shift in the win-curve in the case of erosion (Royals)—baseline revenues decline. Analyzing chronically winning or losing teams makes to possible to estimate the long-term effect, in the form of a change in baseline revenue, of a team that suffers three or more successive seasons of fewer than 70 wins or three or more successive seasons of more than 95 wins.

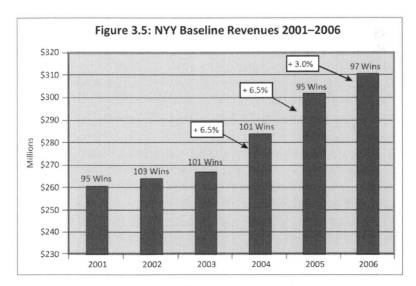

FIGURE 3.5 **N.Y. Yankees baseline revenues and wins.**

The recent Yankee teams are an example of the accretion to baseline revenues effect. As a chronically high-performing team their on-field success has helped increase the demand for the product among fans. That demand can come in the form of either additional tickets sold, higher viewer ratings, or fans' willingness to accept higher ticket prices. Using the 2006 Yankees as an example, the team won 101, 101, and 95 games for 2003, 2004, and 2005. In exchange for these successive 95+ win seasons, the team can expect a 3% increase in baseline revenues—0.6% for each win over 90 for a third consecutive year. In the context of the Yankee ticket price increase prior to the 2006 season, fans are willing to fully absorb three percentage points of the 3.4% increase in 2006 ticket prices without a negative effect on ticket sales.[3] Had the Yankees not raised ticket prices in 2006, we could have expected a 3% increase in attendance (assuming the team performed at the same level as in 2005). Figure 3.5 illustrates the changes in Yankee baseline revenues beginning with the effect of their 95 win season in 2001.

Baseline revenue accretion or erosion is not actually contained in the sloping win-curve, but it affects the *starting point* of the win-curve. An increase or accretion to baseline revenues from a perennial winning ball club will affect the *total* revenue of a team but not directly affect the marginal revenue—the value of any individual win.

To better understand the win-curve, we can break out its component parts and examine the layers. Some teams' win–revenue relationship is dominated by their win dollars (fan response to changes in regular season wins), while other teams' win–revenue relationship is driven by postseason dollars. (Later in this chapter we will describe how postseason revenue dollars are affected by how recently and how often a team has reached the postseason.) Another way to characterize each team's win-curve is by ranking teams in the top, middle, and bottom one-third across both marginal and baseline revenues (see Figure 3.6). The three-by-three grid tells us which are the low-revenue teams (the lower-left corner of the grid) and the high-revenue teams (the upper-right corner of the grid). There are not many surprises in the nine low-revenue teams, other than possibly the Tigers, whose residence in the lower-left corner is probably due to their chronic losing over a number of years until their stellar 2006 season. A few more 90-win seasons and they will no doubt extricate themselves from the low marginal–low baseline revenue category. One potential surprise in the top-right, high marginal revenue–high baseline revenue box is the Seattle Mariners. However, on nearly every dimension the Mariners behave like a high-revenue team, sometimes referred to as a "large market team." Having one of MLB's most popular stadiums and the strong tradition of winning during the early A-Rod, Griffey, Jr., and Randy Johnson years have contributed to their success. Their recent poor teams threaten their status in the top tier, but the Mariners certainly have the financial incentive to improve the club and watch the fans come streaming back to the ballpark in droves.

The White Sox, Indians, Astros, and Cardinals have a somewhat

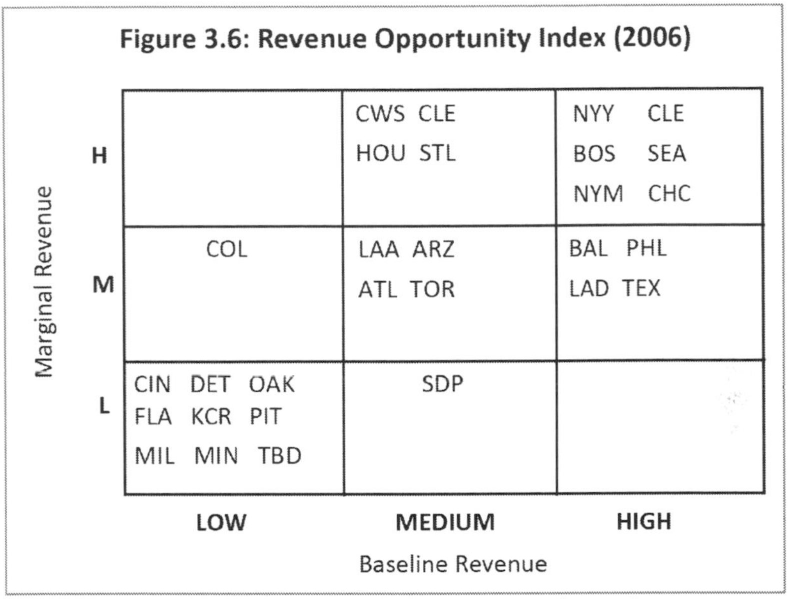

Figure 3.6: Revenue Opportunity Index (2006)

Marginal Revenue	LOW	MEDIUM	HIGH
H		CWS CLE HOU STL	NYY CLE BOS SEA NYM CHC
M	COL	LAA ARZ ATL TOR	BAL PHL LAD TEX
L	CIN DET OAK FLA KCR PIT MIL MIN TBD	SDP	

Baseline Revenue

FIGURE 3.6 **Profiling each team's win-curve through revenue opportunity.**

smaller fan base than the big boys but do not lack fan responsiveness when their teams perform well. This high marginal revenue–medium baseline revenue category can be termed, "if you win, they will come." Conversely, the Orioles, Phillies, Dodgers, and Rangers have a substantial, strong baseline level of support, but fans are somewhat less responsive to supporting a winner. Revenues increase with winning, but for fewer than one-third of the teams, some of which reside in smaller markets. These teams tend to have a high level of competition from other sports teams, which have solid, loyal followings, such as the Cowboys and Mavericks in Dallas, and the Lakers in Los Angeles.

POSTSEASON: THE GAME CHANGER

The pot of gold awaiting a team for a trip to the postseason is a component of the economic equation that can have a dramatic effect on a team's win-curve and, ultimately, the value of its players. The methodology used to estimate the postseason revenue stream follows sound logic and was validated by observation, publicly available information, and discussions with baseball insiders. It begins with the model's estimates of a team's baseline revenues but incorporates increases in revenues based on the team's achievement of playoff status. Using the Chicago White Sox as our example, the baseline revenues (the local attendance, broadcast, concessions, merchandise, and all other revenue the team could be expected to generate from a 70-win season) were estimated at approximately $100 million heading into the 2005 season. The kicker for reaching the postseason is estimated to be 8.5% of *baseline revenues* for the first year following a team's *first* postseason appearance. (Later we will discuss the impact of successive postseason appearances and the diminishing impact on revenue growth.) For the White Sox, 8.5% of baseline revenues would translate into the sale of about 4,000 incremental full-season equivalent (FSE) tickets, generating incremental revenues of about $17 million in the first year.[4] The assumption is that reaching the postseason generates an increased level of interest, excitement, and enthusiasm among the local fan base, including businesses, *equivalent to a 13% increase over 2005 per-game attendance*.[5] The revenue increase could come in the form of more tickets sold *or* fans absorbing ticket price increases.

Over the past 15 years, teams that have reached the postseason have increased ticket prices for the following year by an average of 10%, compared to teams that did not reach the postseason, whose ticket prices rose less than 6%. This spread of over four percentage points in ticket price increases can be attributable to a strategy to monetize the value of the increased fan demand from reaching the playoffs. Since the White Sox did not return to the postseason in 2006, despite a 90-win season, we would expect some level of attrition on these new-found FSE's. A portion of them may drop off for each of the next three years, until the fifth year following the postseason appearance, when there is no residual value remaining, and the team's revenue is back to where it would have been had they never reached the playoffs. The net present value of this revenue stream is one of the motivating factors (beyond ego) that inspire teams to spend in the free-agent market and strive to reach the playoffs. For teams with larger baseline local revenues—usually larger markets—the spoils of October baseball can be even greater.

For the White Sox, the value of reaching the postseason in 2005 is estimated to be approximately $28 million, with over 60% of the benefit realized in 2006 (this does not include the value of winning the World Series, which will be discussed separately).[6] The teams with the greatest impact from reaching the postseason for the *first time* are the Yankees ($55 million), Cubs ($39 million), Mets ($37 million), Dodgers ($34 million), Red Sox ($34 million), and Mariners ($31 million).[7] In the case of the Cubs and Red Sox, owing to limited stadium capacity, much of the increased demand would be monetized via ticket price increases, increased broadcast ratings on NESN, or means other than substantial attendance increases. On the other end of the spectrum, the teams that have the lowest return from reaching the postseason for the first time are the Royals and Twins ($14 million), Brewers ($17 million), A's ($18 million), and Pirates ($19 million). Even in the case of the smaller-market clubs, the postseason can generate a revenue stream with a net present value equivalent to 20–25% of their annual local revenues.

What happens when a team reaches the playoffs in successive years, or in the case of the Red Sox, three or four years in a row, or in the extreme case, the Atlanta Braves' run of 14 consecutive seasons? Is the impact the same in each successive year? While reaching the playoffs in successive years does add to the revenue stream, clearly there are diminishing returns. The validation of a team's efforts that comes with reaching the postseason for the first time can shape fans perceptions about a team's ownership, its management, and its players. The second time around is much less of a revelation, but it does reinforce that the team is a winner and, more importantly, has a successful formula to reproduce a winning season. When measured against the value of a *first playoff appearance,* there is an approximately 75% effect for the second consecutive playoff appearance, 50% for the third, and about 30% for the fourth and any consecutive playoff appearances thereafter.[8] An exception to that is the Atlanta Braves, who at 14 straight postseason appearances test the limits of this logic. There is no longer any incremental revenue for each successive Braves appearance in the postseason.[9] With their difficulty selling tickets for playoff games, there hardly appears to be a positive carryover to the following season.

By analyzing the revenues of World Series winners in the years following their championship, we can also estimate the value of "winning it all" to each team's revenue opportunity. The teams with greatest financial impact from winning a World Championship are the Yankees, Mets, and Cubs, all of which are in the NPV range of $25–35 million. This is in addition to the postseason revenue stream. For the 2005 Champion White Sox, an additional $18 million for winning it all can be added to their $28 million for simply making the playoffs. Chicago's glamour season of 2005 generated an estimated total NPV of $46 million in additional revenue.

WHICH TEAMS ARE IN THE DRIVER'S SEAT?

Each year a handful of teams have a chance, or at least the economic motivation, to dominate the market for free-agent players, based on the postseason revenue opportunity that faces them. This list of teams changes from year to year, based in part on whether or not a team has recently made the playoffs. If they have, they may drop down on the incremental revenue opportunity ranking. The Yankees are an example of this. Despite being the most popular, highest-value team brand in MLB and residing in the largest market, the Yankees continuous presence in the postseason has clearly reduced their incremental revenue opportunity from returning yet another time. Each successive postseason appearance by the Yankees results in *only* $34 million in incremental revenue, approximately 7.5% on a base of nearly $400 million in total revenues.[10] The size of the Yankees' revenue opportunity ranked them sixth in postseason revenue opportunity among all MLB teams in 2006. Figure 3.7 shows the value of successive playoff appearances by Yankees.

When the Yankees leadership, from Steinbrenner to Cashman to Torre to Jeter, proclaim that the season is not a success unless they win the World Series, they are speaking not only emotionally, but also with an implicit understanding of their team's economics. Since the club is destined to generate an estimated NPV of about $27 million if they win a Championship, nearly double the amount of revenue from just reaching the postseason, they are an "economic failure" when they do not bring home the trophy, particularly when measured against their league highest payroll.[11]

While the Yankees have the steepest and richest Win $ revenue curve (the amount of incremental revenue generated from improving regular season wins), who benefits most from reaching the postseason? While this can vary each year, in 2006 it was clearly the New York Mets. Having been absent from the postseason since 2000, they finally regained the attention of local fans with their strong finish to the 2005 season, setting up high expectations going into the 2006 season. Converting this optimism into their first postseason appearance in five seasons is destined to unlock some serious pent-up demand for tickets, broadcasts, and merchandise. The fact that much of the Mets success is built around young players (Beltran, Reyes, and Wright) who are each under contract thorough 2011 gives fans even more reason to be excited about the team's future.[12]

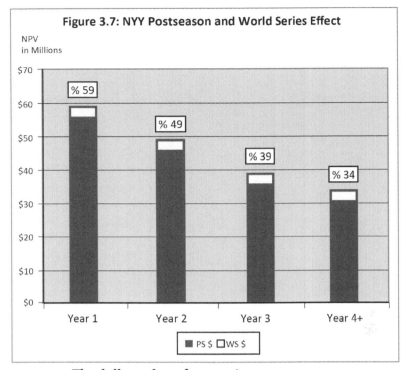

FIGURE 3.7 **The dollar value of successive postseason appearances by the N.Y. Yankees.**

Since reaching the 2006 postseason was worth a league-leading $37 million NPV in future revenues for the Mets, they clearly were aggressiv in adding the "last piece of the puzzle"—the player who would vault them into October baseball. Prior to the season they outbid rivals for star closer Billy Wagner, made the highest offer to catcher Bengie Molina (which he declined, only to sign for less with the Blue Jays), and traded for high-priced slugger Carlos Delgado. With Pedro Martinez and Tom Glavine ripening on the vine, the Mets realized it was now or never to make their move for the playoffs. When combining the Mets' location on the win-curve—arguably a preseason pick to win 88+ games—with the size of their market and their league-leading playoff bounty, it's no wonder that the Mets were in the catbird seat as they approached the free-agent market in early 2006. If there was a player they wanted, they had better financial justification than any other team, but since there are diminishing returns from successive playoff appearances, the power is apt to shift from year to year based on several factors, including the length of a team's dry spell from the postseason. With the Mets' appearance in the 2006 postseason, the power shifts for the 2007 season. The teams that stand to gain the most from returning to the postseason are the Cubs, Giants, and Mariners. While they each have significant ground to cover to thrust themselves into contention, doing so would financially justify the bold moves that could get them over the top and into the playoffs.

WIN-CURVE LEADERS

Evaluating which teams generate the most marginal revenue at different points on the win-curve helps us understand which teams are economically advantaged or disadvantaged. If we assume teams behave rationally, then teams that can generate the most incremental revenue at various points on the win-curve could afford to pay the most for those wins in the player market. There are two distinctly different ways to assess the amount of marginal revenue a five-win improvement in a team will generate: standardizing the number of wins for each team, or using a *forecast or expectation* of each team's win level. Figure 3.3 shows the marginal revenue from a five-win improvement for each team as an 86-win team improving to a 91-win team. This five-win improvement is located at the "sweet spot" on the win-curve—the portion of the curve that has the steepest slope and represents the highest dollar value—representing the impact from increasing the odds of reaching the postseason.

To get a sense of a team's location on the win-curve heading into a season, we can look at the value of each team's five-win improvement beginning with a *preseason prediction* of a team's win level. Using the familiar over–under betting line from one of the popular betting services, we can get a more realistic snapshot of how a team's marginal revenue opportunities may evolve over the course of the season.[13] Figure 3.8 divides the MLB teams into highest, middle, and lowest with respect to the marginal revenue opportunity from a five-win improvement, using the 2006 preseason win expectations as the location on the win-curve. This is a potentially more realistic way of valuing a team's *next five wins*, rather than looking at each team's estimated marginal revenue from the same point on the win-curve.

Dominating the lowest third of revenue opportunity are teams that are expected to win 64 to 77 games and are out of contention, with one notable exception—the Yankees, who have the opposite problem. At a preseason expected win total of 100 for 2006, there is very little value in improving the team to 105 wins. The result is a five-win value of approximately $1 million for the mighty Yankees. However, let's not ignore another potential

Figure 3.8: 2006 Value of a Five-Win Improvement Based on Pre-Season Predicted win Total								
Highest Value			Middle Value			Lowest Value		
Team	$ Wins	$ Value	Team	$ Wins	$ Value	Team	$ Wins	$ Value
CHC	85	14.8	SFG	81	8.1	SDP	77	2.9
LAD	85	13.9	OAK	88	8.0	ARZ	74	2.5
NYM	91	13.4	PHL	81	6.8	BAL	76	2.4
TOR	86	12.6	STL	94	6.6	CIN	74	1.9
LAA	88	12.4	SEA	75	4.7	PIT	75	1.8
BOS	90	12.4	MIL	80	4.3	COL	68	1.6
CLE	90	10.8	TEX	80	3.6	NYY	100	1.1
CWS	91	10.6	MIN	80	3.5	TBD	67	1.0
ATL	89	9.6	DET	77	3.0	FLA	67	0.7
HOU	83	9.3				KCR	64	0.4

$ Value in Millions. Wins based on pre-season over-under from sportsbettingstats.com

FIGURE 3.8 **Value of five wins based on preseason predictions.**

interpretation of the Yankees fate. While the Yankees stand to gain little from *improving* the team's win total. They have a much larger incentive to *protect* the 100-win level. Should they backslide by five wins to 95 wins, they stand to *reduce their revenues by $12.5 million* and reduce their probability of reaching the postseason by eight percentage points. Given the high financial stakes that surround the Yankees' business proposition, it seems like there will always be a way to justify their high spending level—if not for revenue gain, then at least for protection of revenue.

Teams that produce wins at the extreme high end of the win-curve may challenge the model's ability to measure the marginal value of a win. The argument could be made that if a 100+ win team produces a runaway division title, it could contribute to reduced attendance at September home games. Since the games are not expected to be meaningful, star players can be rested to prepare the team for the postseason and fans will be focusing on attending games in October, when they are once again meaningful. Comparing the Yankees' 2004 and 2005 seasons seems to validate this point. In 2004 the 101-win Yankee team won its division but, more importantly, qualified for the postseason by 10 games. The 95-win, 2005 team qualified for the postseason on the next to the last day of the season, in a nip and tuck battle with the Red Sox. The 12 home dates after Labor Day in the 2005 "nail-biter" season produced an average of 52,600 fans, while the last 12 games in the 2004 "cake-walk" season yielded an average of 42,000 fans. Using this example and the specific circumstances surrounding it, the Yankees arguably generated $3 million *less* revenue with their 101-win season than the 95-win season.

Estimating the value of a win, using the win-curve, can be an insightful tool for MLB teams' decision makers. At a minimum, it will give the baseball executive an understanding of the sensitivities of each of the complex variables (location on the win-curve, size of market, loyalty of local fans, and performance of a player) when making a player personnel decision. For example, this analysis would allow the Blue Jays to say, "For B.J. Ryan to be worth $9.5 million per year, he would need to deliver an incremental five wins to what already was an 84-win team, or six wins to an otherwise 82-win team." This information could enable a team to better match player salaries with revenue expectations. This does not mean a team should be a slave to the marginal revenue estimates and decline to sign a player solely on the basis of the costs exceeding the revenues. To the contrary, it may be appropriate under certain circumstances to consciously pay a player more than he can deliver in marginal revenue. If a sought-after player becomes available while the team is moving up the win-curve, it may make sense to overpay him for a year or two while the team is still in its building phase. Investment spending can be a logical well-thought-out approach to ultimately assembling a winning team and can contribute to building the long-term value of the franchise. (The notion of value-creation measures, other than the revenue categories included in the win-curve, will be discussed further in the final chapter.) There is a big difference between understanding the degree to which your team is investment spending versus acquiring a player with the hopes that "it all comes together" and he delivers a return on your investment. The best-managed teams, at a minimum, evaluate the cash flow, or franchise value implications, of a player acquisition, even if it is purely a judgment exercise without the use of any analytical models.

Endnotes

1. The win curve is the statistical estimate of the relationship between a team's revenues and its regular season wins.

2. When valuing the *postseason* or *World Series dollars* prospectively, I use the probability of the event occurring times the value (NPV) of the revenue stream. However, when valuing either on a retrospective basis, I add the entire revenue stream if the "event" is achieved.

3. Yankees 2006 ticket price increase from TMR's web site, *www.teammartketing.com/fci. cfm?page=fci_mlb2006.cfm.*

4. All public reports indicate that this estimate is conservative and that incremental attendance due to the postseason and World Championship run may be low.

5. This increase could come in the form of, say, 1,500 full season ticket sales and 6,000 partial season tickets or any other combination that ultimately adds up to 3,900 additional fans per game for the 2006 season.

6. For the White Sox, the $28 million also imputes an increase in broadcast revenues. Because the length and terms of contracts vary, it is difficult to generalize about the impact. However, I generally assume that broadcast revenues will increase by 20% for a duration of two years.

7. A first-time appearance in the postseason is defined as reaching the postseason after an absence of three consecutive years.

8. The Yankees are an outlier, as the value of the postseason declines at a slower rate. Their sustaining value of reaching the postseason is approximately $34 million, about 57% of the value of reaching the postseason for the first time. One reason the decline is less steep than most other teams is the inclusion of a high ($32 million) value of winning the World Series, which does not decline with successive wins.

9. I estimate there to be no incremental revenue in future years from reaching the postseason. However, there are direct revenues associated from playing the postseason games (i.e., concessions, merchandise sales, etc.).

10. This estimate includes an NPV of $30 million for reaching the postseason, plus an additional $4 million (12.5% of the potential $32 million) the Yankees would gain if they won a World Championship.

11. Figure 3.7 reflects only $3.4 million as the value of a World Championship to the Yankees, which reflects a one-in-eight probability of a $27 million payoff for winning the World Series.

12. Beltran is signed through 2011; Reyes through 2010, with a club option for 2011; and Wright is signed through 1012, with a club option for 2013. Data from Cot's Baseball Contracts, *http://mlbcontracts.blogspot.com/2004/12/new-york-mets.html*.

13. Preseason 2006 over–under betting line from *sportsbettingstats.com*.

PART TWO

PLAYER DOLLAR VALUE

Everyone inside and outside of baseball has an opinion on how much a player is worth. With millions of young people aspiring to someday vie for approximately 800 jobs in Major League Baseball, one would think those who do make it to the "big show" would play for nominal wages. While the Players Association will no doubt take some credit for state of ballplayer salaries today, the reality is that a player's value is highly sensitive to his skill level and ultimately his performance. One reason why ballplayers can demand multimillion dollar contracts (and teams pay them) is simple math—the best players help teams win, and wins generate revenue.

Chapter 4, "Player Valuation: The Model," combines the win-curve analysis (discussed in the previous section) with a player's ability to generate wins for his team. In doing so we examine the situational nature of a player's dollar value. A nine-marginal win outfielder on a 67-win Pirate team may have less value than a 3-marginal win outfielder on an 88-win Dodger team. Despite Jason Bay's impressive performance, he may have contributed less revenue to his team than Andre Ethier's performance earned the Dodgers.

In Chapter 5, "Player Value: Loaded with Options," we discuss aspects of a player's value other than his pure performance, such as his marquee value, a star player's gate appeal and his power to contribute to building his team's brand. We also quantify a player's trade value and discuss how the year-to-year variation in a player's performance and his injury propensity could affect his worth to a team.

In Chapter 6, "Valuing the Babe in his Yankee Years," we apply much of the player valuation discussion to a treasure trove of financial data from Babe Ruth's Yankee years to estimate his dollar worth to the club for his 15 years of stardom.

4 | Player Valuation: The Model

At a time when sabermetric tools can diagnose a player's performance better that an MRI can detect a rotator cuff tear, measuring the dollar value of a player seems to have lagged far behind on the analytical priority list. Admittedly the topic is a bit on the periphery of mainstream sabermetrics—so much so that there does not seem to be a consensus as to the methodology or metric to establish a player's dollar value. There are essentially two fundamentally different analytical approaches to the issue—the cost approach and the marginal revenue approach—each with several variations. Using the cost approach, one would calculate the going rate for a certain level of performance by comparing players' salary levels and their performances. An example of this approach is employed by Bill Felber in his book *The Book on the Book*. In his chapter "What a Player is Worth," Felber discusses a concept he calls "earned value" (EV).[1] He examines the salaries and win contributions of all shortstops (stipulating that value metrics should be position specific) and uses the average compensation per unit of performance as a benchmark. Felber's earned value is the player's performance times the benchmark going rate. This leads to an EV for Alex Rodriguez's 2003 season (his last with the Texas Rangers) of nearly $11 million. One of the shortcomings of this approach is the implication that average value can be defined as the amount a club is willing to *pay* for a player's performance, on average. (Felber does acknowledge that this methodology presumes that players at any particular position are collectively compensated reasonably.)

Several factors blemish the relationship between salary and player value. First, there are three salary classes of players: restricted players (less than three years of MLB service), arbitration-eligible players (between three and six years of MLB service), and free agents (more than six years of MLB service). These classes lead to dramatic differences in pay, even for similar performances. For example, in 2005 arguably two of the top shortstops in the American League were Jhonny Peralta (8.1 WARP [Wins Above Replacement Player]) of the Indians and the Yankees' Derek Jeter (9.5 WARP). The salaries of Peralta and Jeter were $316,700 (the MLB minimum) and $19,600,000, respectively. For a player like Peralta, who has less than three years of service and has not yet reached arbitration or free-agent eligibility, salary has no relationship to performance. Perhaps if the MLB player market consisted entirely of one-year agreements and all players were free agents after each season, salaries would be a more reasonable proxy for value.

Applying the cost-based approach exclusively to the free-agent market could be called a market-based valuation. While the market-based approach to player valuation eliminates the problems mentioned above, because it deals only with free agents, it still raises some questions. If two players perform at the same level, but one is in the first year of a new contract while the other is in the fifth year of a free-agent agreement, we might expect significant differences in pay. Prior to the 2001 season, both Manny Ramirez and Alex Rodriguez signed mega-deals worth more than $20 million per year over the life of the contracts. Through the 2006 season, no deals have matched the magnitude of these agreements. Two of the highest-profile position players to sign free-agent agreements since Ramirez and Rodriguez are Miguel Tejada and Vladimir Guerrero. While all four players are high-impact talents who have the potential to have a dramatic impact on a team, the agreements signed prior to the 2004 season are clearly at a lower compensation level than those of A-Rod and Manny. Signed one month apart prior to the 2004 season, Tejada signed with the Orioles for $72 million over six years, while Guerrero signed with the Angels for $70 million over five years.

Has the market softened since 2001, or have less-worthy players come into free agency? With the 2002 CBA and its robust revenue-sharing provision and luxury tax, one could make the argument that team's economics have been altered, with the revenue-sharing tax reducing teams' marginal value of a win. For teams taxed at a 39% marginal tax rate, the value of each additional dollar of revenue is only 61¢. A player whose marginal wins generate $10 million in gross revenue only delivers $6.1 million to the team's coffers. No doubt, the 2007 CBA will once again alter the economic landscape and affect player value. The early assessment of the new agreement suggests that the marginal tax rates will be reduced, and, more importantly, reduced by a greater amount for the lowest-revenue teams. It is expected that teams will pay approximately 31% in revenue sharing, down considerably from the estimated 39 to 47% resulting from the 2002 CBA. A player's value to a team that was paying 47% and will now pay 31% will increase substantially. Under the new agreement, the $10-million marginal-revenue player will now generate $6.9 million in net revenue for his team, rather than $5.3 million.

Another factor working against player salaries as a benchmark for value is the differing mindsets across team ownership groups. Every team will not take the same approach to free-agent signing decisions. Some may take the marginal value approach and attempt to estimate the true economic value to the team and make a salary offer accordingly. Others may react to a windfall of revenue, such as from the sale of the Washington Nationals, the dramatic success of MLBAM, or the new Fox television contract. If the team asked, "How can I spend $20 million more on payroll in the most productive way?" they might take a different approach to free-agent bidding. These two approaches could translate into very different salaries for comparable players. In the latter example, the team may be closer to the "winning is everything" end of our continuum that balances winning versus financial returns. However, assessing an owner's motivations is a dangerous business, better left to psychologists. Even actions that appear to be financially irrational may be due to a different set of assumptions regarding the team's economics. For example, when Jeffrey Loria invested aggressively to produce a winner in South Florida, he expected the financial windfall from his World Championship to include a publicly funded stadium. Had he been correct, his costly actions to assemble his 2003 Championship team, along with the resulting revenues, might have been viewed as economically rational.

Applying our learning from the win-curve models in the previous chapter, we can recognize other disconnects between salary and value. If a general manager is unrealistically optimistic about his team's quality (i.e., he views them as an 85-win team rather than a more realistic 80-win team), he may likely overpay for a player in the free-agent market. Furthermore, the win revenue curve analysis indicates that a player's value is situational and varies by team and level of competitiveness. Therefore, a player's salary at best would represent a player's value to only one team, at one point on the win-curve.

While the cost-based and market-based approaches *imply* a player's value (based on a salary a team is willing to pay), the marginal revenue approach used in this chapter attempts to directly measure a player's economic value. This approach also has its challenges, as it requires considerably more detailed analysis built on a set of fragile assumptions. The foundation of this approach is dissecting a team's revenue components and estimating how they fluctuate with the team's on-field performance (discussed in detail in the previous chapters). This chapter focuses on the core of a player's marginal value or worth: the *marginal revenue a player's performance is expected to generate for his team.* (The next chapter will discuss additional measures to develop a more complete picture of a player's value and the risk factor of his expected performance and his trade value.) By converting a player's on-field performance into his impact on his team's wins and then translating those wins into attendance and revenue, we can quantify his dollar value to his team (see Figure 4.1).

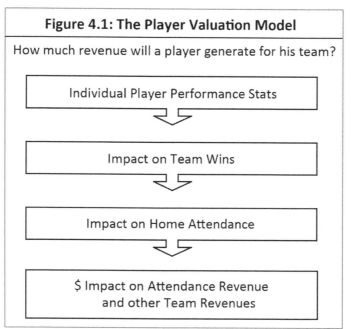

FIGURE 4.1 **The player valuation model.**

This player valuation model answers the question, "How much more revenue are the Angels expected to earn because Vladimir Guerrero is their right fielder (and sometimes designated hitter)?" For the 2005 season, the model estimates the Angels' revenue with Guerrero's 594 plate appearances versus what the Angels' revenue would have been without Guerrero, but with a replacement player playing right field and taking his 594 plate appearances.

The first portion of the player valuation equation—measuring a player's performance in terms of his impact on team wins—has been the subject of much debate in the sabermetric world. As a result, many measures have been developed to convert a player's offensive stats into team wins. Win Shares (Bill James), Win Shares Above Bench (Dave Studenmund), Win Expectancy (Tangotiger), and Wins Above Replacement Player (WARP1) (Keith Woolner and the team at *Baseball Prospectus.com*) are some of the options. Indexing performance to replacement level simplifies the valuation process, as it provides a benchmark against which to measure a player's marginal value. This chapter uses WARP as the benchmark, but includes WSAB as the metric for valuations in the sidebar, The Replacement Level Dilemma, and Figure 4.B. (For a more detailed discussion of replacement level measures, see the sidebar.) These benchmarks allow us to translate any player's performance in *marginal wins* above that of a replacement player.

The next portion of the player valuation equation focuses on converting a team's wins into a team's dollar revenue. More specifically, it translates *marginal wins* attributable to a player into expected *marginal revenue* for the team, net of any revenue-sharing tax payments. This portion of the model builds on the work discussed in the previous chapters—the establishment of win-curves for each team. Each win-curve is a team-specific estimate of the relationship between a team's win total and the revenue it can expect to generate, based on market size, the loyalty of a team's fans, and ticket prices, while adjusting for other revenue drivers, such as a new stadium, player strikes, and work stoppages.

To illustrate how the player valuation model works, let's continue with the example of Valdimir Guerrero's value to the 2005 Angels. Guerrero's WARP value for the 2005 season is listed at 8.2 (at *Baseball Prospectus.com*), implying that his offensive and defensive performance (versus that of a replacement player) were responsible for 8.2 of the 95 Angels' wins for 2005. In other words, if the Angels gave his 594 plate appearances and his innings in right field to a replacement player, they would have won approximately 87 games. Plugging his performance into the estimated win-curve for the 2005 Angels, estimates Guerrero's value to be $17,143,000[2] (see Figure 4.2). Had the Angels employed a replacement player instead of Vladimir Guerrero and everyone else had performed at the same level, the Angels would have generated about $17 million less in revenue from ticket sales, broadcast, concessions, parking, and so on, net of revenue-sharing taxes.

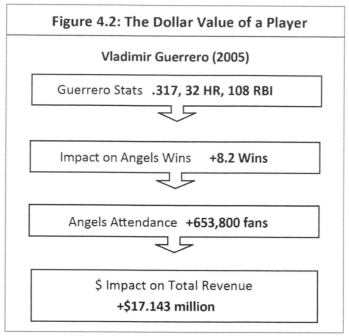

FIGURE 4.2 **The value of Vladimir Guerrero to the 2005 Angels.**

By expanding on the Vladimir Guerrero case study, we can better understand the components of a player's value. A player's performance contributes to revenue in three ways: revenue associated with an increase in regular season wins, the NPV of the potential revenue stream from improving the probability of the team reaching the postseason, and the NPV of the potential revenue stream from the probability of winning the World Series. By fielding a competitive, 95-win ball club with Guerrero (versus an 87-win team without Guerrero), Angels fans rewarded the team with approximately $9.9 million in incremental revenue. In addition, Guerrero's 8.2 wins raised the Angels' probability of reaching the postseason by 68 percentage points (from 24% at 87 wins to 92% at 95 wins). The NPV of the multiyear revenue stream the Angels are expected to generate from a 2005 postseason appearance is approximately $10.3 million. By improving the probability of achieving the postseason revenue stream by 68%, Guerrero generated an additional $7 million in expected value.[3] Finally, by simply improving his team's chances of reaching the postseason, Guerrero also gives his team a one-in-eight chance of wining the World Series. The World

Series effect is worth another $0.6 million. Figure 4.3 provides greater details for these calculations.

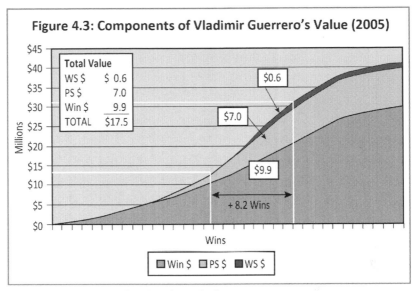

FIGURE 4.3 **Layers of value for Vladimir Guerrero.**

Another approach that bears some resemblance to our analytical framework is employed by Baseball Prospectus author Nate Silver in *Baseball Between the Numbers.*[4] While Silver focuses on measuring the dollar value of a player based on the marginal revenue the player generates, he does not differentiate a player's value based on the team for which he plays. While Silver acknowledges there is likely a difference in a 5-win player's value if he plays for an 80-win Kansas City Royals team or an 80-win New York Mets club, he stops short of estimating what those differences may be. One of the underpinnings of the analysis discussed throughout this book is to differentiate the value of a win, and hence a player's value across markets, as well as differentiating teams within a market. In our analysis each team's win-curve is unique, and a five-win player would have a different value to each team—even the Mets versus the Yankees.[5] Furthermore, the market-to-market differences in the value of a win are not driven only by market size. Fan loyalty, rather than market size, helps explain the strength of the win-curve in markets such as St. Louis and Seattle. (This effect is discussed in more detail in Chapter 10, The Value of Fan Loyalty.)

THE TEAM FACTOR

The team for which he performs has a significant impact on a player's value. In the previous chapter we saw the differences in the value of a win (or the same group of wins) across teams, reflecting a unique win-curve for each team, which translates directly into differences in player value. This uniqueness is driven by the size of the market, the loyalty of a team's fans, and management's ticket pricing practices, among other factors. To demonstrate the impact of team on player value, let us compare the value of a 5-marginal-win (WARP) player responsible for improving his team from 84 to 89 wins. For example, Orlando Cabrera's 2006 season added 5 wins to the Angels, helping them achieve 89 wins for the year, leading to a value of $9.9 million. If we compare his $9.9 million value to the Angels with every other team *at the same point on the win-curve,* we can see the wide range in value, measured by estimates of the marginal revenue his performance would generate for each team (see Figure 4.4). The New York Mets and the Yankees are at the high end of the scale with a value of $14.6 million, while the Minnesota Twins are at the low end of the value scale at $5.6 million.

Figure 4.4: The Value of a 5-Win Player on an 89 Win Team

Team	$ Value	Team	$ Value	Team	$ Value
NYM	$14.6	BAL	$10.6	COL	$8.1
NYY	$14.6	HOU	10.5	TBD	7.4
SEA	12.9	CLE	10.1	FLA	7.3
CHC	12.4	TOR	10.0	MIL	7.1
SFG	12.3	LAA	9.9	OAK	6.2
CWS	11.8	ARZ	8.8	KCR	6.2
LAD	11.6	TEX	8.6	CIN	6.0
PHL	11.3	ATL	8.5	PIT	5.7
STL	11.2	SDP	8.4	MIN	5.6
BOS	11.1	DET	8.2		

FIGURE 4.4 **The value of a five-win player on an 89-win team.**

A team-by-team analysis allows us to understand differences in win-curves for teams in the *same* market. By comparing teams in the same market, at comparable win levels, we can determine which team rules the market. We can answer the question "Who rules Chicago?" by playing "what if?" What if Joe Crede were to become a free agent but declared it was a two-team race because he couldn't bear to leave the Windy City? If we assume the Cubs and White Sox were both 85-win teams, anxious to bolster their chances for a playoff run by bidding for a six-win third baseman.[6] Crede would be worth $18.4 million to the Cubs and $17.3 million to the White Sox. Shifting our intra-market comparison to New York, a five-win player added to an 85-win team would add $20.9 million in marginal revenue to the Mets and $21.2 million to the Yankees. While the Mets' ability to hang in the same stratosphere as the Yankees might come as a surprise to some, it reflects the reduced value of the Yankees' postseason revenue stream, resulting from repeated consecutive appearances in the postseason. If the Mets were amidst a run of 10 consecutive playoff appearances like their cross-town rivals, the value of a five-win player would be approximately $16 million, about $5 million *less* than the Yankees.

SITUATIONAL PLAYER VALUE

Going back to our example of Vladimir Guerrero's value, we can see how much of a player's value is situational. It is a dangerous generalization to declare any player to be a "$10-million player," as a player's value depends on the size of his team's market, the loyalty of the team's fans, the team's location on the win-curve (i.e., level of competitiveness), and the player's performance. If Guerrero or Alex Rodriguez or any star player were playing for a 56-win K.C. Royals team, the case could be made that they would have *no performance value.* As legendary general manager Branch Rickey allegedly once said to Pirate slugger Ralph Kiner after another year of leading the National League in home runs, "We could have finished last without you." Since our analysis indicates that there is very little revenue impact from improving from 56 to 62 wins, one could argue that the value of the player in this specific situation is negligible. If we compare the example of the Royals to backup outfielder Gabe Kapler's value to the 2006 Red Sox, we can once again see the power of the situation. Despite a weak .340 OBP, only 103 at-bats, and his modest 0.9 WARP, Kapler's value to the Red Sox was $2.1 million. This means that Kapler, who comes from a limited pool of available player talent, performs beyond the level of a standard replacement player by nearly one full win, which in turn is expected to generate $2.1 million in marginal revenue for the team.

In any given situation, which factors we have discussed have the greatest impact on a player's value—the team and its market, the team's location on the win-curve, or variations in the player's performance? To shed light on this intriguing question, let's use the model to examine several what-if scenarios. To test the sensitivity of the market, or more specifically the team, we can rank all teams from highest to lowest in win value and then compare three team variations: the team at the 25th percentile in win value, the team at the 50th percentile, and the team at the 75th percentile. (To ensure that we are using the same point on the win-curve for all teams, the analysis is standardized to account for six wins, from the 81st to the 87th.) The value of six wins for the lowest-win-value team is $6.34 million; for the mid-level teams six wins are worth $9.13 million, and for the highest-win-value teams six wins are worth $13.26 million. The average variation across the three market groupings (low, medium, and high) is $3.46 million. We will compare this average variation to the average variations of location on the win-curve and player performance scenarios to determine which factor has the greatest sensitivity and, hence, the greatest impact on player value.

To examine the sensitivity of the impact of a player's value to variations in his performance, we can compare the value of a six-win player to two potential variations in his performance: as a four-win player and as an eight-win player. On the average team, with a baseline of 81 wins, the value of a six-win player is $9.13 million, while a four-win player is valued at $4.80 million and an eight-win player at $15.36 million. The average variation across the three performance levels is $5.28 million.

Finally, we can examine the sensitivity of a team's location on the win-curve and its impact on a player's value. Using a six-win player for all teams, we can compare the value of three levels of team competitiveness: a noncompetitive team (improving from 75 to 81 wins), a competitive team (improving from 81 to 87 wins), and a playoff-contention team (improving from 87 to 93 wins). Six wins are worth $3.79 million for the average noncompetitive team , $9.13 million for the competitive team, and $17.89 million for the playoff-contention team is worth. The average variation for the three locations on the win-curve is $7.05 million. While this analysis is in no way conclusive (because arbitrary ranges were used for each variable), it does show the power of the team's level of competitiveness in determining a player's value. Figure 4.5 summarizes the results of this sensitivity test.

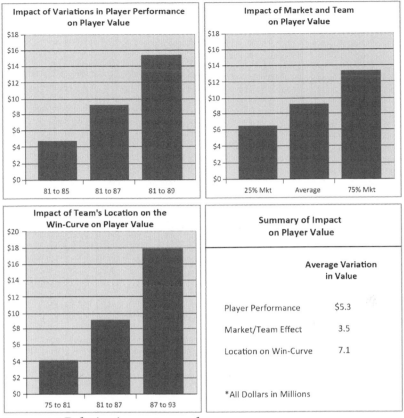

FIGURE 4.5 **Relative impact on value.**

MO$T VALUABLE PLAYERS

Given the importance of a team's location on the win-curve, it will come as no surprise that the players with the highest dollar value to their teams are clustered in the playoff-bound teams. Since the highest-value wins for any team are generally 89 to 92, a team whose players helped them get to that win total will benefit in the form of a higher valuation. Strangely, in 2006 only one NL team (Mets), but six AL teams, reached 89 wins or more. From time to time, a division winner can sneak in at a low win total, as the 2006 Cardinals and 2005 Padres did, but seldom does a wild card team make it to the postseason with just 88 wins, as did the 2006 Dodgers.[7] The highest-value players were clustered in the Mets and Yankees—the two highest-win-total teams in the largest market. Topping the list is Derek Jeter, whose stellar year, coupled with the Yankees strong regular season performance, enabled him to generate $33.7 million for the team with his 9.8 marginal win (WARP) performance. A couple of boroughs away, Carlos Beltran's 10.4 marginal win season for the 97-win Mets was responsible for $31.6 million in incremental revenue to the ball club.

The remaining players in the top 10 of player value are dominated by Yankees, except for David Wright ($25.7 million) of the Mets and Jermaine Dye ($18.5 million) of the White Sox. The other high-value Yankees are Rivera ($26.8 million), Posada ($25.1), Cano ($24.7 million), Wang ($22.6 million), and Mussina ($20.0 million). Noticeably absent from our top 10 is baseball's highest-paid player, Alex Rodriguez, whose mere 5.5 marginal wins in 2006 generated a relatively low $16.8 million. The highest-value players on the remaining 2006 playoff teams are Detroit's Justin Verlander ($14.1 million), the Twins' Johan Santana ($12.8 million), the Dodgers' Rafael Furcal ($12.1 million), the Cardinals' Albert Pujols and Oakland's Frank Thomas (each at $10 million), and San Diego's Adrian Gonzalez ($7.2 million) (see Figure 4.6 for the top 10 highest-value players).

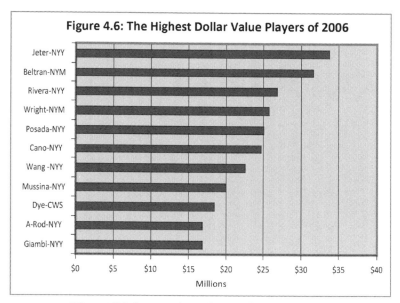

FIGURE 4.6 **The 10 highest-value players for 2006.**

What does the composition of the most valuable player list tell us about player value? By analyzing the player valuation model, there are several clear conclusions regarding the value of players:

Players who help improve their teams along the "sweet spot" on the win-curve (the 85- to 95-win range) have a distinct advantage in creating value. From the previous analysis we concluded that location on the win-curve trumps the size of the market when measuring player value. In other words, value is largely situational—it is dependent on the circumstances. A seven-win player on a 90-win team will generally generate greater value than a seven-win player on a 79-win team. This is based on the logic (and supporting data) that fans are more motivated when their team improves from 83 to 90 wins than when their team improves from 72 to 79 wins. The incremental revenue from improving a noncompetitive team pales by comparison to the incremental revenue generated by a team reaching for a playoff spot. In many cases a three-win player on a 90-win team will create more value than a seven-win player on a 79-win team. For an example of this let's look back to the 2005 season. The Braves' Johnny Estrada, a 3-marginal-win player, generated $5.9 million in marginal revenue for the Braves, while Michael Young, the Rangers All-Star shortstop was winning the AL batting title and playing at a 7.1-marginal-win level, only to generate a modest $2.3 million in revenue for his 79-win team. This is not suggesting that Young should be *paid* less than half the amount of Johnny Estrada. Much of the responsibility of Young's relative low value lies with the Texas Rangers' management. The Rangers failed to surround Young with sufficient talent to make a run at the division title, which would have greatly enhanced his value. If the Rangers were a 90-win team, challenging the Angels for the division championship, Young's value would be approximately $12 million, underscoring the point that the team's location on the win-curve is a key driver of a player's dollar value to his team.

It is a challenge for great players who play on mediocre teams to create significant value. In 2006 Grady Sizemore had a standout season, performing at the 8.5-marginal-win level, while his Indians were finishing four games under .500, 18 games behind the first-place Twins. If a replacement player had taken all of Sizemore's at-bats, the Indians might have won 69 or 70 games. While Indians' fans most likely would have noticed his absence, the estimated difference in revenues would have been only about $2.7 million. However, had the Indians been a 93-win playoff contender in 2006, as they were the previous season, Sizemore would have been worth $15.9 million in incremental revenue. Other standout seasons that did not generate top dollar value in 2006 are listed in Figure 4.7.

As a team improves, particularly above the 85-win level, the value of all *of its players tends to rise. The reverse is also true. As a team gets worse, the value of* all *of its players tends to decline.* Using the 2006 New York Mets

Figure 4.7: Key Players Not in the Top Ten of "Value"

	Marginal Wins	$ Value
• Pujols -STL	11.9	10.0
• Santana-MIN	10.6	12.8
• Berkman -HOU	9.0	5.1
• Mauer -MIN	8.9	10.9
• Howard-PHL	8.6	8.1
• Oswalt -HOU	8.6	4.8
• Morneau -MIN	8.0	9.8
• Ortiz-BOS	7.9	10.2

FIGURE 4.7 **Top-performing seasons that were not the highest in dollar value.**

as an example, let's look at how a player's value changes when team performance changes. The 2006 Mets were a 97-win playoff team, with some key performances from a nucleus of young stars: David Wright (8.6), Jose Reyes (5.6), and Carlos Beltran (10.4). What if things were a bit different in 2006? Suppose the supporting cast underperformed and the team won only 86 games, despite the same performances by their three young stars. As the team moves down along the win-curve, the value of *all* its players declines. Figure 4.8 shows the value of the same Mets players, in a 97-win versus a 86-win scenario.

The fact that the *team's performance* greatly affects player value underscores the logic of *not* trying to match value with salary in all situations. A team's management and ownership are largely responsible for team performance, which is beyond an individual player's control. If a team enters a season with the ownership and management's expectation that it is an 83-win team, but it finishes the season at 75 wins, the value of all of its players will be lower than expected. Even a player who performed at his expected level will contribute less to a 75-win team than to an 83-win team. It is unreasonable to ask players to bear the risk of team performance, since the ownership and management are responsible for overall team performance. When a team underperforms its management's expectations, it is reasonable for the *team* to bear the risk of overall team performance and the resulting decline in the value of all of its players.

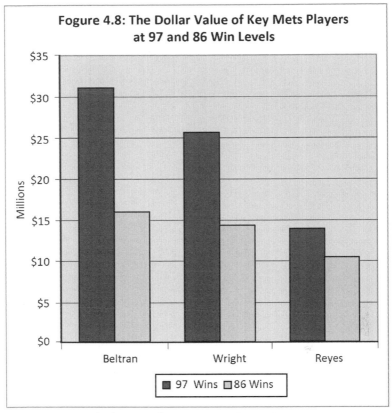

FIGURE 4.8 **Mets' player values at 97 and 86 wins.**

We can also look at player value from another vantage point: the difference between the player's compensation and the amount of revenue he generates for his team. This surplus value is the dollar return the team makes on the player's performance, *net of his compensation*. While high-performing players on playoff-bound teams have a high valuation, they may not top the list of surplus value. Let's look at the Yankees Mike Mussina as an example. Mussina's 6.3 marginal wins in 2006 were worth $20 million in revenue, but the Yankees paid Mussina $17 million for his services, yielding a modest surplus value of only $3 million. On the other hand, the Phillies' Ryan Howard generated $8.1 million in revenue, but with his $355,000 salary, his surplus value is $7.7 million.

The most common profile for high-surplus-value players is star rookies (low compensation) on playoff–contention teams (high marginal revenue). The Red Sox' Jonathan Papelbon was an 8.2–marginal-win performer in 2006, yielding $11.2 million in revenue, at a salary of only $350,000. The star free-agent player is more of an exception on the high-surplus-value list. Carlos Beltran is the most notable exception, with a surplus value of $18 million. Deducting Derek Jeter's $20 million salary from the revenue he generated yields a surplus value of $13.7 million. However, many free agents, particularly those with teams that are out of the running for the postseason, have salaries that *exceed* the incremental revenue their performances generate. The highest-surplus-value players of 2006 include David Wright at $25.3 million and Robinson Cano at $24.3 million (see Figure 4.9 for the highest-surplus-value players).

Figure 4.9: Highest Surplus Value Players (2006)

Player-Team	Surplus $	Player-Team	Surplus $
Wright-NYM	$ 25.3	Reyes-NYM	$ 13.4
Cano-NYY	24.3	Jeter-NYY	13.1
Wang-NYY	22.2	Granderson -DET	13.0
Beltran-NYM	18.0	Verlander -DET	12.3
Rivera-NYY	16.3	Proctor-NYY	11.0
Posada-NYY	16.1	Papelbon -BOS	10.8
Valentin -NYM	14.0	Mauer-MIN	10.5
Dye-CWS	13.5		

Dollars in Millions

FIGURE 4.9 **Highest-surplus-value players for 2006.**

THE LAST PIECE OF THE PUZZLE

The economics of winning dictate that a team's level of competitiveness has a dramatic impact on a player's value. There is little glory or marginal revenue from improving a 69-win team by six wins. The revenue gains from improving a 79-win team by six wins are somewhat larger but pale in comparison to improving an 89-win team by the same six wins. In the latter case the player acquisition that generates the six-win improvement can be considered the last piece of the puzzle—the elusive bullpen stalwart, power hitter, position player, or starting pitcher who, when added to the roster, can add five or more wins and elevate an 85- to 90-win team into serious contention for a postseason spot. A disproportionate number of five-plus-win free agents tend to gravitate to teams seeking the last piece of the puzzle. These can be teams that are legitimately one potential player away from contending for the postseason or teams that *perceive* themselves as being one player away. Possibly falling into the second category are the 2005 Toronto Blue Jays. Despite finishing the 2004 season with an 80–82 record, the Jays' GM, J.P. Ricciardi, approached the off-season determined to thrust his team into contention in the highly competitive AL East. In addition to trading for power-hitting third baseman Troy Glaus and solid first baseman Lyle Overbay, Ricciardi aggressively attacked the free-agent market. He landed two notable, high-profile free agents, left-handed closer B.J. Ryan and right-handed starter A.J. Burnett, signing both players to five-year contracts for $47 million and $55 million, respectively. These signings caught many baseball insiders by surprise as they wondered how the Blue Jays could possibly justify the apparent premium paid for the two pitchers.[8]

A look at the Blue Jays' win-curve and the expected performance of the two stars may shed some light on Ricciardi's thought process. Let's start by assuming each pitcher can perform at the six-marginal-win level over each of the next five years. This is comparable to Ryan's last year as an Oriole and a bit higher than Burnett's historical performance, but is certainly consistent with his perceived upside. The key determinant of the players' value is the Blue Jays' location on the win-curve. If both Ryan and Burnett perform at the six-win level, and the supporting cast plays at a level that allows the Blue Jays to win 93 games, the value of Ryan and Burnett would be $11 million each per year. However, if the supporting cast performs at a lower level, and despite six-win performances by both pitchers the team wins only 83 games, then each star pitcher generates only $3.2 million in value to the Toronto club. Figure 4.10 shows the value of a six-win player at various win levels for the Blue Jays.

The financial justification for Ricciardi's signings hinges on the win level for the Blue Jays over the five-year term of the Ryan and Burnett contracts and the performance levels of the two stars. If the team wins 91 games or fewer, the value of a six-win player is less than the average annual salary of either player. If either star performs at the five-win level, it would take a 93-win performance by the Blue Jays to generate a value of $10 million, which would exceed Ryan's average annual salary but fall short of Burnett's. Since these numbers include the value of *reaching the postseason for the first time,* another factor to evaluate when weighing a long-term contract is the reduced value of reaching the postseason in successive years.

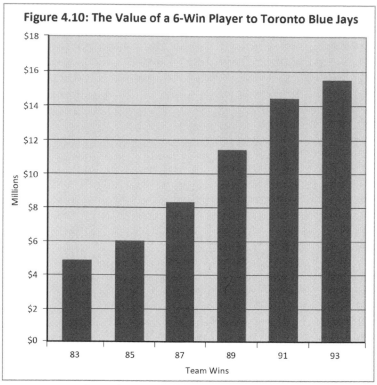

FIGURE 4.10 **Value of a six-win player to the Blue Jays.**

Since there is a diminished value for consecutive postseason appearances, reaching the playoffs for three consecutive years could reduce the value of a Blue Jays' six-win player by $1.5 million.[9] This analysis may imply that J.P. Ricciardi judges his team to be a 93-win club ready to challenge the Yankees and Red Sox for the AL East title, or at least a wild card spot in the postseason, as a 93-win team would seem to justify the compensation he has paid these two sought-after free agents.

When a team signs a free agent who played for a division rival, there is an additional dimension to incorporate into the value calculation. In addition to potentially strengthening the signing club, the signing may weaken the rival team. The signing of closer Billy Wagner by the New York Mets prior to the 2006 season illustrates this "double effect" of an intra-division free-agent signing. Let's assume Wagner to be a six-marginal-win player, replacing a two-WARP Braden Looper as closer for the Mets. Additionally, let's assume other off-season moves made by the Mets management—trades for catcher Paul LoDuca and slugger Carlos Delgado—elevated them to an expected 85-win team for the 2006 season prior to the Wagner signing. To value Wagner, we would calculate the value of a six-win player on an 89-win Mets team, yielding a value of $16.4 million. Now let's incorporate the expected impact of the Wagner defection on the Phillies into *his value to the Mets*. Assuming the Phillies were expected to be an 88-win team with Wagner, if he is replaced by a four-marginal-win Tom Gordon, Wagner's defection to New York would relegate Philadelphia to being an expected 86-win team. Taking into consideration the error rate of preseason estimates, by weakening the Phillies, Wagner's signing improves the Mets' probability of reaching the postseason by an *additional 5 percentage points* beyond the normal probability at 89 wins. The additional 5 percentage points lead to $1.9 million in additional value to the Mets for the Wagner signing, raising his total value to $18.3 million.

Understanding the value of a player, as measured by the marginal revenue he generates by improving his team, can provide important insight for managing the financial aspects of an MLB team. By deepening their understanding of their team's win-curve and translating it into player value, a team will better understand when they are investment spending rather than generating ample revenue to cover their player compensation costs. While the analytical framework outlined in this chapter adds considerably to the dialogue on how much is a player worth, it focuses mainly on the core of a player's value, his *performance value*. The following chapter will introduce other potential components of a player's value that are not directly related to the playing-performance impact on his team's wins. These factors include the *drawing card* aspect of a player—his *marquee value*—as well as his trade value, reflecting his potential worth to teams other than his current employer. The next chapter will also address the historical variability in a player's performance (i.e., not all five-marginal-win shortstops are the same) to quantify the risk factor associated with the variability in a player's performance.

Endnotes

1. Bill Felber, *The Book on the Book* (Thomas Dunne Books, 2006), pp. 193–196.
2. The model calculates the marginal revenue from Guerrero's performance to be $15,162,000. His value equals the marginal revenue, less the cost of a replacement player, $317,000, the approximate ML minimum salary in 2005.
3. Expected value is equal to the probability of an outcome times the value of the outcome.
4. Nate Silver, *Baseball Between the Numbers* (Basic Books, 2006), edited by Jonah Keri, pp. 174–198

5. Another unique aspect of my model is that I have defined the relationship between regular season wins and attendance as nonlinear. As wins increase (between 75 and 95), revenues increase at an increasing rate.

6. This Assumes that both teams' alternatives to Crede at third base were replacement players.

7. The implication of the distribution of wins in 2006 is that few NL players (other than Mets players) are credited with high dollar values, as their teams were not in the sweet spot on the win curve.

8. Ryan and Burnett contract details from Cot's Baseball Contracts web site, *http://mlbcontracts.blogspot.com/2005/01/toronto-blue-jays_05.html*.

9. A six-WARP player for a 93-win Blue Jays team in the season following 3 consecutive playoff appearances would have a value of $10.5 million versus $11 million in value for a team that had not previously reached the postseason.

The Replacement Level Dilemma

In one of his many moments of brilliance, Bill James, the father of baseball statistical analysis, was able to distill a player's on-field performance stats—batting, fielding, and pitching—into the player's contribution to his teams wins, elegantly called "win shares." At the time, this new metric answered so many questions that it inspired the *next* generation of questions, such as, "If Miguel Tejada is responsible for 10 of his team's wins, how many of those games would the Orioles have won if Tejada were not in the lineup?" Replacing Tejada with Chris Gomez or Brandon Fahey, the backup shortstops on the 2006 roster, versus going into the mid-season trade market or late-season waiver-wire market, might yield significantly different answers. If Tejada were to be the victim of an off-season injury that would shelve him for a season, the Orioles would have the luxury of time and even more options, including the free-agent market, to seek a replacement. Defining the standardized quality level of a replacement alternative is an important analytical tool for baseball analysts. Developing a commonly accepted performance level metric that is representative of widely available players, taking into account positional differences, provides a useful baseline for a broad range of analyses.

To say there is no consensus on a metric to capture "replacement level" is an understatement. There is ongoing debate and controversy among expert sabermetricians and baseball analysts even as to its definition. Baseball Prospectus' (BP) WARP comes under criticism from those who feel it sets the baseline too low, primarily from overstating the gap in defensive skills between the regulars and replacement players. We can compute the implicit baseline or replacement level defined by WARP by subtracting a team's WARP from their actual win total. By doing so for all MLB teams for the 2005 season, replacement level is defined as 24 wins, the equivalent of a .148 winning percentage team.

In an effort to advance the industry's collective knowledge and understanding, even the experts at BP are willing to challenge their own (and each other's) thinking and continuously improve their metrics. BP author Nate Silver has developed a concept he calls "Freely Available Talent" (FAT), which may improve upon the definition of replacement level. This metric captures the higher degree of defensive difficulty, and hence fewer substitutes for high-skilled positions, namely shortstop. While FAT adds to the list of potential definitions of replacement level, it has yet to be converted into a published stat with individual player values. Fortunately, BP does not have a monopoly on sabermetric concepts

→

and measures. Dave Studenmund at *The Hardball Times* has developed his own version of baseball's baseline level of performance, Win Shares Above Bench (WSAB), a lineal descendant of Bill James' original work defining Win Shares. Putting WSAB to the same 2005 test—subtracting a team's WSAB from their actual win total—results in an implicit bench level defined as 53 wins, the equivalent of a .327 winning percentage.

Beyond the usual supply differences by position (e.g., the scarcity of shortstops because of the physical demands of the position, etc.), replacement player availability is influenced by multiple factors: the duration for which the replacement player is expected to fill in and the time of year the unexpected need arises. Teams can tolerate nearly any alternative in a pinch and for a short period but are apt to set the bar considerably higher if the replacement player is needed for a longer duration, as he will have a greater impact on overall team performance. If the need arises in the off-season, as in our hypothetical Tejada example, a team can pursue a wider range of options in a relatively "efficient market," than if the need were to occur after the mid-season trade deadline. If a need arises in August, and a team wants to look outside its existing roster and its minor league system, MLB's waiver process serves as a barrier to player movement and market efficiency, limiting the available pool of talent. Figure 4.A is a graph of the *conceptual relationship* among three key factors in the replacement level equation: the duration of the replacement need, the timing of the replacement need, and the quality level that will be acceptable to the team. The horizontal axis represents the overall impact of the replacement choice on team performance—in a crude sense a demand curve for the replacement player. The vertical axis represents the supply side of the replacement player equation, particularly the barriers to efficient player movement.

Our goal is not to settle the debate over the right metric for replacement level, but rather to pick a meaningful measure of "opportunity cost" to use as a calibration point—a baseline against which a player's value can be benchmarked—as an important input into several analyses included in this book, particularly a player's dollar value. It seems that Dave Studenmund's WSAB measure pegs the baseline closer to the "off season need/full season replacement" section of the curve, while BP's WARP stat might be closer to the "immediate need/short-term fix" portion of the curve. While it is likely that neither measure is ideal, and that the best baseline for our purposes may be somewhere in between, WARP seems to be an acceptable choice for player dollar valuation, and the necessary choice for much of the analysis later on in this book. It is an acceptable choice for player valuation because it is more likely

$\longrightarrow$

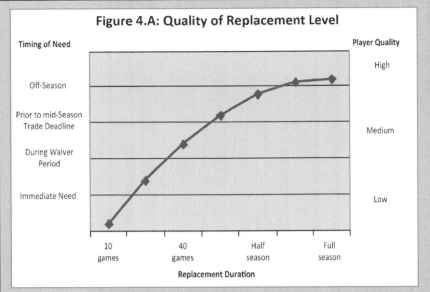

FIGURE 4.A **The timing, duration, and quality of replacement-level players.**

to come with a known cost, the MLB minimum salary, versus the much wider range of talent that populates the bench definition in WSAB. Analyses in later chapters delve into player performance levels over a much longer time frame, making it difficult to find WSAB data. For those staunch supporters of WSAB, a player valuation calculation is included (Figure 4.B) that reflects the use of WSAB as an alternative baseline.

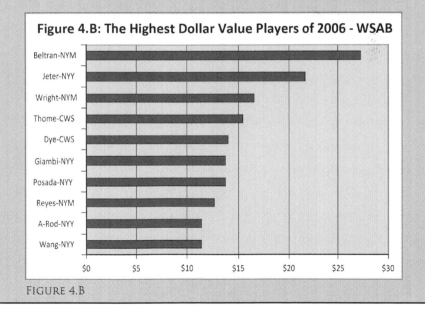

FIGURE 4.B

5 | Player Value: Loaded with Options

In the previous chapter we discussed the player valuation model that focuses exclusively on translating a player's *on-field performance* into the impact on revenue dollars to his team. The other potential source of value, particularly for a star player, is his *gate appeal*, or *marquee value*. Certain players are magnets for fan attention and adoration and have the power to bring people to the ballpark. Pedro Martinez is an enormously popular New York Met with charisma and a palpable intensity that captivates fans. His value to the Mets (at least prior to his injury) goes beyond winning games. Pedro is an admired public figure whose personality and image are assets to the Mets' brand. He sells tickets and merchandise and improves television ratings. Players like Pedro are brand builders. Their positive image carries over to their ball club, and they help contribute to the overall value of the brand and the franchise. An approach to measuring a star player's marquee value is the first topic discussed in this chapter.

Beyond marquee value, two other factors can affect a player's value, particularly when assessing his *future value*: his *expected performance*, including the historical *variation* in performance and his potential value in the trade market—his *resale value*. In previous chapters, much of our discussion regarding player value focused on valuing past performance, using actual performance measures. When evaluating a player's future performance, we must estimate his expected performance in the form of his impact on team wins. The most straightforward prediction may be a point estimate (a mean) such as five marginal wins. If we go beyond a mean performance estimate to forecast a range, we are generating additional information that can be incorporated into the expectation of a player's overall value. A five-marginal-win player who we expect to perform between four and six wins is different than one who shows a historical range that leads us to expect him to perform between three and seven wins. In the latter case, there is greater variation, or risk, for the club, potentially resulting in an adjustment to his value to his team. It may also be important to differentiate the *source* of a player's performance variation, such as the good year–bad year syndrome versus a propensity for injury. A *performance risk factor* can be an important piece of the value equation when evaluating a player's future value.

Finally, it may be important to recognize a player's value to *other teams* in his valuation. The player valuation model discussed in the previous chapter focuses on measuring the player's value in the context of his current team—measuring on-field performance value—and ignores the potential for additional value from owning the player's rights, or his *resale value*. The supply–demand realities of certain positions (e.g., pitching) may increase a player's external value, independent of his performance. Estimating a player's value in the secondary market for players—his value as a liquid asset—requires an understanding of the dynamics of the trade market for players, both during the off-season and at the mid-season trading deadline. In aggregate, these three additional factors—marquee value, expected performance variation, and resale value—can add depth and richness to the measurement of a player's value, with the latter two components being particularly relevant when assessing future value. (For a discussion of the critical variables to consider when valuing a player see the sidebar, Five Musts to Consider when Valuing Players.)

MARQUEE VALUE

This dimension of a player's value is at the core of an ongoing debate that can be summarized by the question, "Do we identify with and root for the *player* or the *laundry*?" As long as we concede that there is *some* relationship between fans and individual players, in addition to fans' attachments to their favorite teams, we are implicitly acknowledging players' marquee value. Some players contribute to their team beyond their on-field performance in ways that don't necessarily translate into wins in the standings. These popular, likeable players have fan appeal and are one reason fans come to the ballpark or tune in their televisions. Who are these players? The easiest way to answer the question is to gaze around the stands at the ballpark and count the names on the backs of the team jerseys worn by fans. In Yankee Stadium you will see Jeter, A-Rod, Matsui, Rivera, and even a few that read "Giambi." In U.S. Cellular Field on the south side of Chicago, it will be Konerko, Thome, Dye, and a sprinkling of Crede and Pierzynski.

Marquee value is the point where the baseball department and the marketing department intersect. Players with marquee value contribute not only to their team's win total, but also to the value of the team as a brand. They personalize the image of the team and provide a face and a personality to go with a logo, often enabling fans and teams to connect with one another in a meaningful and potentially enduring way. Incorporating this component of a player's worth into his valuation is a delicate exercise with little precedent. In the late 1970s a study was conducted to estimate the gate value of one of baseball's first notable free agents, Catfish Hunter, then of the Yankees. The statistical analysis of game-by-game attendance of the 1975 season yielded an impact of over 4,100 additional fans attributable to Hunter, independent of his impact on team wins.[1]

A more current example is Roger Clemens in 2004—his first season as a Houston Astro. Returning to his hometown late in his celebrated career, with an unusual arrangement allowing him to forego certain road trips, Clemens was a hot attraction at Minute Maid Park. Clemens did not disappoint. In 33 starts he turned in an 18–4 record with a 2.98 ERA and 218 strikeouts. This was good enough for his seventh Cy Young Award. In his 20 starts at home, attendance was 1,525 fans per game higher than in the 61 games when other starting pitchers took the hill. At an average ticket price of nearly $25 per seat, that amounts to incremental revenue of over $38,000 per start, or $762,500 for the season. Clemens' drawing power in Houston pales by comparison to the charismatic Pedro Martinez's ability to fill seats at Shea Stadium. In his first year in a Mets uniform, his 16 home starts averaged 5,270 fans *more* than the Mets home attendance when he did not pitch. The popular Pedro Martinez generated nearly $2 million in incremental revenue for the Mets by taking the mound on 16 occasions at Shea Stadium in 2005.

This method of quantifying the marquee value of starting pitchers (attendance on pitching days compared to nonpitching days) is not viable when evaluating an everyday-position player. Also, the method may be a bit too literal, as it attempts to measure fans' short-term response in the form of day-to-day attendance changes.[2] Unlike performance value, which is a derivative of fans' up and down responses to the team's wins and losses, fans' relationships with their favorite players are usually more enduring than yesterday's box score. A marquee player's impact can even transcend his playing career. Any Yankee fan growing up in the 1950s and 1960s can still feel emotion when they conjure images of Mickey Mantle. He is inextricably linked to the image of the Yankees for his generation of fans. The same can be said for Roberto Clemente for Pirates fans in the 1960s, Brooks Robinson for Orioles fans in the 1960s and 1970s, or George Brett for Royals fans in the 1970s and 1980s. Even after a marquee player is traded, he can have a lasting impact on the franchise for which he made his mark. The Mets' Tom Seaver, arguably the greatest player in the history of the franchise, is an example of a player whose value transcends his days in a Mets uniform. As the leader and star pitcher who led a young franchise to a memorable World Championship, Seaver helped personalize the great memories for Mets fans of his era. Despite his trade to the Cincinnati Reds in 1977, with half of his Hall of Fame career still ahead of him, it is impossible to think of the 1969 Mets and *not* think of Tom Seaver.

When attempting to quantify the enduring value of star players, we need to account for their long-term impact. It may make more sense to relate a player's marquee value to the overall brand value of the franchise than to its annual revenues, which can fluctuate based on the team's wins and losses. This approach begins with an estimate of the value of the team as a brand and then assesses the impact of a given player on the brand value. (For more on the brand value of a team, see Chapter 10, The Value of Fan Loyalty.) The team brand value is linked to the baseline revenues a team generates (the revenues associated with a 70-win season), which are independent of a current season's win total. Baseline revenue is the answer to the question, "Even if the team is not competitive in a given year, how many fans will attend games, watch and listen to broadcasts, buy merchandise, etc.?" It's one way to quantify the equity and loyalty intrinsic to the team as a brand. Since MLB teams are thought to be valued at two to three times total revenues, this formula applies a 2.5 multiplier to *baseline revenues* to estimate the brand value. In aggregate the brand value represents about 69% of the total market value of the average MLB franchise.[3]

With the brand value calculation as a backdrop, how do we estimate which players have marquee value, and how do we assess their dollar impact on brand value? First, a player must have the personal qualities that appeal to fans—the "X" factor. Does a player have a positive image? Is he recognizable, articulate, and accessible? These are important considerations in determining his marquee value. A second criterion is a minimum level of performance. It is rare to think of a bench player who has gate appeal or marquee value. We'll use the four-marginal-win level as the line of demarcation—a performance level that generally indicates a regular (everyday) player who makes a substantial contribution to his team. Players with four marginal wins or more are candidates for having marquee value, while players below that level are not.

The third factor is the player's continuity with his current team. It takes time for players to assimilate into a new ball club and be identified with the image of the team. In Alex Rodriguez's first year as a Yankee, he continued to enjoy enormous popularity and maintain his perch as one of baseball's best and most popular players. However, in his first season, he was not thought of as a true "Yankee," but rather as a transplant from Seattle and Texas. The designation of true Yankee was reserved for Derek Jeter, Bernie Williams, and a handful of others. While he possesses *some* marquee value today, it remains to be seen if A-Rod will ultimately come to be identified with the Yankees. In one possible scenario his image will become merged with the Yankee tradition, and his personal popularity will ultimately translate into benefits for the New York Yankee brand. In this scenario we can expect his value as a Yankee asset to go beyond his playing performance.

Finally, in order to quantify a player's marquee value, each of these three factors is considered in relation to the overall brand value of his team. Figure 5.1 captures the formula for measuring a player's marquee value to his team.

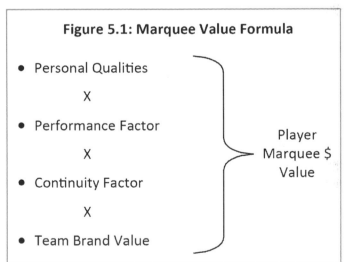

FIGURE 5.1 **Formula for marquee value.**

Delving deeper into the formula, the four criteria for gauging a player's personal qualities are:

Positive image: Usually a player needs to be scandal free and generally thought of as a solid citizen.[4] This can be reflected by his level of community involvement. Fortunately for baseball and baseball teams, many players fit this criterion. Thinking of this attribute evokes images of Bernie Williams touring the shelters in lower Manhattan in the days following the 9/11 attacks on the Twin Towers. His sincerity toward bewildered family members of missing workers from the World Trade Center are emblazoned in the minds of many New Yorkers as a tribute to his genuine care and concern for his fellow citizens.

Recognizability: The player must have an already established identity with fans. The player might be identified with an outstanding attribute, such as being an extraordinary speedster and base stealer or a Gold Glove–caliber defender. He may also be a credible baseball veteran, having achieved some notoriety, perhaps for his past accomplishments with another team.

Accessibility: It is important for the player to be willing to engage the media, the public, and the fans. An example of the ultimate accessible player is Curt Schilling, the Red Sox hurler, who not only answers any question he's asked, but also volunteers answers to questions the media may have forgotten to ask. On the other end of the accessibility scale we have the former superstar pitcher Steve Carlton. At some point during his career, Carlton zipped his lips and refused to comment to the media on virtually any matter. While players like Carlton can have gate appeal and marquee value, it is clearly diminished by their lack of public persona.

Articulateness: A player's marquee value is enhanced if he is an effective communicator and has a solid command of his language.

Players who meet these criteria can enhance the image and brand value of a team. In markets with demographic diversity, certain players can be brand representatives to specific demographic or ethnic segments of the market. Pedro Martinez may be an example of a player who has gate appeal in New York's Latino community beyond his appeal in the non-Latino community. In our marquee value formula, a player need not have a check mark in every one of the four criteria; however, if a player does meet all of the criteria, he will contribute even greater value than a teammate who may have only three check marks. Further, there is a limit to the number of players per team who can truly contribute to the value of the brand. For example, the seventh most popular player on the team most likely has a relatively small impact on brand value. This is not to say that the community service work he does at the local children's hospital is not recognized and appreciated by fans, but that the attention it gets is dwarfed by his higher-profile, more popular teammates. To deal with this issue, we will limit the marquee value to a maximum of six players on any one team.

The formula for quantifying marquee value incorporates two additional factors: a player's level of performance and his tenure on his team. Although a player's performance value is measured separately through on-field performance measures, the marquee value framework does account for the interaction between a player's popularity and his performance.[5] For example, if Albert Pujols and Cardinal catcher Yadier Molina were judged to have the same personal qualities (positive image, recognizability, accessibility, and articulateness), Pujols would still have greater marquee value, based on his overall level of performance as one of the premier players in baseball. The performance factor component of the formula awards a value of 0.1% of the team's brand value for each gate appeal factor the player possesses.[6] Also, continuity can enhance the marquee value of a player, as longer tenure builds a stronger link between the player and his team.[7] Figure 5.2 shows estimates of Derek Jeter's annual marquee value.

To place this valuation approach in perspective, consider that the maximum marquee value generated by the players on any team would be 2.8%

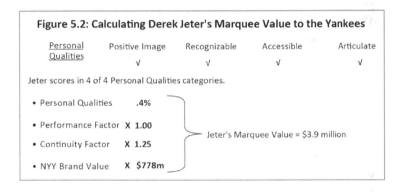

FIGURE 5.2 **Derek Jeter's marquee value.**

of the brand value of that team. Keeping in mind that the brand value is typically less than the total value of the franchise, this approach suggests that possibly 1.5 to 2 percentage points of the annual appreciation in a team's franchise value can be attributed to the marquee value of its marquee players.[8] In recent years MLB teams have been appreciating at a 9.25% rate per year, leaving approximately three-quarters of the appreciation in a team's value to be attributed to such factors as growth in national MLB revenues, the marketing efforts of the team (independent of these marquee players), and the on-field performance of the team.[9] In other words, 75% of the appreciation in the value of a franchise is attributable to the "laundry," while the other 25% is attributable to its most beloved and identifiable players.

While this methodology clearly requires judgment, it is an attempt to quantify a player's public appeal by relating it to the base value of the team he is representing. If, for example, Jeter played for the Kansas City Royals, he would generate only about $680,000 of gate value (0.625% × $109 million). It is no coincidence that when the highest-priced players are floated onto the market for potential trades, such as then–Texas Ranger Alex Rodriguez in December 2003, teams with the highest brand value become the logical acquirers. Teams like the Yankees, Mets, Red Sox, Cubs, and Dodgers stand to gain more in the form of marquee value than teams like the A's, Twins, or Pirates.

In some cases the teams with high brand value are also the teams with the steepest win–revenue curve, benefiting the most from a star player's on-field contribution. This double effect (marquee value + performance value) gives them an edge in the top-tier free-agent market. Several teams, most notably the Dodgers and Orioles, maintain the unusual combination of a high brand value (baseline revenues) but a somewhat flat win–revenue curve. These teams tend to harvest proportionately more value from marquee players than performance value from their stars' on-field contributions. Also, as teams slide backwards down the win-curve (i.e., an 80-win team, rather than a 90-win team), marquee value becomes a larger portion of a player's value, as his performance has relatively less impact on revenues. For example, if Miguel Tejada is responsible for making the Orioles an 80-win team rather than a 72-win team without him, his performance value is $3.2 million. However, his marquee value is not affected by the team's poor performance and is stable at approximately $1.2 million per year. Figure 5.3 shows how players' performance values and total values are affected by their team's on-field success, while marquee value remains stable.

The star players who can claim to have marquee value are an essential ingredient in building the brand value of a team. These players extend the team beyond a logo and a nickname and provide faces to go with the brand. In much the same way that products utilize celebrity spokespersons to promote the brand, a team brand benefits from the positive attributes of its most notable players. These players personalize the team at a level that is more likely to emotionally connect with fans. Of course, this is a double-edged sword. When a star player is connected with a scandalous

Figure 5.3: Performance Value and Marquee Value*

	Team Wins	Performance Value	Marquee Value	Total Value
• Miguel Tejada, Baltimore	90	$15.9	$1.2	$17.1
	80	$3.2	$1.2	$4.4
• Jim Edmonds, St. Louis	90	$17.0	$1.2	$18.2
	80	$6.1	$1.2	$7.3
• David Ortiz, Boston	90	$17.0	$2.6	$19.6
	80	$6.2	$2.6	$8.8
• Chipper Jones, Atlanta	90	$13.3	$1.1	$14.4
	80	$8.3	$1.1	$9.4
• Jim Thome, Chicago WS	90	$18.0	$1.0	$19.0
	80	$6.0	$1.0	$7.0

* $ in millions and assumes 8 WARP for each player

FIGURE 5.3 **Effect of a team's performance on performance value and total value.**

incident, such as Jason Giambi's or Barry Bonds' alleged steroid use, it can negatively impact fans' perceptions of their teams. This is even more likely if the teams are perceived to be complicit in the incident or in any way failed to intervene in the matter. The damage to the team will relate directly to the player's association with that ball club. In Giambi's case he was a Yankee for only a couple of years before the buzz about his alleged steroid use filled the newspapers. The damage to the Yankees is certainly less severe than if the scandal had been associated with Derek Jeter, the immutable Mr. Yankee, whose image is completely intertwined with the identity of the ball cub. Giambi's case is even more complex, as he issued an ambiguous apology to his teammates and fans, presumably (although never explicitly) for using steroids. His apology combined with his resurgent performance has resurrected his image considerably and even made him a somewhat sympathetic figure with many Yankee fans.

In addition to capturing the nonperformance value of a player, marquee value has another logical and important place in the player valuation equation. It is the one component of the player valuation framework that reflects the *change in value of the franchise*. Performance value is measured by the change in *revenues* and does not directly measure any implied appreciation of the franchise. Conversely, because of the enduring effects of prominent players, the marquee value is not focused on annual revenues, but rather on the appreciation in brand value. When combined, the performance value and the marquee value reflect key players' impact on both their team's cash flow (revenues) and market value (brand value).

PERFORMANCE RISK FACTOR

When evaluating a player's dollar value retrospectively, we have the benefit of a player's stats to reflect his on-field performance. We can debate the accuracy or validity of statistics such as WARP or win shares, but we are not forced to guess if the player missed 50 games owing to injury or had an off year that was far below his expected performance. When using the player valuation model to measure past performance, we simply translate on-field performance into financial value. When dealing with *future* performance, we have the additional challenge of estimating the player's *expected* performance before estimating his dollar value. For example,, not all five-marginal-win players are created equal. When a GM assesses the future value of a player, he must forecast both the player's expected performance and the player's *performance risk factor*—the potential variation from his expected performance. If the GM expects a player to generate five wins for each season of a contract, how should the GM view, and more importantly value, the potential deviation of actual performance from his estimate? The financial markets have addressed this question for many years. If two assets have an expected return of 6% per year, but one has virtually no historical variations in its returns, while the other tends to vary wildly from year-to-year, the more stable asset has a higher value. The riskier asset is generally cheaper in order to compensate the owner for the added risk.

Let's delve into this issue and its implications on player value by examining the risk profile—the average WARP and average annual variation in WARP—of selected starting shortstops over a recent five-year period. In Figure 5.4 the *y*-axis is each player's five-year average WARP, while the *x*-axis represents the percent standard deviation of the player's WARP. The upper-left portion of the graph represents high performance (WARP)/ low risk (variation). Two distinct data points that stand out: Alex Rodriguez (from his days as a shortstop) and the Phillies' Jimmy Rollins. Rollins is one of the higher-performing shortstops, averaging five WARP over the past five years (2001-2005), with a miniscule 6% average variation. Conversely, the lower-right section of the graph represents low performance/high risk.

Former shortstop Nomar Garciaparra averaged approximately the same overall performance level as Rollins, but with an astronomical 70% average variation in performance. Another shortstop with a similar average WARP level but high variation is Edgar Renteria. During his last five years (four with the Cardinals and one with the Red Sox) Renteria's average year-to-year variation was 50%.

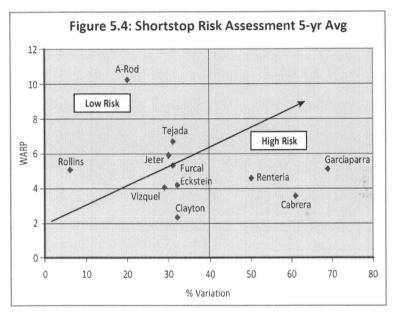

FIGURE 5.4 **Shortstops' WARP and risk.**

INJURY RISK FACTOR

Is there a difference in value for players who are expected to perform at the same level but have significantly different risk profiles? In an academic journal article, two economists empirically evaluated "risky workers" in baseball.[10] One of the hypotheses they set out to test is the notion that the "riskiness of the worker (such as variation in performance) should be positively related to earnings of that worker, just as the variance in the past performance of the stock is positively associated with the price of a call option".[11] They suggest that higher performance variation, equals *higher* player value (although for free agents they conclude there is little correlation.) In this study the authors do not distinguish between the two different sources of variation in player performance, or risk: the *quality* of a player's performance and the *quantity* of his playing time. We can measure *quality* as a rate statistic, such as .05 WARP per game played, while *quantity* can be measured in terms of the number of games played.

The two risk factors have very different characteristics. The variability of the *quality* of a player's performance may be symmetrical if there is an equal chance of a player over-performing or under-performing his expected WARP per game. It's called a good year or bad year. On the other hand, the variability in the *quantity* of playing time for an everyday player is not symmetrical. When evaluating the productivity of an everyday player, a team assumes he will play virtually the full season, say 155 games. Therefore, while injuries can *reduce* his playing time by 20, 30, 40 or more games, his upside is limited to only seven additional games. *The injury risk factor nearly always has a negative effect on expected performance.* (One exception could be the signing of a pitcher during his recovery phase from Tommy John surgery, for example, the Yankees' signing of Jon Lieber in 2003. In this case the pitcher may be paid for two years while expecting to be active for only the second year. Should the pitcher's recovery accelerate, he could provide *upside* to his expected performance.)

In light of this analysis of performance risk, what is the potential impact on player value? A historical variation in the *quality* of a player's performance may have a counter-intuitive effect on a player's value. Even though a player with significant variability might present a greater risk, his potential upside *may more than offset* his potential downside because of the nonlinear shape of the win-curve. When considering only the *quality* of a player's performance, higher variation may even be *preferred* by teams because of the accelerating value of wins as a team moves up the win-curve. However, if a player has a history of missing playing time *owing to injury* (greater than the average injury rate for other players at his position), this will have negative implications for player value. Let's look at three shortstops from our sample to place injury risk in perspective. By comparing the average variation in playing time (number of games played per season) for Rollins, Renteria, and Garciaparra, with the average variation in WARP (from Figure 5.4), we can better understand each player's *source* of variability and determine whether an adjustment to a player's valuation is warranted (see Figure 5.5).

Garciaparra is clearly an outlier on the high side, with much of his variation in year-to-year WARP being attributable to playing time variations from his string of injuries. Jimmy Rollins is an excellent example of

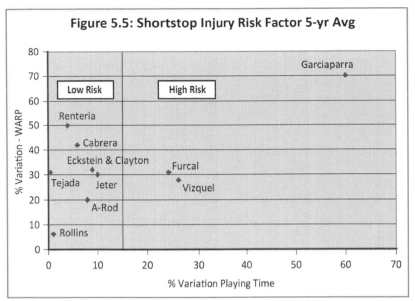

FIGURE 5.5 **Playing time versus WARP variation. (The left side of the figure represents low injury risk and the right side represents high injury risk).**

the low-risk side (as is Tejada), as his playing time has been remarkably consistent over the five-year period. So how do we assign a dollar value—premium or discount—to the risk assessment? The reduced uncertainty regarding playing time clearly has some value to a team. Let's treat past variation in playing time not as a perfect predictor of risk, but as an indicator of future risk and classify historical performance variation (risk) into three levels: high, normal, and low risk. High risk is defined as performance variation that is 50% higher than the position average. Using our shortstop example, the average shortstop five-year average variation in playing time is 14%. A player whose variation is greater than 21% is considered high risk, while a player whose variation is less than 7% is considered low risk. Any shortstop in the range between those levels is considered normal or average risk.

The valuation adjustment coinciding with each of the risk categories is as follows: a low-risk player's value to a team is adjusted up by 10%, while a high-risk player's value is adjusted down by 22%.[12] There is no adjustment for the average-risk player. The valuation adjustment is based on the average dollar value of a win that a high-risk player is apt to cost his team and a low-risk player is apt to preserve for his team. The discount for high-risk players cushions the team's risk in the event of injury. Conversely, greater performance certainty from low-risk performers is worth a premium to the team, despite the player's upside being limited by the 162-game schedule. Figure 5.6 shows the player value calculation for Rollins and Garciaparra—one low injury risk and one high injury risk player.

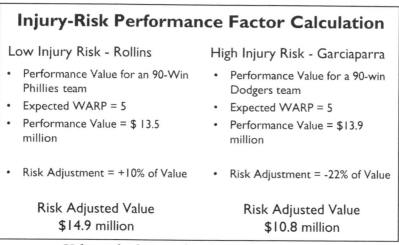

Injury-Risk Performance Factor Calculation

Low Injury Risk - Rollins

- Performance Value for an 90-Win Phillies team
- Expected WARP = 5
- Performance Value = $ 13.5 million

- Risk Adjustment = +10% of Value

Risk Adjusted Value
$14.9 million

High Injury Risk - Garciaparra

- Performance Value for a 90-win Dodgers team
- Expected WARP = 5
- Performance Value = $13.9 million

- Risk Adjustment = -22% of Value

Risk Adjusted Value
$10.8 million

FIGURE 5.6 **Value calculations for shortstops Jimmy Rollins and Nomar Garciaparra.**

RESALE VALUE

Another component of a player's value that goes beyond his performance or marquee value is his resale value. Depending on the time of year, there can be an active, somewhat fluid secondary market for players' services. We observe it constantly in the form of trades. The highest level of trade activity seems to occur in either the off-season or in July as the mid-season trade deadline approaches and teams reset their rosters for the second half of the season run or to shed salary dollars and begin positioning their team for success in future seasons. If a team decides that a player no longer fits with their plans, they will make that fact known and try to begin a dialogue with interested suitors. Conversely, if a team has a need to fill and cannot accommodate it from within their organization, they will scour the market and look for attractive players and their sellers.

The primary reason two teams are able to consummate a trade is simply that the player is *worth more to another team than to his current team*. This is not always because the current team is dissatisfied with the player. A player could have solid value to his current team but even greater value to another team. Let's assume the player was signed on the free-agent market several years earlier, so that every team had the chance to bid for him.[13] There are four potential explanations (beyond personality-related issues, such as "clubhouse chemistry") as to why the player is now worth more to another team—four sources of a change in his valuation. (See Figure 5.7)

Figure 5.7: Four Sources of Change in a Player's Valuation Leading to a Potential Trade

- Player "financially" underperforms...two potential reasons
  - Current team moves down the win-curve and player's value declines
  - Player's on-field performance is worse than expected
- Another team is searching for "last piece of the puzzle"
  - Other team moves up the win-curve and player's value increases
  - Other team develops pressing, urgent need
- Impending expiration of player's contract
  - Player's future value is approaching zero
- Change in the depth chart of player's current team
  - New emerging talent creates substitute for current player, changing value equation

---

FIGURE 5.7 **Four sources of change in a player's valuation.**

One potential source of change is the player's *financial underperformance*. This may occur through no fault of the player. The team may have misjudged his financial value at negotiation time and overpaid. Alternatively, they may have set their price for the player assuming they would be a 92-win team with him, but poor team performance has made them to an 83-win team. Since a team's location on the win-curve has a dramatic impact on player value, their noncompetitive status has significantly reduced the player's value to them. When the Florida Marlins signed Carlos Delgado prior to the 2005 season, they anticipated being a contending team, with a new stadium in the works. Once the Marlins decided to bail on their quest for their third World Championship in their short history, they no longer could tolerate Delgado's five-year, $55 million deal. If the Marlins had been a 90-win contender, the contract would have been reasonably valued. However, with their strategic choice to be noncompetitive and build for the future with younger players, Delgado's value to the Marlins dropped precipitously, and he was traded to the contending Mets.

Another source of a player's financial underperformance may be related to his on-field performance. The Cubs had every reason to expect a five-WARP season from LaTroy Hawkins, coming off a five-plus WARP year in 2003 with Minnesota. After being signed to a three-year, $11-million deal with the Cubs, he had one strong season and then promptly plummeted to being a one-WARP player for the 2004 season and was dealt to the Giants. He continued his sub-par performance in 2005, and the Giants traded him to the Orioles, while paying a portion of his salary. In both cases (the team misjudging the financial value of the player's performance and the player having a poor season), the financial value of the player has changed. As a result, if the player were to become a free agent today, his current team would not likely win the bidding war for his services.

Another source of the change in a player's valuation is that another team is searching for the last piece of the puzzle, and your player is an ideal fit. The acquiring team may have had an untimely injury to a key player, or they may simply see themselves in a position to make a run at the post-season and have a need at a key position. As the trade deadline approaches each July, the market changes daily. A six-game winning streak in mid-July could make a team a buyer as they recalculate their chance of reaching the postseason. On the other side of the coin, a mid-season slump coupled with an injury to a key player may be enough to convince a club to conserve their financial resources and focus on mounting a charge next season.

One reason a team employs a particular player is the belief that he fits in their long-term plan. In other words, a player provides value in the form of his current performance as well as his future expected performance. Once a player nears the end of his contract, the second form of value becomes moot. Hence, a third source of a change in a player's valuation is the *impending expiration of his contract.* As a player nears the end of his contract, his expected future value to his current team, as well as his trade value, approaches zero. The last year of a player contract is like a stock option contract speeding toward its expiration date. If a player is not creating financial value for his team through his performance (the marginal revenue he generates is less than his compensation), he is tantamount to an "out of the money" option. He is a likely candidate to be dealt away, since he will no longer have any value to his team once his contract expires. If he is creating value for his team, the team may attempt to preempt his free agency by offering a somewhat competitive contract for the certainty of a signed deal. If the player declines the club's offer and insists on free agency, it may make more sense for the club to trade him to a team that is filling an important need. His current team can always bid for his future services in the open market following the season.

We often witness this affect in July for players who are in the last year of their contracts. A classic example was the 1998 trade of Randy Johnson from Seattle to Houston. At the July trading deadline, the deal was consummated, with the Mariners sending the "Big Unit" to the Astros for Freddy Garcia, Carlos Guillen, and John Halama. Johnson had three months left on a $6 million per year contract when he became a free agent. In the midst of a 76-win season, Seattle felt that Johnson's contract was beyond their financial means. They believed they could get excellent value from a team who needed him to compete for the postseason—as the last piece of the puzzle. The Astros were in the middle of the playoff chase and in need of a top pitcher. They also knew that Randy was pitching to impress his off-season suitors and expected that he would be at the top of his game. Not to be disappointed, the Big Unit went 10–1 in his 11 starts, with a 1.28 ERA and four shutouts. He led Houston to a division title, generating a healthy return on their $3 million (half a season at $6 million per year). Johnson also benefited, as his stellar performance earned him a long-term contract (from the Arizona Diamondbacks) that paid approximately twice the amount per year of his 1998 compensation. This trade created value for both the Mariners and the Astros. Seattle shed $3 million of salary that would not yield them even one-third of that amount in revenue and received three excellent prospects in return. The Astros paid Randy Johnson $3 million, and he delivered five WARP (in a half-season), earning Houston about $6 million in incremental revenues; all they gave up were three untested prospects.[14] Johnson also served as an insurance policy to reach the postseason and provided greater hope for the team to go deep into the playoffs.

A fourth source of change in a player's valuation is a *change in the depth chart of the seller's team*. A team may want to deal a high-value player if they have a top prospect waiting in the wings. Their high-value player can be dealt to a team that sees him as filling an important need. For example, the value of Lyle Overbay to the Milwaukee Brewers changed over the course of the 2005 season as Prince Fielder emerged as a viable replacement. Fielder was thought to have greater long-term potential and a higher ceiling than Overbay. A new substitute emerged, changing the Brewers' value equation for Overbay. Even if Lyle performed exactly as expected, his value to the Brewers declined simply because of the presence of Fielder, but Overbay's "external" value—his value to other teams—did not change. Overbay was nearing the end of his arbitration-eligible phase and was one year away from free agency. In an open-market bidding war, it is likely that the Brewers could not justify a competitive offer. The result was Milwaukee's trade of Overbay to the Toronto Blue Jays prior to the 2006 season and the insertion of the less expensive and potentially more talented Prince Fielder into the starting lineup as the everyday first baseman for the Brewers. (An interesting alternative that goes against the grain of conventional baseball thinking would have been to trade Fielder, rather than Overbay. In Chapter 8, A Strategic Approach to Assembling the Roster, we discuss the "asset value" of young, validated Major League–ready players such as Fielder and how their value can be monetized via a trade or sale.)

To better understand the dollar value created by a trade, let's examine the Diamondbacks trade of Curt Schilling to the Red Sox in November of 2003. In 2003 Schilling played for an 84-win D-Backs team and contributed about six WARP, a significant decline of about 30% from his 2001 and 2002 performance. If we anticipate an improvement in his next season's performance (seven WARP), given Arizona's position on its win-curve, Schilling could be expected to generate about $5 million in value (including gate value) in 2004, while drawing a salary of $12 million. On the other hand, Boston was in need of a frontline starter to complement Pedro Martinez in their chase for an AL pennant and an elusive World Championship. Coming off a 95-win season, they probably viewed a potential seven-WARP ace as worth about $16 million. Add to the evaluation that seven WARP might have been a conservative estimate, as Schilling was coming off a down year. If he returned to his 2001 or 2002 performance (nine WARP), his value to Boston could be about $20 million. This trade created significant value for both teams, erasing a potential $7-million deficit for Arizona while creating a $4- to $8-million opportunity for Boston.[15] By reallocating Schilling to a team where his value was higher, $11 million of value was created, split between two teams. Figure 5.8 shows these calculations for both sides of the trade.

With these logical sources of motivation to trade players, why don't trades occur with greater frequency and regularity? Several impediments create an inefficient secondary market for players. The July 31 trading deadline makes a trade more difficult in August, when teams striving for the postseason may have emergency needs to fill. Since a player must clear waivers in order to be trade eligible, the player might be claimed by a team

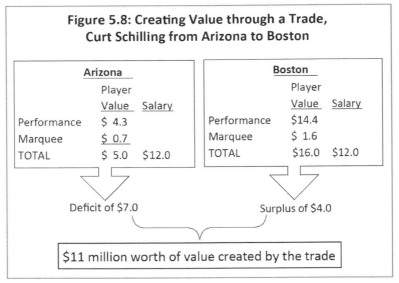

FIGURE 5.8 **The Schilling trade.**

lower in the standings than his intended destination team. Sometimes the waiver process can lead to unintended consequences. In August of 2000, while the Yankees were in the throes of their "paranoid years," fueled by the intimidating hand of Steinbrenner on GM Brian Cashman's shoulder, they entered a claim for 48 players who were put on waivers, for the purpose of preventing a team with a better record—Oakland, Seattle, or Boston—from acquiring any of them. One of the players was Tampa Bay's Jose Canseco, who at the tail end of his career was hardly the Yankees last piece of the puzzle. Much to Cashman's dismay, the Devil Rays' then-GM Chuck LaMar informed him that the Yankees won the "Canseco sweepstakes," requiring that they take possession of Canseco for the meager price of $20,000.[16]

Other barriers to trades include "no trade" clauses in some players' contracts (which can sometimes be overcome with cash) or differing perceptions regarding a player's talent level. Teams who have a key player at a position are often not candidates to trade for someone else. The Yankees will not likely be in the market for a shortstop while Derek Jeter, their captain and resident legend, is in uniform, unless he can switch positions, à la Alex Rodriguez. An incumbent player also changes the math on a prospective trade. While some teams would consider Jimmie Rollins a five-marginal-win shortstop, to the Baltimore Orioles he might be three marginal wins *less than* Miguel Tejada, while to the 2006 Boston Red Sox, he could be viewed as a two-plus-marginal-win player. A player's compensation also weighs heavily on a player's trade prospects. Should the Orioles choose to unload Miguel Tejada, at a salary of $12 million in 2007 and $13 million in 2008 and 2009, his compensation may only make financial sense to teams looking for the last piece of the puzzle.[17]

Often casual fans will ignore a player's compensation as an important variable in the value equation. (A player's compensation and its effect on his value as a team asset is discussed in more detail in Chapter 8, A Strategic Approach to Assembling the Roster.) In the summer of 2005 New York sports talk radio was filled with speculation that Mike Piazza should be traded, as he was in the final year of his hefty contract and the Mets were not contenders. Various names were bandied about on Mets fans' wish lists, nearly all of them denying the economic reality that the only fair trade for Piazza might not have included anything in return. Piazza was two-thirds through a three-WARP season, so it's reasonable to assume he was capable of adding one marginal win to an acquiring team over its last 55 games. The problem was in the price—$5 million, or one-third of his $15 million agreement. Rather than asking for something in return, it might have been considered a good deal if the Mets *gave* the acquiring team and additional player, say, Miguel Cairo, to reduce the acquiring team's cost per marginal win and bring it back to a reasonable level. Instead of receiving someone in exchange for Piazza, the Mets were more likely to be required to give another player in order for a team to be willing to take Piazza.

A player's resale, or asset, value is directly related to his expected performance, his compensation, the length of his contract and the going rate to purchase the same marginal wins in the free-agent market. An example of a star player with high asset value is the Yankees star closer, Mariano Rivera, who will be in his option year in 2007, at a compensation of $10.5 million.[18] Assuming Mariano performs at the seven-WARP level in 2007 (slightly below his 7.9 in 2006), benchmarked against free-agent contracts for pitchers, a team would expect to pay approximately $17.9 million for seven marginal wins. (This analysis and methodology is discussed in more detail in Chapter 7, The Economics of Player Development"). This leaves a surplus, or asset value, of $7.4 million for Rivera, based on the price of replacing his performance in the free-agent market.

Evaluating BJ Ryan's five-year deal with the Blue Jays, thought to be an outrageously expensive deal at the time, may shed some light on the importance of a player's asset value. Based on the economics of the deal, the Jays will likely have the possibility of "bailing out" if they no longer realize their value from the Ryan contract. Perhaps they will slide down the win-curve to be an 83-win team. At that point he might be worth only $4 million in performance value to Toronto, but they may be able to offer him on the trade market, as his $10 million salary in the last three years (2008–2010) of his contract could be less than his asset value. At current market rates, a six-marginal-win relief pitcher would be expected to cost about $17.4 million in the free-agent market, making Ryan a good value to a team looking to add the last piece of the puzzle.

The heart and soul of a player's economic value to his team is his performance value—the impact of his playing performance on team wins converted into the marginal revenue his team is expected to earn from those wins—but the discussion of value" does not end with performance value. A player's marquee value, his resale value, and the overall risk level of his expected performance, particularly his propensity for injury, can all have an impact on his ultimate value to his team. The player with the highest marquee value, Derek Jeter, benefits from the "perfect storm" of being the highest-profile All Star, on the highest-revenue club in the largest market— all of which add up to mega-marquee value. Players with a high injury risk factor, such as Nomar Garciaparra, Mark Prior, and Carl Pavano, may find that their next contracts will have low base salaries and be loaded with incentives to stay healthy. One example of this is the reported 2006 contract between the Oakland A's and often-injured Frank Thomas. Thomas signed as a free agent for a base salary of $500,000, with incentive clauses focused on his health and playing time allowing him the potential to make an additional $2,600,000.[19] On the matter of resale value, any player who's compensation, relative to his performance, is discounted to the market rate for free agents is going to command the most value in a player exchange.

Endnotes

1. For road games Hunter also drew an average of 2,600 additional fans. In 1975 a portion of road revenues (20% in the AL) were shared with the visiting team.

2. An exception to this limitation is evaluating selected high-profile players to gain a historical perspective long after their careers have ended. Chapter 6, Valuing the Babe in His Yankee Years, shows the benefit of pre- and post-Ruth attendance and revenue figures and estimates his *annual* marquee value by contrasting Yankee attendance in the Ruth compared to the non-Ruth years. In this situation using regression analysis to measure Ruth's impact on Yankee annual attendance can be an effective method to quantify his marquee value.

3. According to Forbes MLB Team Valuations for 2006, the team average value was $376 million. My estimates of brand value yield a team average of $259 million.

4. One exception may be Barry Bonds. Although many fans would characterize him as a villain, many others still pay to see a unique high-profile player.

5. Performance factor is a multiplier equal to .75 for a four- to seven-WARP player, 1.0 for a seven- to 10-WARP player, and 1.25 for >10-WARP player.

6. The formula credits the top three gate-appeal players per team with 0.1% for each attribute they possess, while the fourth- through sixth-highest gate-appeal players are credited with 0.05% for each attribute. Determining whether they possess an attribute is subjective.

7. The continuity factor is a multiplier equal to 0.75 for less than three years with current team, 1.0 for three to five years, and 1.25 for more than five years with current team.

8. The top three players can each be credited with up to 0.625% of the team's brand value. The next three players can be credited with half that amount for a possible maximum for six players of 2.8%.

9. Forbes valuation for 2002–2006 for franchise values increased by an average annual rate of 9.25%.

10. Christopher R. Bollinger and Julie L. Hotchkiss, "The Upside Potential of Hiring Risky Workers: Evidence from the Baseball Industry," *Journal of Labor Economics*, Vol. 21, No. 4, 2003.

11. Ibid.

12. Any valuation adjustment should reflect the reality of less upside from a low-injury risk player (capped at 162 games) than the downside of a high-injury risk player. The low-risk outliers in our shortstop sample represent 10% more playing time than the average, while the high-risk outliers represent 22% less playing time as a downside.

13. In reality, even in a free-agent environment, the player may have declined to consider several teams, regardless of the terms of their contract offers, owing to personal preferences.

14. Johnson is not credited with any playoff dollar value, since Houston won their division by 12.5 games over the Cubs.

15. This calculation excluded the value of the four players shipped to Arizona in exchange for Schilling. The value of Fossum, Lyon, de la Rosa, and Goss would not materially change the valuation of the trade.

16. Buster Olney, "The Yankees Get Canseco, But the Question is Why?" *The New York Times*, August 8, 2000, p. D1.

17. Tejada's contract data are from Cot's Baseball Contracts, *http://mlbcontracts.blogspot.com/2005/01/baltimore-orioles_112321768568552760.html*.

18. Rivera's contra

Five Musts to Consider When Valuing Players

Any team that simply converts a projection of a player's performance into his value is taking a dangerous shortcut that leaves far too many important variables out of the player value equation. At least five key variables, beyond the projection of a player's performance, are critical in ultimately determining a player's dollar value to a team:
- The team's *location on the win-curve*
- The team and the market in which the team plays
- The potential *variance in the player's projected performance*
- The *duration* for which the player is being valued
- The demand for the player by a *rival* team

The team's location on the win-curve has the greatest impact on a player's value. Players who fill the role of last piece of the puzzle and increase their team's odds of playing October baseball can generate millions of dollars more than a similar player with a 75-win team. The marginal revenue generated by a player who elevated his team from an 87-win to 92-win team is $12.4 million, across all teams, for the 2006 season. If that same player helped an 80-win team become an 85-win team, he would generate $5.1 million in marginal revenue.

The team and the market also have a big impact on a player's value. Playing for a team whose fans are highly responsive to changes in the team's on-field performance can add to a player's value. Playing for a team that reached the postseason for the past four years can lessen a player's value, as the potential marginal revenue from returning to the postseason is lower with each successive appearance. A five-win player added to an 87-win team would generate an estimated $9.8 million for the 2006 Braves, compared to $15.1 million for the Phillies.

The potential variance in a player's projected performance can affect his value to a team. Not all five-win players are created equal. Some players' track records are similar to the reliability of a treasury bill, while others resemble a lottery ticket. The differing levels of uncertainty surrounding a player's potential performance impact his value. Players with a high *injury risk* present more downside from lost playing time, earning a lower valuation than their injury-free counterparts. Some players have an iron-man profile but significant *performance* variation year-to-year. If a five-win player is equally likely to perform at the three-win or seven-win level, the penalty or reward for his performance variation depends entirely on where his team is on the nonlinear win-curve. Taking two wins away from an 85-win

→

Astros team reduces revenue by an estimated $2.9 million, while adding two wins would generate $4.1 million in revenue. If the Astros are a 92-win baseline team, losing two wins would cost a hefty $5.6 million, while adding two wins is worth only $4.2 million.

When determining a player's value, a team must answer the question, "For how long?" Injury and performance and risk increase with duration, as do risks associated with the business environment and MLB rules under which teams operate. The economic framework becomes a *variable*, rather than a constant, when analyzing a player's value several years into the future. The terms of the Collective Bargaining Agreement (CBA) are one of many examples of how a business climate can change. Multiyear player valuations made in 2001, without knowledge of the impending changes in the revenue-sharing provisions contained in the 2002 CBA, were made with great peril. The significant increase in the revenue-sharing tax and the resultant reduction in marginal revenues from winning is one reason why contracts at the Manny Ramirez and Alex Rodriguez stratospheric levels were not duplicated during the reign of the 2002 CBA. Not until the recent announcement of the current CBA (which runs through 2011) and its lower revenue-sharing tax did we see a return to the contract values of five years earlier. Players on a team whose revenue-sharing tax was reduced from 39 to 31% under the current CBA will generate 13% more marginal revenue (eight percentage points of revenue on a base of 61%) at the same level of on-field performance.

Players who are in demand by direct *rival* teams—teams that compete directly for a spot in the postseason—can have a premium attached to their value. Most front-of-the-rotation pitchers, as well as star free-agent position players who fill a void for a rival team, fit this description. The straightforward valuation methodology we've used quantifies the impact of the added wins on a team's revenue. The additional dimension of *value* that comes from poaching a rival's player is the result of *reducing* the opponent's win total, thereby *adding to your probability of reaching the postseason*. The Padres signed Greg Maddux to improve their win total. If it also reduces the Dodgers wins and increases the Padres' probability of reaching the postseason by five percentage points, it would result in an additional $1.3 million in value for Maddux.

Factors beyond our top five include a player's marquee value and the position he plays. The inclusion of a no-trade clause in a player's contract limits a team's ability to trade a player, adding another dimension of risk to the team and detracting from his value. A more thorough valuation of a player includes other factors, but the five musts are the minimum any team should consider in valuing a player.

6 | Valuing the Babe in His Yankee Years

Perched at the pinnacle of baseball annals is its mythic figure, Babe Ruth. No person has ever defined a major sport the way Babe Ruth defined America's pastime. Ruth's emergence in the early 1920s was the equivalent of baseball's perfect storm of three phenomena converging to create maximum impact and, hence, maximum value. He was a game-changing force, as he literally transformed the way in which baseball was played by making the home run fashionable. Second, he was emerging as baseball's biggest star at a time when the sport was rising to dominance and becoming a virtual American obsession. Finally, he landed in the epicenter of media and commerce—where all "bigness" begins and ends—New York City. The confluence of these circumstances may have led to popularity and adoration unrivaled by any American athlete, before or since.

In baseball's early days, when history and tradition were just being formed, baseball's stars became immutably linked with the identity and image of their teams. Christy Mathewson and manager John McGraw were as much the New York Giants, as the team itself. For the first quarter of the twentieth century, the New York Giants were synonymous with New York baseball. From 1903 to 1925 the Giants won three World Championships and 10 National League pennants, in addition to seven second-place finishes. By contrast, their American League siblings, the Yankees, experienced a dismal first two decades. Their crowning achievement was three second-place finishes in the AL while playing under .500 baseball for the 20-year period.

On a national level a dark cloud was hanging over baseball as allegations of the Black Sox scandal were swirling in the early 1920s. The turmoil culminated with the dean of Northwestern Law School calling for the U.S. government to take control of baseball. Colonel John H. Wigmore advocated for a "federal department of sport," with a seat in the cabinet.[1] He claimed baseball "should be declared a public service" and run by the state in order to "expel the mercenary cynics who have exploited it for private gain."[2] Amidst this crisis, baseball was in need of at least a jolt, if not an image makeover. In the winter of 1920 the Yankees' acquisition of Babe Ruth was the perfect tonic, changing the course of not only New York baseball, but Major League Baseball, as well. Ruth, twice a 20-game winner for the Red Sox, was permanently converted to a Yankee outfielder and home run machine, forever setting America's game on a new trajectory. (Ruth made 95% of his career mound appearances as a Red Sox, but hit 92% of his career home runs as a Yankee.) His majestic and prolific home runs mesmerized baseball fans and redirected their attention from the World Series "fix" and back to the playing field.

Some even credit Ruth as the impetus for an evolution in stadium design.[3] In the early days playing fields were open in the outfield, so that long fly balls were often chased down and caught in dramatic fashion. Some reasoned that the enormous popularity of Ruth's home runs led to a demand for additional seating, and what better place to locate these new seats but behind a shortened outfield fence, which in turn, would lead to more home runs. However, since Fenway Park, Wrigley Field, the Polo Grounds, and Ebbets Field were already constructed when Babe began his home run tear, he may not deserve much credit for the completely encircled playing fields. He does deserve credit for being the driving force behind the construction of Yankee Stadium. In Ruth's first year with the Yankees, they outdrew the Giants *at the Polo Grounds*, prompting their unfriendly landlord to ask the Yankees to vacate the premises.[4] Yankee owners Rupert and Huston treated their eviction as an opportunity to build a massive new ballpark in the Bronx. No doubt their confidence was boosted by Ruth's arrival, by the recent change in local laws to allow lucrative Sunday home games, and by the opportunity to add concession sales to their revenues. Major League Baseball hit the jackpot as the trade of Babe Ruth placed baseball's marquee star and greatest talent in the nation's center of public attention: New York City.

To analyze Ruth's value to the Yankees we can apply a methodology, similar to that discussed in the previous chapters, to a unique data set that was unearthed by Michael J. Haupert and Kenneth Winter, economics professors at the University of Wisconsin–La Crosse. They discovered a most unusual artifact at the National Baseball Library at the Hall of Fame in

Cooperstown: archives of New York Yankee financial records coinciding with the ownership of Colonel Jacob Rupert, from 1915 to 1937.[5] The data consisted of journals and ledgers covering a wide variety of Yankee revenues and expenses. Since no financial statements existed, Haupert and Winter diligently totaled closing entries from journals, essentially constructing (or reconstructing) income statements, which included ticket revenues, concessions, advertising revenue, and stadium rental revenue.[6] Gaps in the data prevent a detailed revenue breakdown for each of the 23 years, but enough data exist to create a win–revenue curve for the Yankees for this time period and ultimately create a dollar valuation for Babe Ruth.

Despite playing in the reserve clause era that indentured a player to his team, and without a union or player agents to coach him, the Babe clearly understood the concept of a player's ability to generate revenue. Following the 1926 season he asked the Yankees for a $100,000 annual salary but was rebuffed when the team countered with a $52,000 offer. Ruth lamented, "If I were in any other business I would probably receive a new contract with a higher salary without request, or rival employers would bid for my services." He continued, "Baseball law forces me to work for the New York club or remain idle, but it does not prevent a man from being paid for his value as a 'business getter' as well as for his mechanical services."[7] Even if the commentary was ghost-written for the Babe, it was an excellent summary of baseball's reserve clause and its implications, as well as an acknowledgement of a player's ability to bring crowds to the ballpark as a business getter.

Considering the mindset of Major League Baseball in the early twentieth century, Ruth might have defined his role as a business getter to mean two sources of value, his performance value and his marquee value. The concept of a player's performance value, his impact on a team's win–loss record converted into dollars of revenue, was supported by at least the owner of the New York Giants, John T. Brush. Brush had a conviction that the primary ingredient in building a successful baseball business was the team's on-field performance. "The organization and upbuilding of the team must be given first place. Without this, baseball ownership fails," said Brush.[8] As baseball's most successful franchise in the 1900s and 1910s, both on and off the field, Brush was generating up to $300,000 per year in profits.[9] He also had an affinity for acquiring star players and was a strong advocate for the concept of marquee value. He believed that the mere announcement that future Hall of Famer Rube Marquard was the scheduled starting pitcher would ultimately generate gate receipts well in excess of his $11,000 purchase price.[10]

Ruth's performance value was unparalleled in the 1920s and 1930s. His highest impact season was 1923, when he led the Yankees to their first World Championship. With 41 HRs, 131 RBI and a career best .393 batting average, Ruth was responsible for 19 of the team's 98 wins according to Baseball Prospectus' WARP statistic.[11] Had a replacement player been installed in the outfield in Ruth's place, the Yankees might have finished in third place behind Detroit and Cleveland, instead of winning the AL pennant by 16 games. If his performance value was legendary, his marquee value might have been even greater, dwarfing that of any present day player. The Yankees rode the Babe to the top of the attendance standings in 1920, his first season, by drawing a record 1,289,422 fans with a third-place team. Even more impressive was that it represented *an increase of nearly 900,000 fans per season from the average of the previous five years.* In Ruth's first year they outdrew the next highest team, the second-place New York Giants, by nearly 40%, after being outplayed and outdrawn by the Giants for most of their existence.

THE WIN-CURVE FOR THE YANKEES OF THE 1920S AND 1930S

The process of estimating Ruth's dollar value to the Yankees begins by quantifying the relationship between winning and revenues for the team. In a process similar to the win-curve estimates of today's MLB teams (discussed in detail in Chapter 3), a win-curve was estimated for the Yankees during the Ruth years using regression analysis.[12] The regression model was driven by three variables: a measure of team wins, a variable to capture Babe's presence (in an effort to measure his marquee value), and the number of World Series games played, since they were a substantial revenue generator for the team.[13] Much like the dollar valuation of a present day player, Ruth's *performance value,* the portion of his value attributable to his impact on Yankee wins, is affected by the Yankees ultimate annual win total. For years in which Ruth was the Yankees' last piece of the puzzle (e.g., 1921), his value is greater than in a year when the Yankees won the AL in a runaway (e.g., 1932). Similar to our present day findings, the win-curve will generally have a steeper slope when the team is in a pennant race, winning between 88 and 98 games. The dollar value of each five-win increment, between 75 and 100 wins, ranges from $48,000 to $90,000. The highest-value five-win segment is the 92nd to 97th wins, and the lowest value segment is the 75th to 80th wins. Figure 6.1 shows the estimated win-curve for the Yankees based on data from the 1915 through 1937 seasons.

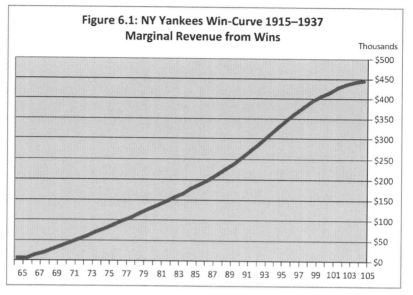

FIGURE 6.1 **Yankees win-curve.**

The estimated win-curve focuses on one component of Ruth's dollar valuation, his performance value, and includes the model's estimate of the revenue impact of the Yankees participation in the World Series. The model indicates that each World Series home game was worth about $43,000 in revenue to the team, assuring $86,000 for the requisite two home games for each Yankee World Series appearance.[14] One significant difference between the Ruth era and the present day wild card era is the number of wins needed to qualify for the postseason. Despite a regular season schedule with eight fewer games, a team generally needed more wins to reach the postseason in the Ruth era. Today, a 98-win club is virtually assured a position in the playoffs, while in the Ruth era a 98-win team had an estimated 68% probability of winning its league's pennant. A 93-win team, which today has an 84% chance of winning its division or being the wild card, had only a 32% chance of reaching the postseason in the Ruth era. Figure 6.2 shows the probability of reaching the postseason in the wild card era versus the Ruth era.[15] The third and final component of the regression model is the estimate of Ruth's marquee value, measured by a variable to capture his presence (or absence) in the Yankee lineup. The results indicate that Babe's presence for a full season was worth approximately $398,000 in incremental revenue to the Yankees.

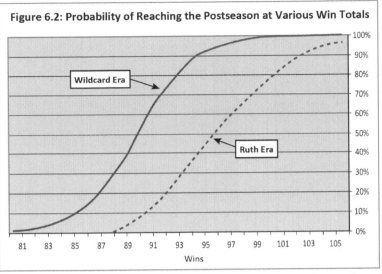

FIGURE 6.2 **Probability of reaching the postseason in the Ruth and wild card eras.**

A RUTHIAN VALUATION

The dollar value of the Babe is the sum of three factors: his performance value, World Series value, and marquee value for each of his 15 years in New York. The following is a further breakdown of the three components of the estimate of Ruth's dollar value to the Yankees:

Performance value: The win-curve is the key component in determining a player's performance value. This is calculated by applying Ruth's annual win contribution (WARP) to the Yankees' estimated win-curve, which places a dollar value on each win (the same process discussed in detail in Chapter 4) As a 16-win player on a 95-win team, as he was in 1920, Babe gets credit for the team's last 16 wins and the revenue they generate. Presumably, if the Yankees employed a replacement player in Ruth's position, the replacement would have produced zero wins and the team would have won 79 games. Ruth's performance value for 1920 is $170,000, an amount equal to the estimated revenue generated by the 80th through 95th wins. Ruth's highest performance value came in 1923, when he had a 19.1 WARP for a 98-win World Championship team, for a dollar value of $206,000. His lowest–dollar-value year is estimated to be in 1925, when he accumulated a career low 5.7 WARP on a seventh-place Yankee team that won only 69 games. For 1925, Ruth's performance value is estimated at $23,000.

World Series value: This represents an attempt to quantify Ruth's impact on a separate and significant revenue stream that accrued to pennant winning teams in this era: World Series gate receipts, concessions, and other related revenues. For example, in the 1928 World Series sweep of the St. Louis Cardinals, the first two games were played in front of a combined 122,000 fans at Yankee Stadium. (A total of about 200,000 fans viewed the four games, including the two played in St. Louis.) Yankee financial records show revenues of over $97,000 from the 1928 Series.[16] For all Yankee World Series appearances in our data set, the model estimates a revenue impact of $43,000 per home game.[17] Generally Ruth is given credit for the mandatory two home games for each World Series. Using our marginal approach to player valuation, the Yankees arguably would not have won the AL pennant and qualified for the World Series if not for Ruth's performance.[18] Exceptions to the two home game guideline were applied in 1927 and 1932. In these seasons the Yankees were arguably singing the refrain, "We could have done it without you." Since these formidable teams would likely have won a pennant and garnered their two home games even if Ruth was a spectator, the revenue attributable to the Babe is reduced to 25% of the World Series receipts.[19]

Marquee value: Perhaps the most controversial of the three valuation components is marquee value, which is intended to account for the presence of Babe Ruth on the Yankees and the number of fans and the amount of revenue he would attract by simply being "the Babe."[20] Ballplayers are more than mechanical performers who compile stats that aggregate to their teams' wins and losses. Star players can have a highly public image that engenders strong reactions from fans. Babe Ruth's star power, or marquee value, is possibly unmatched in baseball history. Ruth burst onto the national scene when the universally popular sport had few competitors. In addition, he fundamentally changed the way in which the game was played by introducing the home run as a daily or weekly occurrence. The nature of this transformation—a manifestation of strength and brawn—made the change even more engaging, appealing, and eye-catching to the ripe American public. Furthermore, as a 25-year-old entering his prime, Ruth relocated to the center of the sports universe in 1920—New York City. This adds up to possibly being the highest-profile athlete in the history of American professional sports. His ability to command the public's attention was unparalleled, and since he predated broadcasts of baseball games, his mystique translated into ticket sales—at home games (first at the Polo Grounds then at Yankee Stadium), on the road, at in-season exhibition games on scheduled off days, and in barnstorming tours across the United States and abroad.[21]

The model estimates the average marquee value for a full season of Babe Ruth as a Yankee to be $398,000. In years when Ruth played in fewer games owing to a suspension or injury (e.g., 1925), his marquee value was a low of $318,000. While this valuation may appear unrealistically high, it appears more reasonable when comparing the Ruth years with the pre- and post-Ruth years. Total revenue for the Yankees for the first five years (1920–1924) of Ruth's tenure ranged from a low of $1.11 million to a high of $1.38 million. For the five years immediately preceding Ruth's arrival (1915–1919), the Yankees' revenues ranged from a low of $196,000 to a high of $446,000. *This staggering difference in the average between the five-year periods is $966,000 in annual revenues.*

Some of this difference in revenue is attributable to the improved record with Ruth as a Yankee. The Yankees averaged 73 wins for the five years pre-Ruth and 95 wins for the first five years with Ruth. According to our estimated win-curve, the 22-win gap is worth about $226,000 in total revenues per year. (Add another $40,000 to $80,000 in World Series revenue that can be attributed to improved performance for seasons in which the Yankees reached the World Series.) A portion of the gap between the pre-Ruth and early Ruth years can be attributed to the new Yankee Stadium and its increased capacity, which debuted in 1923, the fourth year of Ruth's tenure as a Yankee.[22] It is reasonable to imagine the stadium effect to be worth several hundred thousand dollars per year.[23] This provides perspective and supports the model's estimate of $398,000 in value for a full season

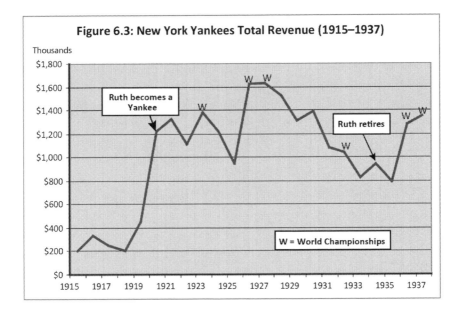

FIGURE 6.3 **Yankees total revenue.**

of the Babe as a drawing card. In the year following Ruth's departure (1935), despite an 89-win, second place, Gehrig-led Yankee team that challenged the Tigers for the pennant, the Yankees revenue fell to $786,000, providing further support for the estimate of Ruth's marquee value. (Despite finishing seven games behind the AL champion Tigers, the 1934 *Ruth-led* Yankees generated 19% more revenue than the 1935 club.) Figure 6.3 shows estimated total revenue over the 1915 to 1937 period.

Babe Ruth's total dollar value to the Yankees over his 15-year career is estimated to be nearly $8 million, with a high of $688,000 for the 1923 season and a low of $341,000 for the 1925 season. In four of Ruth's seasons his dollar value was over $600,000, and in only six seasons his value was less than $500,000. There are two common ingredients for Ruth's highest value seasons (1921, 1923, 1926, and 1928). First, they are all AL pennant winning teams. In addition, Babe's win contribution made the difference between a first- and second-place finish. On the other hand, for the 1927 and 1932 World Championship teams, Ruth's value is estimated to be $509,000 and $456,000, respectively. In both seasons, the Yankees won the pennant by more games than Ruth's win contribution, suggesting that they would still have made it to the World Series even if a replacement

Figure 6.4: Summary of Babe Ruth Valuation

Year	Performance Value	Performance Marquee	World Series Value	Total Value
1920	$170,000	$ 398,000	-	$568,000
1921	$190,000	$ 398,000	$42,000	$630,000
1922	$104,000	$ 318,000	$42,000	$464,000
1923	$206,000	$ 398,000	$85,000	$688,000
1924	$151,000	$ 398,000	-	$549,000
1925	$ 23,000	$ 318,000	-	$341,000
1926	$154,000	$ 398,000	$85,000	$636,000
1927	$ 90,000	$ 398,000	$21,000	$509,000
1928	$137,000	$ 398,000	$85,000	$619,000
1929	$115,000	$ 358,000	-	$473,000
1930	$136,000	$ 398,000	-	$533,000
1931	$151,000	$ 398,000	-	$549,000
1932	$ 77,000	$ 358,000	$21,000	$456,000
1933	$103,000	$ 358,000	-	$460,000
1934	$ 79,000	$ 358,000	-	$437,000
Total	$1,886,000	$5,645,000	$380,000	$7,912,000

FIGURE 6.4 **Summary Of Ruth valuation.**

player substituted for the Babe. In addition to 1925, when Babe appeared in only 98 games, his lowest-value seasons are clustered at the end of his career (1932–1934), when his performance slipped and fans realized he was well past his prime. Figure 6.4 summarizes Babe Ruth's year-by-year dollar value to the Yankees.

VALIDATING THE VALUATION

We can test the model that estimates the Yankees win-curve, and ultimately Ruth's value to the Yankees, for reasonableness by dissecting its results. Since Ruth provides two primary sources of value—performance value in the form of his annual win contribution and marquee value from his popularity and image—we can create scenarios to *exclude* these effects and consider the reasonableness of the result. (To simplify this exercise we will add World Series value into the definition of performance value.) The simplest way to depict this evaluation is via a four-box grid, to look at the projected attendance and revenues under the various scenarios. The upper-left corner of Figure 6.5 represents the real-life scenario of Ruth from 1920 to 1934, leading the Yankees to seven AL pennants and four World Championships and averaging 94 wins per season. The lower-right corner represents a scenario in which the Babe was never a Yankee. The Yankees would gain no attendance or revenue from his marquee value, nor would they have benefited from his performance on the field. In the top-right quadrant Babe is not a Yankee, so the Yankees receive no benefit from his marquee value, but the equivalent of his on-field performance gets re-distributed to his teammates so that the Yankees still win seven pennants and four Championships. In our final scenario, Babe is present with all his grandeur intact, and the Yankees realize the fruits of his marquee value, but the Babe performs only at replacement level, and the Yankees win–loss record is as if Babe was absent from the lineup. Figure 6.6 shows the model's estimates of the revenue impact of each of these scenarios, and Figure 6.7 shows the home attendance impact.[24]

If Babe never arrived in New York, represented by the lower-right box, the Yankees would have been the virtual equivalent of the Washington Senators for the time period 1920–1934. The Yankees would have likely averaged 81 wins per season and won two AL pennants and one World Series. During the same years, Washington averaged 82 wins and won three AL pennants and one World Series. The Yankees' projected average attendance of 455,000 compares reasonably to Washington's 473,000, with a 4% difference. The larger New York market might increase the Yankees' attendance

Figure 6.5: Babe Ruth's Dollar Value - Playing "what if"

1920-1934	SCENARIOS	
	With Ruth's Marquee Value	Without Ruth's Marquee Value
With Ruth's Performance Value	• Actual NYY performance • Averaged 94 wins • Won 7 AL Pennants and 4 World Championships	• No Ruth as a drawing card, but his performance is redistributed among teammates • Same 94 wins, 7 AL Pennants and 4 Series Wins
Without Ruth's Performance Value	• Babe's personality makes him a "drawing card", but he performs at "replacement level" • Average 81 wins • Wins 2 AL Pennants and 1 World Championship	• No Ruth Performance and no Ruth as a drawing card • 81 Wins per year with 2 AL Pennants and 1 World Championship

FIGURE 6.5 **What if . . . scenarios.**

expectations, but might be offset by dividing baseball interest and attendance among three local teams. Considering that the Yankees would have averaged a third- to fourth-place finish and been a distant second, as measured by on-field success, to the New York Giants, and still had to compete for fans with Brooklyn, the estimate seems plausible.

To evaluate the marquee effect of the Bambino, which is estimated at $398,000 (see Figure 6.4) we can compare the Yankees' revenues for the Ruth years (1920–1934) to the pre- (1915–1919) and post-Ruth years (1935–1937). The Yankees averaged $1,235,000 in total revenue during the Ruth years, while averaging $679,000 for the pre- and post- years, a difference of $556,000. While some of the difference in revenue is attributable to a higher-performing team in the Ruth years (averaging 94 wins versus 82 wins), the estimated marquee value of $398,000 for Ruth seems plausible. Further evidence to support the Babe's unique marquee value is contained in the Yankees' financial data.[25] Revenue from in-season exhibition games, generally played in non-American League cities on travel days, increased nearly tenfold following Ruth's arrival on the Yankees. Prior to the Babe, the Yankees netted an average of a meager $2,500 per season, while during the Ruth years they averaged over $22,000.[26] Spring training revenues followed a similar pattern, but on a larger scale, rising to nearly $45,000 in

Ruth's presence, up from $4,700 for the years preceding Ruth.[27] The total impact of these peripheral line items represents over $60,000 in annual Yankee revenue, largely attributable to the Babe.

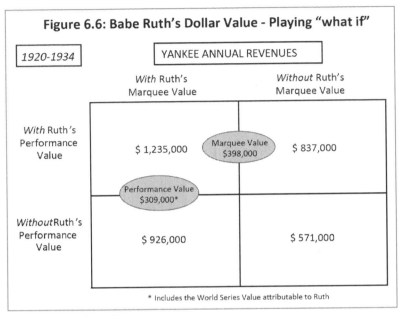

FIGURE 6.6 **What if . . . revenues.**

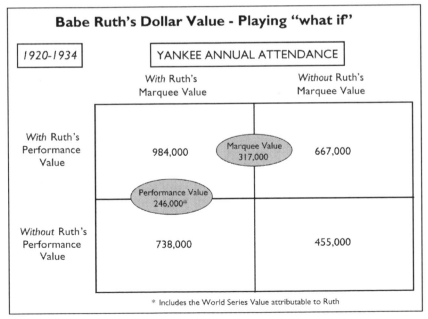

FIGURE 6.7 **What if . . . attendance.**

THE BABE'S VALUE: YEAR BY YEAR

The following is a year-by-year account of Ruth and his contribution to the Yankees:

1920: The previous year, his last in Boston, Ruth set the Major League record for home runs in a season with 29. He accomplished this while playing in only 130 games, 17 as a pitcher. Even before he arrived in New York, the Babe was being heralded as a revolutionary force in the game. In Ruth's first year in pinstripes he completed his transition to a full-time-position player, with only one mound appearance in his 140 games played. He banged an unthinkable 54 homers, nearly double the single-season record he established just one year earlier. With his record breaking 30th homer coming on July 20, the anticipation of the next Ruth homer was the driving force behind new attendance records in six AL ballparks.[28] His slugging percentage of .849 was the best of his career and stood for more than 80 years as the all-time record until Barry Bonds topped it in 2001. The Yankees finished in third place for their second straight season, three games behind the World Champion Cleveland Indians, despite winning a franchise-high 95 games. With the excitement that Ruth generated and an exciting pennant race, the Yankees drew a league-leading 1,298,422 fans at the Polo Grounds as a tenant of the rival New York Giants. Ruth's dollar value to the Yankees in his inaugural season in New York is estimated at $568,000, about 30 times his $18,750 salary.

1921: Ruth continued to rewrite baseball's record books as he set the single-season homer mark for the third consecutive year, crushing 59 round-trippers. The Babe had many stellar, record-breaking seasons as a Yankee, but 1921, along with 1923 and 1927, represents one of his greatest seasons. He added 171 RBI and contributed 17.5 wins to a Yankee team that won 98 games and won its first pennant by 4.5 games over the Indians. Ruth's feats captivated the baseball world and stole the New York fans' attention from the rival Giants. The fanfare reached a peak in mid-June when the Babe became the first person to homer into the centerfield bleachers at the Polo Grounds.[29] For the nonbelievers, he did it again, *the next day,* amidst a seven-home run binge in a five-game stretch.[30] To no one's surprise, the Yankees once again drew over 1.2 million fans, for the second year outdrawing their landlords by more than 250,000 fans. The NL pennant–winning Giants would extract revenge as they beat the Yankees to win the World Series. Nonetheless, the Yankees were growing a bit too popular for the Giants to tolerate, so the Giants demanded that the Yankees vacate the Polo Grounds as soon as possible. Two years later Yankee Stadium would open across the river in the Bronx. Ruth's 1921 dollar value to the Yankees is estimated at $672,000, his second highest in his career and still 17 times his salary.

1922: Ruth's strong-willed personality and extracurricular barnstorming tour following the 1921 World Series posed a problem for baseball's hierarchy. He ignored a rule that forbade players who had participated in the World Series to barnstorm (for fear that players would create an informal rematch and upstage the Series).[31] Insisting on earning additional pay, Ruth met his match when he defied Commissioner Landis and was subsequently suspended for the beginning of the 1922 season. After two otherworldly seasons, Ruth came back to earth, playing in only 110 games, precipitating an attendance revenue decline of about 17%. For any other player in baseball, it would have been an MVP-type season, but Ruth's team-leading 35 home runs, 99 RBI and .672 slugging percentage were a decline from the standards he set in his previous Yankee seasons. Nonetheless, the Yankees won the AL pennant by a mere one game over the St. Louis Browns but lost another World Series to possibly the greatest New York Giants team in their illustrious history. For the third straight year the Yankees outdrew the Giants, with over one million fans as they laid plans for the next year's debut of Yankee Stadium. Despite contributing fewer than 10 wins to the Yankees' season, Ruth's value is estimated at $507,000 for the 1922 season, with a substantial portion of his value attributable to his bigger-than-life persona and the power to draw people to the ballpark.

1923: On April 18th Yankee Stadium debuted to a standing-room-only crowd of over 70,000, with an additional 25,000 fans turned away.[32] The largest crowd in baseball history (at the time) saw their stadium christened with a Ruth home run, and the Yankees and the Babe were on their way to their first World Championship. Ruth had possibly his greatest season that year. Babe, who played in every Yankee game, hit .393 with 41 home runs and 131 RBI. Combined with 170 walks and 17 stolen bases, he contributed more than 19 wins to the 98-win Yankees that won the AL pennant by 16 games over the Tigers.[33] Ruth bombed three World Series home runs, and the Yankees toppled the mighty Giants in a six-game Series that drew over 300,000 fans.[34] With their brand new ballpark and their first World Series triumph, the 1923 Yankees officially dethroned the Giants as the kings of New York baseball, a position they would hold until the Giants and Dodgers ultimately left the city and moved to the West Coast 54 years later. Ruth's value for the 1923 season is estimated at $688,000, the highest of his 15-year career in pinstripes.

1924: Babe turned in another stellar season (.378, 46,121) and was narrowly denied the Triple Crown by Washington's Goose Goslin, who led the AL with 129 RBI. Locked in a tight pennant race with Washington, the Yankees fell two games short despite winning 20 of their last 23 games. The Yankees rode the momentum from their previous season's World Championship to outdraw the NL pennant–winning Giants by over 200,000 fans. This supports the same "carryforward effect" that we observe today. While winning nine fewer games than the previous year and finishing in second place, the 1924 Yankees increased attendance over 1923 by 4.6%. Babe contributed 15 wins to the 89-win Yankees, at an estimated dollar value of $549,000 for the 1924 season.[35]

1925: Ruth and the Yankees had a disappointing year. Babe had health problems and missed the first two months of the season. Later, he had a run-in with manager Miller Huggins and was suspended. The result was a seventh-place finish for a team that turned in an uncharacteristic 69–85 record. Attendance was down dramatically, as Yankee fans' had apparently given the team only a one-year reprieve from losing the AL pennant. A second year removed from a World Series appearance, attendance declined by more than 30%. Babe appeared in only 98 games and batted a meager .290 with only 25 HRs. Given his poor conditioning and his lack of self-discipline, some wondered if the 30-year-old Ruth was at the tail end of his career. Ruth's contribution to Yankee revenues is estimated to be the lowest of his career, at $341,000.

1926: The Babe proved his naysayers wrong as he led the Yankees to a bounce-back year. Starting with an 18-game winning streak during *spring training*, 1926 had all the makings of a turn around from the Yankees dismal 1925.[36] Ruth, at 31 years old, led the club, batting .372, with 47 HRs and 150 RBI. Two youngsters, Tony Lazzeri and Lou Gehrig, pitched in with over 100 RBI each, and the Yankees returned to the World Series, winning 91 regular season games, finishing three games ahead of Cleveland. With their on-field success, and these two bright young stars to complement Ruth, their attendance returned to over one million fans, while the Giants and Dodgers were both sub-.500 teams that drew 700,362 and 650,869, respectively. It was a very successful year for Ruth and the Yankees, up until the last play of the seventh game of the World Series against the St. Louis Cardinals, which may still be the most unusual conclusion of the Fall Classic. (In Game 4, the Babe became the first player to hit three home runs in a World Series game.) In the late innings of Game 7, the Yankees struggled against Hall of Fame pitcher Grover Cleveland Alexander, who had come in from the bullpen in an effort to quell a Yankee rally. With two out in the ninth, Alexander, who had retired all seven batters he faced, issued a walk to the Babe. On the next pitch, Babe, convinced the Yankees could not string together enough hits to score him, attempted to steal second and was thrown out, to give the Cardinals the 1926 World Series. (This would be the Babe's last *losing* World Series game, as New York would be champions three more times before he would hang up his spikes.) His "caught stealing" notwithstanding, Ruth's dollar value to the 1926 Yankees is estimated at $636,000, second only to his dollar value in 1921.

1927: Many have called this Yankee team the greatest baseball team of all time. Led by Ruth and his remarkable feat of 60 home runs, the Yankees clobbered the AL with 110 wins, finishing 19 games ahead of the second-place Philadelphia A's. The Babe's supporting cast had come of age, with Gehrig leading the Yankees in batting average (.373) and RBI (175). The heavily favored Bronx Bombers went on to sweep the Pirates in the World Series. Fans flocked to see the legendary team, as well as witness baseball history as Ruth sought to top his own single-season home run record. With 1.1 million fans, the Yankees were flourishing both on the field and at the box office. When estimating Ruth's dollar value for this historic season, he is penalized because of the expectation that the team may have accomplished much of their success even without him. Statistically, Ruth had one of the top three seasons of his career. His 16-win contribution was an integral part of the make-up of the 1927 Yankees.[37] However, if Ruth had been replaced by a replacement player, the Yankees would have been expected to still win 94 games and the AL pennant and very possibly the World Series. Also, the dollar value of the 94th through 110th wins is less than, say, the dollar value of the 84th through 100th wins, further lessening the financial impact of the Babe's great season. The result of the analysis places an estimate of Ruth's dollar value at $509,000 for his record-setting 1927 season.

1928: The Yankees followed their legendary 1927 season with an encore, winning the AL pennant with 101 wins and finishing 2.5 games ahead of the Athletics. They also matched their four-game sweep in the World Series, this time over the Cardinals, to whom they had lost two years earlier. Ruth was remarkably productive at age 33, with 54 HRs and 142 RBI, while batting .323. His 13-win contribution to the 1928 Yankees proved to be more valuable than his previous year's performance, as the Yankees were in a tight pennant race much of the season. His dollar value is estimated at $619,000 for the season.

1929: The Yankees failed to "three-peat" in 1929, as they finished a distant second to the Philadelphia A's. As the country entered the Depression, the Yankees' attendance remained healthy at an AL-leading 960,148, although the NL pennant–winning Cubs outdrew the Yankees by more than 50%. Despite missing 19 games, Babe still led the AL with 45 HR's. His .345 average and 154 RBI allowed him to contribute 11 wins, worth an estimated $473,000.

1930: Ruth delivered another monster year in 1930 (.359, 49, 153), yet the Yankees finished in third place, 16 games behind the repeat World Champion Philadelphia A's. With Babe as baseball's biggest drawing card, the Yankees drew an AL-leading 1,169,230, narrowly outdrawing the 86-win Brooklyn Robins, who topped 1 million fans for the first time in Brooklyn history. Ruth's salary reached its career peak of $80,000, and his 14-win contribution to the 86-win Yankees is estimated to have been worth $533,000

1931: For the third consecutive year, the A's won the AL pennant without much of a pennant race as the Yankees finished in second place, 13.5 games behind. The Babe had arguably his last great year, as he hit .373 with 46 HR's and 163 RBI. The Yankees 912,437 fans were still more than any AL team, by a margin of 45% over the second-best A's. Ruth's 14-win contribution to the 94-win team is estimated to have been worth $549,000.

1932: The Yankees returned to the World Series for the seventh and final time in the Ruth era with a 107-win dominating performance. It marked the third time the Yankees exceeded 100 wins in the Ruth era. The Yankees turned the tables on Philadelphia by winning the AL by 13 games. Their sweep of the Chicago Cubs in the World Series was the Yankees third sweep in their last three appearances, having not lost a Series game since Ruth was thrown out trying to steal second in 1926. While the Babe's season was respectable (.341, 41, 137), Gehrig led the team in batting average and RBI. Gehrig also had a four-homer game, an accomplishment never matched by Ruth, further symbolizing the passing of the baton to the next generation of Yankee greatness. Babe also relinquished the league HR title to the A's Jimmie Foxx, who challenged Babe's single-season record but fell two short to finish his season with 58. The Yankees drew 962,320 to lead the AL, and Ruth's nearly 12-win contribution is estimated to have been worth $456,000 to the Yankees.

1933: Depsite winning 91 games, the Yankees finished in second place, seven games behind the Washington Senators. With the country mired in the Great Depression, the Babe agreed to a substantial pay cut to $52,000. He hit just .301, with 34 HR's as a 38-year-old aging superstar. The Yankees drew just 728,014, their lowest attendance in the Ruth era. In a last-ditch effort to boost sagging attendance, Ruth agreed to be the Yankees starting pitcher in the season finale. His complete victory against the Red Sox, in which he also homered, marked the last mound appearance of his career.[38] The magnitude of Ruth's career baseball accomplishments can be summed up in the aftermath of a game in which he notched his 94th career victory as a pitcher and hit his 686th career home run. The estimated value of his nearly 10-win contribution is $460,000.

1934: In Ruth's final year as a Yankee, the club finished in second place, seven games behind the pennant-winning Detroit Tigers. Playing in only 125 games, the Babe hit 22 HRs, with 84 RBI and a .288 batting average. Gehrig, clearly the new leader of the Yankees, batted .363 and virtually doubled Ruth's HR and RBI output, with 49 and 165, respectively. The Babe hit his unthinkable 700th career homer in Detroit in July. In his final home game as a New York Yankee, only 2,000 fans attended a Yankee loss that officially handed the AL pennant to the Tigers.[39] Ruth's seven-win contribution is estimated to have been worth $437,000 to the 1934 Yankees.

The impact of Babe Ruth to the New York Yankees is virtually impossible to overstate. It is not an exaggeration to say the franchise was struggling for survival in 1919 under the ownership of Colonels Rupert and Huston and was a distant second in popularity to McGraw's New York Giants. Without the Bambino, the Yankees would likely have been the on-field equivalent of the Washington Senators, a respectable 82-win club with two or three AL pennants and one World Championship. Without the Babe, one can wonder if the Yankees' owners would have had the fortitude and financial motivation to build Yankee Stadium. If the Giants had continued to dominate New York, placing the two franchises on different trajectories, might it not be possible that the *Yankees* would have been the franchise to vacate the city in 1958, rather than the Giants and Dodgers? Finally, would the sport of baseball have reached its present day heights of popularity if the Babe had not landed in the epicenter of media and commerce—New York City? Fortunately, we will never know the answer.

Endnotes

1. "Urges U. S. Operate Baseball Like Mails," *Chicago Daily Tribune,* September 10, 1921.

2. Ibid.

3. William J. Dwyer, "Baseball: An Evolution from a Sport to a National Million-Dollar Business," *The Washington Post*, April 28, 1935.

4. N.Y. Yankee web site, *http://newyork.yankees.mlb.com/NASApp/mlb/nyy/ballpark/stadium_history.jsp.*

5. Michael J. Haupert and Kenneth Winter, "Pay Ball: The Profitability of the New York Yankees 1915-1937," *Essays in Economic and Business History*, XXI, 2003, p. 90.

6. Ibid., p. 90.

7. "Babe Ruth Demands $207,000 Contract: Letter to N.Y. Owner Hits at Baseball Laws," *Chicago Daily Tribune,* February 27, 1927, p. A1.

8. Edward Mott Wooley, "The Business of Baseball," *McClure's Magazine*, Volume XXXIX, July, 1912, p. 244.

9. Ibid., p. 244.

10. Ibid., p. 244.

11. Ruth's WARP1 statistic for the 1923 season was 19.1 according to *Baseball Prospectus. com, http://www.baseballprospectus.com/dt/ruthba01.shtml.*

12. Because there are no reliable ticket price data, "adjusted" total revenues for the Yankees are used as the dependent variable, rather than home attendance.

13. Total revenues from the Haupert and Winter data were adjusted to exclude line items judged not to be attributable to any player on the Yankees, such as revenue from renting Yankee Stadium for boxing matches or college football games.

14. The expected value of a World Series appearance is included in the win curve. It is estimated by multiplying the probability of winning the pennant, at each win level, times the dollar revenue ($86,000) of playing in a World Series.

15. For the purpose of establishing the probability of reaching the postseason at various win levels, the Ruth era is defined as 1915–1939. Data are from both the AL and NL.

16. Haupert and Winter data.

17. The exception was the two years the Yankees played World Series home games at the Polo Grounds, 1921 and 1922. These games carry a different set of economics, as the New York Giants were the landlord. The data suggest that the revenue impact of two home games was approximately $21,000 per year.

18. Some judgment was exercised in determining how much of the World Series revenues should be attributable to Ruth in any given year. In most years when the Yankees reached the World Series, two home games (and their revenue) were attributed to Ruth, as any additional home games resulting from an extended Series can be considered chance and should not be counted in any player's value.

19. Rather than giving Ruth no credit for the 1927 and 1932 World Series, we assign to him a one-half game revenue credit to account for the possibility that the World Series was better attended and popularized by his mere presence.

20. A different approach is used here to estimate Ruth's marquee value than that explained in Chapter 5. this approach includes a variable in the win curve regression model to isolate the revenue impact of Ruth's presence. This variable is a variation of the number of games he played in a given season. It is a way of differentiating between Babe's marquee value

when he played a full season (e.g., 1921) and his suspension and injury-impacted seasons (e.g., 1922), when fans who were considering a trip to Yankee Stadium had no expectation of watching Babe on the field.

21. Leigh Montville, *The Big Bam: The Life and Times of Babe Ruth*, Doubleday Books, 2006, p. 301 indicates that in the early 1930s the Yankees were averaging 33 exhibition games per year.

22. A variable to isolate the revenue impact of the opening of Yankee Stadium in 1923 did not prove to be statistically significant in the regression model to estimate the Yankees win curve.

23. Despite not being statistically significant in the win curve regression model, $200,000 to $300,000 is a reasonable approximation of the impact of the new Stadium and is comparable to the percentage effect we observe in current day teams.

24. The top-left box of Figure 6.5 represents the "actual" scenario of Ruth as a Yankee with his performance and marquee value as estimated in our model. The top-right box assumes the Yankees perform the same as in the actual scenario but do not have Ruth as a drawing card. In other words, Ruth was not present, but his performance was redistributed among his teammates, so as not to reduce the Yankees overall performance. The lower-left box is the inverse of that scenario, in that Ruth's on-field performance would be that of a replacement player, rather than his actual Hall of Fame statistics. The Yankees' team performance would have suffered accordingly. However, in this scenario Ruth's drawing power would still be present. Finally, in the scenario depicted in the lower-right box, neither Ruth's performance, nor his marquee value would exist. It is as if he never joined the Yankees.

25. Haupert and Winter data for selected years for exhibition game revenue and spring training revenue.

26. Haupert and Winter data available for only 1915 through 1922 and 1928 through 1930.

27. Ibid.

28. See Note 21, p. 114.

29. "Ruth's Record Hit Helps Yanks Win," *New York Times*, June 14, 1921.

30. "Ruth Hits 2 More; One a Record Drive,: *New York Times*, June 15, 1921.

31. Montville, p. 143.

32. "74,200 See Yankees Open New Stadium; Ruth Hits Home Run," *New York Times*, April 19, 1923.

33. The *Baseball Prospectus.com* WARP1 value for Ruth was 19.1 for 1923.

34. World Series data from *baseball-reference.com, http://www.baseball-reference.com/postseason/1923_WS.shtml*.

35. The *Baseball Prospectus.com* WARP1 value for Ruth was 15.1 for 1924.

36. Montville, p 229.

37. Ruth's WARP1 statistic for the 1927 season was 16.2 according to *Baseball Prospectus. com, http://www.baseballprospectus.com/dt/ruthba01.shtml*.

38. "25,000 See Ruth Hurl 6-5 Victory," *New York Times*, October 2, 1933.

39. "Tigers Idle, Win Flag as Yankees Bow," *New York Times*, September 25, 1934.

PART THREE

THE PLAYER DEVELOPMENT SYSTEM

One of the keys to running any successful business is to identify and adeptly manage its high-impact leverage points—the one or two levers a leader can maneuver, for which even a small change in direction can lead to a dramatic impact on results. An MLB team would be hard-pressed to define a more important leverage point of its on-field and business success than its scouting and player development system. Nothing a team does will likely have a greater impact on their cost structure than the success or failure of their farm system's ability to feed talent to the Major League club.

Chapter 7, "The Economics of Player Development," begins by dissecting a team's player development and payroll economics. It focuses on the key enabler of an efficient payroll, the productivity of the scouting and player development system, and some of the key attributes and metrics that distinguish between a highest-performing and least-productive player development system. It blends this analysis with a comparison of the cost of "buying wins" in the free-agent market and discusses the key attributes of the best-in-class scouting and player development systems.

Chapter 8, "A Strategic Approach to Assembling the Roster," takes a big-picture look at how a team can artfully construct its Major League roster, from an economic and financial viewpoint, to give it a consistent chance to reach the postseason. In addition to laying out a financial framework around which a team can be modeled, we discuss the key operating principles that form the basis of sustaining a high-performance team at an affordable payroll while discussing the valuation of a team's most important asset, its players.

7 | The Economics of Player Development

The lifeblood of any baseball organization is its ability to select and develop high-quality talent to staff its Major League roster. No other element of the game can give a team a greater competitive advantage than the ability to produce playing talent. The rules of Major League Baseball dictate its prominent role in a team's success formula. The current version of the reserve clause, which indentures a player to a team for a minor league development period, plus a six-year Major League time horizon, provides a team with a healthy salary discount for home-grown players. If baseball (MLB and the MLBPA) were to change its rules and allow players to achieve free-agent status earlier in their careers, draftee signing bonuses could suffer, and investment in player development might be reduced, as teams would have less time to recoup their investments.

Under the current system, players with less than three years of MLB service (the exception is the most senior 17% of 2-plus-year major leaguers who are designated as Super 2's and are eligible for arbitration one year earlier) are considered "restricted" players and are often paid at, or slightly above, the MLB minimum. Arbitration-eligible players (three to six years of MLB service) are generally paid at a discount to free agents, ranging from 33 to 82%, depending on years of service.[1] The teams with the best-in-class player development systems produce playing talent at a decided cost advantage over teams with a poor track record in graduating major leaguers from their minor league system. Since much of the scouting and player development system is composed of fixed costs (signing bonuses are an exception), success is driven by the number and quality of major leaguers produced.

MLB teams, like many other businesses, are faced with a classic "build versus buy" decision. Unlike a telecom company that chooses to outsource the manufacturing of its cell phones, every baseball team has a procurement (scouting) and manufacturing (minor league system) department, which if managed properly, provides a low-cost source of its most important asset—playing talent. So, the question is not whether a team should outsource one of the most important components of its value chain, but "*how many* resources should we devote to the task of developing players?" and "*how much* of our roster can we fill with home-grown players while maintaining a high level of competitiveness?"

For some teams, player development is the focal point of all baseball operations, with player acquisitions and free-agent signings the opportunistic adjustments to put the finishing touches on the ball club. For other teams, player development is a perplexing enigma, which gets a lot of lip service, but questionable results. The process of player development is made all the more challenging because sometimes it takes several years for a team to know if it's on a successful track. It's normal for today's draftee to spend three years in the minor leagues and a couple of years at the Major League level before a team really knows the payoff of their investment. With a lengthy feedback loop, it's tempting for an organization to shift their direction or continuously tinker with their approach, particularly if they lack a well-conceived development strategy.

What is the payoff of a first-class player development system? Does it make sense to put so much focus, resources, and executive attention into the process when a team can dip into the free-agent market each winter in the hopes of assembling a competitive roster? MLB's rules give "build" the inside track versus "buy," particularly the six-year MLB time horizon a team has to recoup its development costs. Some of the key variables that drive the math of developing versus acquiring players include the yield from the annual player draft, the size of signing bonuses for draftees, the length of time a player spends in the minor league system, and his ultimate productivity at the Major League level.

THE COST OF DEVELOPING PLAYERS

Profiling the draft history of a sample of 10 teams gives us a sense of the performance range across MLB, as well as determining which teams performed at the highest and lowest levels. The analysis includes all draft picks of the 10 teams over seven consecutive drafts (1991–1997), as any fair comparison of the build versus buy dilemma would extend the internally developed players through six years of Major League service—the length of time a team has exclusive ownership of a player.[2] The 10 teams in the sample averaged 32 marginal wins produced (prior to a player achieving free-agent status) for each annual draft.[3] Other averages for the sample set include 3.8 players per draft who ultimately graduated to the big leagues *and* had *positive marginal wins.* (Another 1.5 players per team per year reached the Major Leagues but played below the replacement level.) Beyond the data from the sample, in order to calculate the cost of developing and harvesting marginal wins from the draft and develop route, an assumption was made about the annual cost of scouting and player development, including signing bonuses. While this information is not readily available, and any figures that may have appeared in published reports are outdated, we use a $12 million annual cost (including signing bonuses) as the cost of scouting and player development.[4] Because we are dealing with a 10-year timeframe, these costs are meant to reflect a team's average costs in the 1999 to 2002 time window, not present day costs.[5] Combining the net present value of the cost of developing, with the Major League salary dollars the draft graduates would earn, yields an estimated cost per marginal win of $860,000.[6]

Two teams that performed at opposite ends of the spectrum during the timeframe surveyed, the Twins and Dodgers, may give us a sense of the range in draft performance. Compared to the average team's 32 marginal wins, the Twins delivered 44 marginal wins per draft, while the Dodgers supplied only 16. For six of the seven consecutive years measured, the Twins' drafts ultimately provided more than 30 marginal wins, with the 1994 draft class yielding an impressive 75 wins, driven by Todd Walker, AJ Pierzynski, and Corey Koskie. Conversely, the Dodgers delivered over 20 wins only twice in the 7-year period. For three of the seven years they had horrendous drafts that yielded fewer than three wins each for the entire draft class. The Twins had more year-to-year consistency than the average team, as their variation indexed at 79 to the sample average, while the Dodgers' inconsistency translated into a 145 variation index. The bottom line impact reflects the disparate performance. The Twins' dollar cost per marginal win for home-grown, drafted players is estimated at $710,000, while the estimate of the Dodgers cost is $1,330,000 per marginal win, assuming they spent the equivalent dollars on scouting and player development.[7]

The Yankees might have mirrored the Dodgers if it were not for 1992 first-round draft pick Derek Jeter's 33 cumulative marginal wins prior to his eligibility for free agency. Following the success of developing Jorge Posada (1989 draft) and Andy Pettitte (1990 draft), the Yankees struggled thorough the 1991–1997 period, with only two drafts yielding more than

10 marginal wins. The result is a cost per marginal win of $1.5 million. Another team that distinguished itself and rivaled the Twins stellar draft performance was the Indians. From 1991 through 1996 the Indians delivered at least one substantial player each year: Manny Ramirez in 1991, followed by Paul Shuey, Steve Kline, Danny Graves, Sean Casey, and David Riske. The result is a cost per marginal win of $650,000 for home-grown players. Even though players were traded by their original team, the scouting and player development system of the drafting team should still get credit for the players' marginal wins prior to free agency. For example, Sean Casey was traded during spring training of 1998 to the Reds for Dave Burba, but Casey would not have been eligible for free agency until after the 2004 season.[8] Whether or not the original team acquired fair value in exchange for their drafted player is a separate matter and should not reflect on an evaluation of its player development system.

Figure 7.1 summarizes the results of the teams in the sample.

Figure 7.2 shows the leverage against the fixed costs of the player development system, reflected in the relationship between cost per win and marginal wins.

Scouting and Player Development

Productivity and Costs for 10-Team Sample for 1991-1997 drafts*

Team	Marginal Wins /Draft	Marginal Wins Per ML Player	Marginal Wins Per Player/Yr	$ Cost **
ATL	28	7.6	1.1	.950
BOS	39	8.9	1.3	.780
CHC	28	9.4	1.3	.920
CLE	46	12.4	1.8	.650
LAD	16	8.4	1.2	1.330
MIN	44	9.6	1.4	.710
NYM	28	8.5	1.2	.930
NYY	21	6.1	0.9	1.510
OAK	38	7.7	1.1	.820
STL	36	7.3	1.0	.890
10-Team Avg	32	8.6	1.2	.860

* Marginal Win data is cumulative and prior to players free agent eligibility   ** Millions of Dollars per Marginal Win

FIGURE 7.1 **Draft summary for sample teams.**

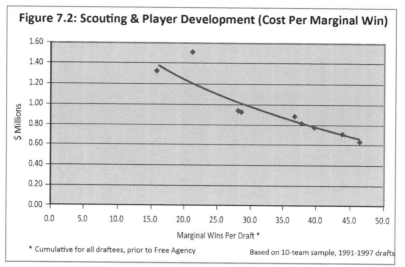

FIGURE 7.2 **Graph of sample teams' costs per marginal win.**

THE COST OF FREE AGENTS

To quantify the average free agent cost per marginal win, we analyzed salary data and marginal win performance data for more than 500 players for the 2005 season and concluded that free agents carried an average cost of $2.4 million per marginal win.[9] The data also show a large variation in the average cost per marginal win by position, with pitchers, particularly left-handers, at the top of the free-agent food chain. First basemen and designated hitters come at cheapest price in the free-agent market, at $1.96 million per marginal win, while pitchers are valued at $2.57 million and left-handed starting pitchers at $3.19 million per marginal win. Figure 7.3 shows the going rate for free agents, based on the sample of the free-agent contracts in effect during the 2005 season.

To compare the cost of development with the cost of purchasing the same wins in the free-agent market, we need to go beyond comparing the out-of-pocket costs of each type of asset. We need to account for the time value of money for the developed players, which includes signing bonuses paid out years before a player ever sees a Major League ballpark, a gestation period in the minors, and ultimately a stream of marginal wins from the handful of players who reach the majors. To create our apples-to-apples comparison, we'll set the clock to the year a draftee makes his Major

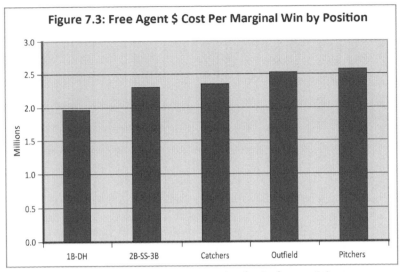

FIGURE 7.3 **Free-agent costs per marginal win by position.**

League debut. In our comparison the draft would have occurred four years earlier, and the player has five additional years (beyond the current year) to contribute to his drafting team prior to eligibility for free agency. To capture the full potential return of the home-grown player, we evaluate the costs and returns over a 10-year period. The free agent, on the other hand, is a "sign and play" model, with a short gap between a signing bonus and the expected marginal wins on the playing field. To evaluate the build versus buy investment tradeoff, we measure the cost of marginal wins from harvesting an average team's draft and compare it to the price of those same wins in the free agent market.

One key component of the comparison between the cost of home-grown and free-agent players is accounting for the elapsed time from when costs are incurred to when wins are produced. The output of the average draft class, determined by the sample data, is 31 marginal wins over the six years of Major League service prior to free agency. The net present value of the average player development system is $860,000 per marginal win, versus $2.4 million per win purchased in the free-agent market (see Figure 7.4 for the detailed cost comparison.)

The cost advantage a team's player development system provides is dependent on the output of the system—the number and quality of graduates it promotes to the Major Leagues. Even in the worst-case examples from our sample teams, the Yankees and Dodgers, the home-grown player is

Figure 7.4: "Build vs. Buy"
Draft and Develop vs. Free Agents

	Develop. Costs	ML-1	ML-2	ML-3	ML-4	ML-5	ML-6	Total
Marginal Wins		8	8	6	3	3	3	31
Draft & Develop	$ 12	$ 2.7	$ 1.3	$ 1.3	$ 2.9	$ 3.2	$ 3.6	$26.5*
Free Agent	---	19.4	21.1	17.5	9.1	9.4	9.7	$78.6*

Development + Payroll
Costs/Marginal Win

Draft & Develop $ 860,000
Free Agents $2,400,000

* Net present value of total costs

FIGURE 7.4 **Cost comparison of build versus buy.**

still a cheaper alternative, but less so. The Yankees' and Dodgers' cost per marginal win for developed players is $1.5 million and $1.3 million, respectively, while the best-in-class teams, the Twins and Indians, are able to produce talent at a cost of $710,000 and $650,000 per marginal win, respectively. A strong player development system creates a double benefit. It allows a team to maintain a *lower cost* of home-grown talent and provides the pipeline that allows a team to field a *higher mix* of the low-cost talent.

We can dissect the cost of a marginal win by separating the development costs and payroll costs to gain deeper insight into a team's economics. Looking at payroll only yields a particularly wide spread between free agents and home-grown players of $2.4 million to $420,000, respectively. Allocating player development costs adds another $440,000 to home-grown players for the $860,000 sample average per marginal win. Figure 7.5 breaks down the cost of development and the average payroll expense by each class of player.

	Development Costs	Payroll Costs	Total Costs
Free Agents	---	2.400	2.400
Home-grown Players	.440	.420	.860
Arbitration Eligible	.440	.880	1.310
Restricted	.440	.200	.640

Figure 7.5: Development Costs & Payroll Costs by Class of Player*

* Costs are in millions of dollars per marginal win

FIGURE 7.5 **Payroll costs and development costs.**

TALENT AS CAPITAL

An MLB team realizes tangible benefits from being a best-in-class talent evaluator and developer. Much of a team's scouting and player development system is burdened with the fixed costs of finding and moving 40 to 50 players per year through their minor league system. Moving the needle on the player development system's output, by yielding more Major League talent per player drafted can substantially reduce the cost of producing marginal wins. Any team that produces more than its fair share of Major League talent can keep a lid on its payroll by shifting its roster mix toward the inexpensive end of the pay scale. The team's return on investment is the gap between the development costs and salary it pays to these restricted players versus the price it would have paid to purchase these wins in the free-agent market.

Can the benefits of being a low-cost producer of MLB-ready talent can extend beyond staffing a team's own roster? What if the best-in-class teams viewed their scouting and player development systems as potential profit centers? Since a player's overall asset value relates to his expected performance relative to his compensation, young players indentured to a team for six years of MLB service can be a valuable asset, with the highest-quality young players being a team's *highest*-value player assets. If a team could build a bank of excess talent—more than they could practically absorb at the MLB level—could they monetize the value by selling the talent to other teams? (Today's Major League rules prevent high-value cash transactions, which we will discuss in the next chapter, A Strategic Approach to Assembling the Roster.)

Another way to receive value for a highly productive player development system is to trade young prospects for seasoned players who can step in and help a team win today. The exchange rate of today's wins for tomorrow's wins is a complex equation influenced by several competing factors. With the advent of the wild card, the increasing number of teams in the playoff hunt each year has placed more teams in the mid-season trade market seeking the last piece of the puzzle. However, the escalating cost of free agents over the past decade has placed a greater value on the "prospect," who has six years of discounted marginal wins to contribute to his team. (For a more detailed analysis and discussion, see the sidebar, The Exchange Rate: Today's Wins versus Tomorrow's Wins.)

To gauge the typical life cycle of a player's asset value, we analyzed over 50 active players who have 10 or more years of Major League service. Indexing the marginal wins (WARP) they delivered each year to their career average made it possible to create a performance arc for their 10 years' of performance. The average salary for the same 10-year cycle was also analyzed, by calibrating their performance against the Major League minimum, typical arbitration awards, and the market rate for free agents. While both lines in Figure 7.6 represent indices, it is clear that a player's highest return to a team—as measure by the opportunity cost of buying the same wins in the free-agent market—is his pre–free agency years. A player's *tenure* is nearly as important as his performance in determining his asset value.

One way for a team to alter the shape of the performance and salary arcs is to consider retaining a young player with a long-term deal. It generally makes sense to take advantage of a young player's inability to negotiate a salary in order to reconcile the overall economics of operating a team. There are exceptions when a team would benefit by paying the player additional dollars for the purpose of locking up his services and gaining salary certainty over a longer period of time. The Cardinals took this route with Albert Pujols. As a prelude to their ultimate long-term deal, the team gave Pujols a $900,000 salary for his third year of MLB service, a record for any third-year player. The Cardinals followed up with a seven-year, $100 mil-

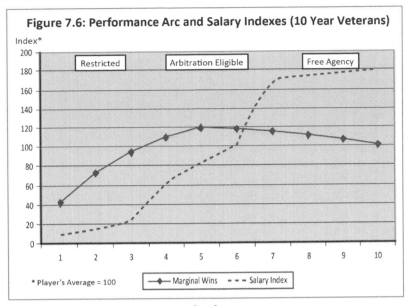

FIGURE 7.6 **Performance arc and salary arc.**

lion deal, beginning when he still had three years of arbitration eligibility remaining.[10] By effectively accelerating Pujols through the pay grades—restricted, arbitration, and free agency—and offering him a competitive free-agent wage earlier than he would have received it, they were able to delay his ability to negotiate with other teams for at least an additional five years. Clearly this approach should be reserved for the truly special player, which Pujols has proved to be.

Another motivation for signing a restricted or arbitration-eligible player to a long-term deal is to lock up a "face of the franchise" player—someone who has marquee value and fan appeal and who the team can utilize to connect the team brand with its fans. In addition to Pujols, players like Derek Jeter and Grady Sizemore fit this description. In addition to their formidable talent, they have enormous fan appeal. The Yankees went two years into arbitration with Jeter (Jeter won a $5 million arbitration award in his first year of eligibility) before signing the marquee player of baseball's marquee franchise to a 10-year, $189 million deal.[11] The Indians struck early with Sizemore, signing him to a six-year, $23.45 million contract, the largest deal ever given to a player with less than two years of MLB service.[12]

DEFINING A STRONG PLAYER DEVELOPMENT SYSTEM

What constitutes a strong scouting and player development system? What differentiates teams like the Twins, Indians (for our sample years), Braves, and A's, who are renowned for their ability to grow talent, from the Yankees and Dodgers? There is a short list of criteria that influence the return on investment of a team's development system and can also serve as goals for the best-in-class organizations:

- *Delivering a high number of marginal wins* to the Major League club, within the window that a player is indentured to a team. All other things being equal, the more marginal wins a minor league system graduates to the MLB club, the more value it creates. However, occasionally a team will draft and develop a player who turns out to be a late bloomer, and much of the player's value is generated *after* he reaches free agency. Unless the player is perceived to be a valuable commodity in a trade, he has little value to the drafting club. Two examples of players who succeeded but did not pay off for their drafting team are pitcher Paul Byrd and ex-catcher turned first baseman Scott Hatteberg. Byrd's was drafted in the fourth round in 1991, but the late bloomer delivered fewer than eight marginal wins prior to reaching free-agent status and more than 20 marginal wins after he became a free agent.[13] Hatteberg, a late first-round pick in the same 1991 draft delivered seven marginal wins prior to free agency, compared to more than 13 after free agency.[14]

- *Year-to-year draft consistency* is another mark of a high-quality development system. It benefits the Major League club to have a steady stream of talent available and ready to graduate to the big league roster. This allows the team to be selective in filling needs and lessens the need to look externally to the high-cost free-agent market to plug a hole. Weak drafts in back-to-back years can have a domino effect and set a team back years in their development cycle. A void of MLB-ready talent in the high minors may force a GM to make a long-term commitment to a veteran free agent, reduce his bargaining power in the trade market, or promote a developing player too early to fill a need. In 1992 the L.A. Dodgers were virtually shut out in the June draft. The only player from their 60 drafted players to reach the Major Leagues was a utility infielder, Keith Johnson, a fourth-round pick who played in a total of six games in his big league career. The Cubs had several consecutive weak drafts in the early 1990s, placing unwanted pressure on the team to make other moves in an attempt to be competitive.

- *Spreading marginal wins across an optimal number of players* is another success variable for a team's player development system. For example, if a team has an average yield of 20 marginal wins per draft (cumulatively for all draftees, for all years prior to their free agent eligibility), the amount of value created will be affected by the *number of players* comprising the 20 marginal wins. If these 20 wins are spread over seven players, efficiency might be low. These too few wins spread over too many players consume a high number of roster spots and major league minimum salaries for the draft graduates. Assuming an average of four years per player, each player would average less than one marginal win per year, making it difficult for the MLB team to productively use their contribution. At the other end of the scale, if the 20 marginal wins are tied up in only one star player (averaging 3.3 marginal wins for each of his six years prior to free agency), the return on investment from the draft may be too concentrated, indicating an all or nothing result from the draft process. In the latter scenario, one serious injury could completely wipe out any value from a particular draft.

- *Development time from draft day to the Major Leagues* is another important variable. A baseball team's development system is like a manufacturing plant dedicated to producing Major League talent. The longer the gestation period, the more capacity is needed to produce a finished product. Higher capacity leads to higher costs and lower productivity. In a sample of all first-round draft picks from the 1995–1998 drafts, the average development time for those who ultimately reached the Major Leagues is 3.4 years, made up of college players at an average of 2.7 years and high school draftees at an average of 4.1 years. If a team developed a strategy to shorten the development cycle so that minor league tenure was one year shorter than the average, they could potentially reduce capacity—the number of minor leaguers or possibly even the number of minor league teams—and ultimately reduce their overall cost of development while maintaining the same level of output.

- *It is critical to capitalize on high draft picks,* as the hefty signing bonuses make these high–risk, high-reward investments. If a team has the fortune of drafting in the top 10 picks in the annual draft, it may be in line to lay out a sizable bonus in the range of $2 million to $5 million in recent years. From the late 1990s drafts, over 70% of the top 10 picks made it to the Major Leagues, and many are today's stars, including Barry Zito, Mark Mulder, Jon Garland, Ben Sheets, and Josh Beckett. One sure way to lower a teams' overall return from its player development system is to have a top 10 pick fail to reach the big leagues. At the top of the draft, say the first three rounds, a team may spend $3 million or more in bonuses plus the "carrying costs" of three players for two to three years in the minor leagues to yield one bona fide major leaguer. If the early rounds can be categorized as a high risk investment, the late rounds can be thought of as a lottery ticket. At the bottom end of the draft a team may need to carry, say, 25 players for four years each to mine one bona fide big leaguer.

- *Focusing scouting and player development resources on the highest-value positions* will improve its contribution to the organization. Based on salaries paid to free-agent players and their contributions to wins, the market places a premium or discount value on certain positions. While the average cost of buying a marginal win in the free-agent market is estimated at $2.4 million, outfielders are estimated to be priced at $2.5 million, pitchers at $2.6 million, and left-handed pitchers at $2.9 million. Left-handed starting pitchers, who presumably would be the cream-of-the-crop of all left-handers, are estimated to be valued at $3.2 million. Conversely, first basemen and designated hitters are pegged at $1.9 million per marginal win. A player development system creates more value for the organization if it biases its output toward the high-priced end of the value scale, particularly pitching. Anything an organization can do to fill a pitching need internally and avoid filling it via the free-agent market will save money and take pressure off of payroll expenses.

Teams that subscribe to these six operating principles, or strategic directions, for their scouting and player development systems have the inside track on building an affordable winning team. Being among the top-tier teams in marginal wins produced from their minor league systems, spread over the optimal number of players with year-to-year consistency while managing minor league development time, along with a high "hit-rate" on draft picks in the first several rounds and a focus on high-value positions all contribute to a top-notch player development system.

THE INTERNATIONAL MARKET FOR PLAYERS

Beyond the draft, the international markets provide a rich source of talent, particularly Latin America and Asia. Of the fertile markets outside the United States, where baseball dominates the sports landscape, only Canada, Puerto Rico, and other U.S. territories are included in the draft. A player residing in another country is eligible to be signed as a free agent, which is the route taken by All Stars Bobby Abreu and Miguel Cabrera. Abreu (Houston) and Cabrera (Florida) were both signed as 16-year-olds in their native Venezuela. More recently two graduates from the Yankees' farm system—Robinson Cano and Chien-Ming Wang—did not come from the amateur draft, but rather as international free-agent signings. The absence of a draft usually means the ability to discover talent and signing bonus dollars are the keys to winning a prospect. As a result, the well-endowed teams have staked claims to foreign markets and elbowed the less-fortunate teams out of the picture. Signing unproven prospects in Latin America has become a focus of a broader range of clubs, but the Yankees have jumped into the fray with checkbook in hand. With their financial advantages, the Yankees do not need to be the first to discover a player; they can simply swoop in at the eleventh hour and top another team's signing bonus and likely win the prospect of their dreams.

Star Japanese players have gravitated to the major markets with lucrative contracts that are beyond the reach of most teams. The latest sensation, 26-year-old Japanese pitcher, Daisuke Matsuzaka, is expected to eventually evolve into a top-of-the-rotation starter for the Red Sox. Matsuzaka, who once threw 250 pitches in a 17-inning high school tournament game, is ready to make his MLB debut in 2007. His former team, the Seibu Lions, landed a $51.1 million fee to part with his services just two years earlier than his free-agent eligibility. On top of the posting fee the Red Sox parted with another $52 million over six years, raising Matsuzaka's total cost to over $103 million, or $17 million per year.

The Matuszaka signing is an interesting case study in baseball economics and negotiating leverage. Under the posting rules agreed on by the Japanese Baseball League and MLB, the Seibu Lions would have retained his rights and not received the $51.1 million posting fee if the player did not sign with the Red Sox. Unlike a free agent, Matsuzaka was not allowed to negotiate with other MLB teams. On a conceptual level, it's as if the Red Sox paid Matsuzaka $103 million, who in turn paid $51 million to purchase his rights from his team, the Seibu Lions. The star pitcher's alternative was to wait two years until he qualified for free agency and negotiate with any MLB team without any money being owed to Seibu. How much money did Matsuzaka leave on the table by not displaying the patience to wait two more years? Did the Red Sox pay more or less than they would have if the pitcher was a free agent? The Red Sox likely saved some dollars on their total cost of Matsuzaka's services in this two-step process by engaging in the competitive bidding at the *posting fee* level, rather than in the player–team negotiation. The competitive bidding occurred early in the process when several important factors were still unclear, such as the player's salary demands, no doubt tempering the bids and restraining the overall cost of Matsuzaka.

International player sourcing has become a game of high-stakes poker, attracting mostly the teams with the biggest bankrolls. While MLB can alter the economics by subjecting international players to a draft, they have shown no inclination to do so. Some teams have pulled scouts out of international markets or scaled back resources, believing they cannot compete against the free-agent bonuses paid by the higher-revenue teams. These teams need to be certain that they are taking a broader view of the international market as a potential niche opportunity to source talent. The search costs, success rate, and bonus levels of each potential international market need to be weighed against the success of their drafts and the cost of buying talent in the free-agent market. A detailed study would require access to information that is not publicly available, such as a team's international scouting cost data. It would be particularly interesting to determine if there is a strong correlation between a team's draft success and their international sourcing track record. One hypothesis suggests that they are *inversely* related. Possibly the Yankees mediocre performance in the draft is a result of a focus on international players, a market that does not require them to stand in line and wait their turn, but instead allows them to deploy their flood of revenue to outbid other teams. It's one arena where their economic advantages can be fully leveraged.

WINNING IS JOB ONE

Building a high-performance player development system requires more than having a strategy. It's also about execution. This is an area where baseball can take a page from the business world's playbook, particularly from the quality initiatives swept through U.S. companies in the 1990s. One of the key underpinnings of delivering product quality is managing the key business processes and using metrics that continuously monitor success. Since one key ingredient to producing wins is talent, the amateur scouting department can be thought of as the raw material procurement department of a baseball team. The efficiency and effectiveness of a raw material purchasing process is a key first step to producing a high-quality product. In baseball terms it would mean holding the scouting department accountable by using a set of measures geared to gauge success and failure in the key area of player selection. A GM can rate his scouting department on the three key measures of player selection: the percent of draftees reaching the majors, development time in the minors, and, ultimately, the draftees' marginal wins in the big leagues. The development time metric would be calibrated against MLB-wide averages. For example, college pitchers drafted in the first round average 2.7 years to the big leagues, while high school pitchers average 4.1 years. For fifth rounders, average development time is 3.5 years and 4.6 years, respectively, for college and high school pitchers.[15] The scouting scorecard does not need to be restricted to a team's draft choices. The scouting department can also be held accountable for its *recommendations* by simply tracking the recommended players' performances through another team's farm system.

Accountabilities can be cascaded through the entire scouting department to maintain consistency and alignment with the organization's objectives. For example, the organization may have a bias toward focusing on college pitchers, with the intention of sourcing the highest-value assets while reducing the development time and path to the Major Leagues. This strategy might result in an organizational guideline of a 60–40 mix of college and high school prospects to be followed and rated. So each scout's metrics would include the number of pitchers, college versus high school, and nonpitchers he would need to scout and rate, using the same type of discipline that a sales team would use to determine the number of prospects they would need to visit to deliver a sale. At the end of the scouting season each scout and regional director would be rated on metrics for efficiency (the number of prospects scouted by category [pitcher/nonpitcher, college/high school]) and effectiveness (the quality of the recommendations, including prospects drafted by other teams, and their signability). By implementing measures at every level of the scouting department, a GM or scouting director can better align a team of scouts and enable them to focus on the specific direction the organization sets. Implementing detailed metrics throughout every level of the scouting organization is the equivalent of measuring quality.

In baseball it is difficult to separate the raw material procurement process—scouting—from the manufacturing process—player development. Extending our quality initiative to the farm system would include measuring the activities necessary to properly develop an important component of the team's asset base: its minor league prospects. In addition to teaching fundamentals, the most valuable development tools an organization can offer are plate appearances and batters faced. The player development system's accountabilities and metrics would include the number of plate appearances for priority prospects. Critical to the development of a young player is the exposure and experience to comparable or higher-caliber players. A minor league organization must create team rosters that appropriately match a player with his "stretch" level of performance, while giving him ample playing time. Mismatching players with teams could result in a logjam at a position and insufficient playing time for a key prospect, stunting his growth and ultimately his path to the Majors. Running a minor league organization is a challenging exercise in asset management. For the best clubs these asset allocation decisions are far too complex to be made on gut instinct. The best-in-class development organizations painstakingly match these learning experiences with the highest potential return assets—all in the name of building a winner.

Our quality initiative can be extended to an often overlooked aspect of player development: health management or injury avoidance. Philosophies vary on pitch counts and the number of innings young pitchers should be permitted to work. Some believe that gradually increasing the annual innings for a pitching prospect will ultimately ready him for a 200-plus inning season in the Majors. While injuries have much to do with luck, the teams who make injury prevention a priority tend to succeed at minimizing players days lost to injury. Baseball Prospectus author and injury expert Will Carroll has helped raise the awareness at the Major League level. He annually awards the Dick Martin Award (named after former a Minnesota Twins trainer) to the team with the best medical staff based on days lost and payroll dollars lost to the disabled list, and year-over-year improvements, among other measures. The award was won by the Tampa Bay Devil Rays in 2004 and the Milwaukee Brewers in 2005. According to Carroll, on average, over 800 man-days are lost to a Major League club each season. That adds up to about 4.5 man-*seasons* from a 25-man roster each year.[16] Reducing lost time by a mere 20% could save a team over $4 million in nonproductive payroll expense.[17]

In teams that make reductions of lost time a priority, that attitude tends to permeate the organization. When considering free-agent signings, they value injury tendency as a more important factor than other clubs. This is particularly important for teams that operate with an economic disadvantage to the mega-market teams like the Yankees. They recognize that a key ingredient to building a winning team is keeping their 25-player roster healthy and available to be deployed, avoiding the need to pay a premium price to fill an immediate need owing to injury.

Nothing has a greater impact on the economics of winning in baseball than a team's scouting and player development. Payroll efficiency is largely determined by the quality and quantity of the finished product turned out by a team's farm system. While most teams analyze roster scenarios several years into the future, the best-in-class approach utilizes a quantitative framework that models the economic impact of alternative scenarios, focusing a team to proactively maintain a mix of productive young players.

Endnotes

1. John D. Burger and Stephen J. K. Walters, "Arbitrator Bias and Self-Interest: Lessons from the Baseball Labor Market," *Journal of Labor Research*, Vol. XXVI, No. 2, Spring 2005, pp. 267–280. On page 275 of this article, Table 2 shows arbitration awards relative to players' marginal revenue product (MRP). The authors conclude that free agents are paid in the range of 78% to 94% of their MRP, so their arbitration award analysis is quoted here *relative to free-agent compensation.*

2. Draft data are from*www.baseballcube.com*, an excellent site replete with volumes of data on every Major League draft. Since the analysis requires an evaluation of a draftee's complete marginal win contribution for the six years that he remains the property of his team, we do not to go beyond the 1997 draft. Evaluating the 1998 (and beyond) drafts would require the additional complexity of forecasting a player's expected performance to calculate the ultimate number of marginal wins he would provide the team that owns his contract. Also, we do not distinguish between a player who remained with his drafting team for the entire period prior to becoming a free agent as opposed to a player who was traded. In both cases the number of marginal wins the drafted player produced prior to reaching free-agent status is evaluated. While free-agent eligibility dates are not explicitly published, it is possible to estimate the time at which a player became a free agent from his playing time statistics at *www.baseball-reference.com*.

3. The 10 teams are the Mets, Braves, Twins, Dodgers, Cardinals, Cubs, Indians, Yankees, A's, and Red Sox. Not all of these marginal wins are "usable" wins on the team's roster. Since the analysis is based on the *draft year*, the wins may not arrive at the Major League level at a time, or at a position for a ML team to realize their full value. In some cases the players were dealt to other clubs because the team that developed the player did not have a roster spot available to capitalize on the graduating player. The average team in the sample is estimated to have produced an average of 31 usable wins per draft. The average team in the sample is estimated to have a 5% "waste factor," with a low of zero (Twins and Indians) and a high of 10% (Cardinals and Yankees).

4. This excludes international scouting and signing bonuses, as foreign players are generally nondrafted free agents.

5. If we were to use present day scouting and player development costs, the analysis would require us to forecast free-agent costs nearly 10 years into the future—an impractical task.

6. While data on teams' scouting and player development costs are difficult to obtain, we assume a combined $12 million per year for the average team is. This includes signing bonuses but is not intended to include dollars spent on international scouting, as foreign players are not subject to the draft.

7. Since the Twins had many early draft picks in the years surveyed, and were aggressive in signing their players, it is certainly possible that they had a higher than average scouting and player development average annual dollar cost when compared to all teams. Even if they spent $3 million per year more than the estimated average of $12 million, their cost per marginal win of developed players would increase to $840,000, still below the sample average.

8. Casey was under contract through the 2006 season, but *could* have been eligible for free agency following the 2004 season if he was under a one-year contract.

9. The 2005 performance data are from Baseball Prospectus.com's WARP1 statistic, which is intended to measure wins over what a replacement player would produce. Salary data are from Cot's Baseball Contracts, *http://mlbcontracts.blogspot.com/2005_01_03_mlbcontracts_archive.html*. The data set includes about 20 players from each team who put in the most playing time. The data were used to calculate the ratio of free-agent compensation, by position, to arbitration-eligible and restricted players. The sample was then "normalized" by adjusting for the overall 2005 payroll for all teams ($2.2 billion), relative to the marginal wins for all teams (1,701 derived from the implicit .150 winning percentage of a replacement-level team versus the average .500 team). The result is an overall payroll cost per marginal win of $1.29 million for all pay grades of players.

10. The Pujols salary data are from Cot's Baseball contracts, *http://mlbcontracts.blogspot.com/2004/12/st-louis-cardinals_111971260115041890.html*.

11. The Jeter salary data are from Cot's Baseball contracts, *http://mlbcontracts.blogspot.com/2005/01/new-york-yankees_111398168678860040.html*.

12. The Sizemore salary data are from Cot's Baseball contracts, *http://mlbcontracts.blogspot.com/2005/01/cleveland-indians_20.html*.

13. His pre–free agency WARP is 7.8, and his post–free-agency WARP is 20.2, thru 2006, from *Baseball Prospectus.com*.

14. Hatteberg's WARP is 7.1 for his pre–free agency years and 13.1 for his post–free agency years, thru 2006, from *Baseball Prospectus.com*.

15. Data are from a five-year sample (1995–1999) of all first-round draft picks who reached the majors through 2005.

16. Will Carroll, "UTK Special: The Dick Martin Award," *Baseball Prospectus*, December 2, 2005, *www.baseballprospectus.com/article.php?articleid=4632*.

17. This assumes the equivalent of one player for a full season at four WARP, which is replaced at the average cost per WARP of $1.63 million.

The Exchange Rate: Today's Wins for Tomorrow's Wins

A secondary benefit of a strong player development system is the accumulation of talent capital—assets that are expected to produce future wins. But what if a team wants *more* from its player development system *now*? If a team has already promoted the players that are Major League–ready, how can a farm system that has been fully harvested of today's "ripe fruit" produce more? By bartering "seeds" for ripe fruit, a team can use its player development system, a presumably low-cost source of talent, to bring in ripe fruit to produce incremental wins today. As an alternative to the pricey free-agent market, a team with a need to fill can choose to sell off minor leaguers (future wins) in exchange for established major leaguers (current wins) who are under contract at a cost that beats the free-agent market.

What is the exchange rate of future wins for current wins, and what factors affect the rate? We know the equation is not one win today in exchange for one future win. Future wins are discounted for several reasons: a win today produces revenue today versus a win next year that produces revenue next year; also, there is a risk factor associated with the expected future wins of any prospect. Prospects show promise; some fulfill the promise and some do not. Generally, we would expect an untested prospect's performance risk to be greater than that of an established player. While there may not be one ideal situation to use as a measuring stick, analyzing the range of circumstances surrounding trades that exchange future wins (prospects) for current wins (established players) may help us determine the value of the player development system's assets as barter for current wins. (In the next chapter, A Strategic Approach to Assembling the Roster, we will discuss the value of young, proven major leaguers as talent capital.)

Two sets of data may provide the boundaries for the exchange rate. The upper limit for the number of future wins exchanged for current wins may be represented by trades occurring at the mid-season trade deadline. As this deadline approaches, teams tend to line up on one side or the other. A team is either a buyer that believes it has a need to fill to make a postseason run or a seller that is not in the race and feels like it can trade a current player to build for the future. The exchange is often a trade of current (immediate) wins for future wins and is driven by the contending team's short-term mentality of "renting" an impact player whose contract expires at the end of the season. The lower limit for the number of future wins ex

→

changed for current wins may occur in off-season trades, or at least in non-deadline deals. In this situation the GM may have a broader range of options to try to improve his team and may be free from the time pressures of acquiring a player to plug into tomorrow's game. By evaluating these two types of transactions we may be able to put a value on future wins produced by the player development system.

It is difficult to draw definitive conclusions from anything short of an exhaustive study, but a few examples show the unpredictability of trading established win producers for future win producers. The 1998 trade deadline deal that sent Randy Johnson to the Astros netted the Houston club 5.3 marginal wins in less than a half-season, enough to earn a spot in the postseason. In exchange, the Astros dealt three prospects, Freddy Garcia, Carlos Guillen, and John Halama to the Mariners. Collectively the threesome generated more than 64 marginal wins in the years prior to reaching free agency. Seattle retained Garcia, who generated more than half the total, for five and a half seasons, before shipping him to the White Sox. One year earlier, a mid-season deadline deal had a similar impact to the team acquiring the young, untested talent. The 90-win Mariners attempted to bolster their playoff push by acquiring Heathcliff Slocum, to fill the role of closer, from the Boston Red Sox. In return, the Red Sox picked up two prospects, Jason Varitek and Derek Lowe. While Slocum earned only 3.5 marginal wins over his year and a half stay with the Mariners, Varitek and Lowe not only became centerpieces of a future World Championship team, but also delivered 70 marginal wins before they reached eligibility for free agency. In both cases the team receiving minor league talent hit the lottery with future stars, while the benefit to the team needing immediate help was fleeting. For the nine deadline deals in 1998, 74 future wins were exchanged for 18 current wins, an exchange rate of about four to one.[1]

For trades occurring outside of the month of July, established players who are traded for minor leaguers tend to have more than a half-year remaining on their contract. The economics change when the established player is not in his "walk year" of an expiring contract, as the acquiring team has more time to balance the exchange. In 13 non-deadline deals in 1998 involving minor leaguers for major leaguers, 49 future wins were exchanged for 44 current wins, for a ratio of about 1.1 to 1.[2] To illustrate the analytical framework for determining the exchange rate between current wins and future wins, let's split the difference of our two scenarios and say that five current wins are worth nine future wins spread over the three years, beginning in the year *following* the transaction year. This scenario implies a discount rate of about 35%,

→

meaning that a win today is the equivalent of 1.35 wins next year, or 1.82 the following year. Based on this type of analysis, we can place an estimated value on the use of player development to generate additional wins today, despite not having any additional Major League–ready players. Following our example, by trading nine future wins, which are expected to materialize over the next three years, a team can acquire five wins today. Taking the analysis one step further, if the Twins' player development system can generate wins at an average cost of $710,000 per win, the *marginal cost* of wins is $1,100,000—the cost of generating additional wins today from a player development system that has already delivered all of its Major League–ready talent to the Twins' roster.[3]

1 For the purpose of this analysis, a deadline deal is defined as trades that are consummated in the month of July.
2 The 44 current wins include all wins produced by traded established major leaguers over the remaining time of their contract.
3 The cost is calculated by the following formula: (the NPV of the cost of developing 10 future wins at $710,000 per win)/(five current wins, which were received in exchange for the future wins).

8 | A Strategic Approach to Assembling the Roster

Building a winning team is more than picking the best 25 players. It has as much to do with economics and finance as it does with baseball talent evaluation. The two major variables that drive a team's cost of winning are the productivity of the player development system and the decisions made in the volatile free-agent market. The 2005 Yankees showed that a team can spend $200 million and still go down to the last weekend of the season to clinch a playoff spot, while the 2004 St. Louis Cardinals, with an $83 million payroll, waltzed deep into October. For an MLB team today, it is not enough to simply field a winning team. If the payroll level is not sustainable, meaning it is not supported by revenue growth, it will drain the team's cash flow, deplete its franchise value, and be abandoned in an accountant's heartbeat.

Given what we know about the way fans reward winning teams with increased revenues, every team's ambition should be to reach the playoffs, or at least consistently be a playoff contender. It's the virtual equivalent of being in MLB's top quartile in wins, which in most seasons translates into 90 or more wins. While being one of the top seven or eight teams in win totals may not guarantee a playoff spot, owing to the way divisions are aligned, it is reasonable to expect to at least be in contention for the postseason. Since the baseline revenues and win curves of most teams will not afford them the luxury of paying top dollar year after year, spending payroll dollars efficiently is critical to sustainable success.

The dream scenario is to deliver first-quartile wins with a fourth-quartile payroll, but the pay structure of MLB makes this combination difficult to accomplish with consistency. Even the cheapest home-grown players become more expensive when they reach arbitration eligibility and can become prohibitively pricey when they reach free agency (after six years of MLB service). Sustaining the dream scenario of first-quartile wins and fourth-quartile payroll year after year may not be practical, as it might require unprecedented forced turnover and an unrealistic flood of young, inexpensive talent from a team's minor league system. A more reasonable ambition for a team may be to set a target of top-quartile wins, combined with *third-quartile payroll* expenses. Based on the win curves and baseline revenue for most teams, this scenario would add economic value to the franchise and produce cash flows to sustain the cycle, even providing a financial cushion if the team failed to be in contention once every three or four years.

We can get a closer look at team performance relative to payroll by using a four-by-four grid (Figure 8.1). The top-right box represents the maximum success and efficiency (it is numbered 1.4 for the highest [first] win quartile and the lowest [fourth] payroll quartile), while the lower-left represents the worst efficiency (4.1 for the lowest-quartile wins and the highest-quartile payroll).

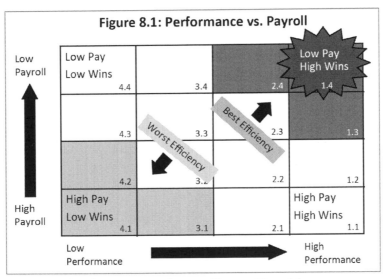

FIGURE 8.1 **Performance and payroll quartile grid.**

Since 2003, only two teams achieved the top-right box: the 2003 Marlins, who went on to win the World Series, and the 2005 Indians, a 93-win team that narrowly missed the playoffs on the last weekend of the regular season.[1] The Yankees and the Devil Rays are the only two teams that have finished in the same box each of the past four years. One could say they both got what they paid for, as the Yankees finished in the highest performance–highest payroll box (1.1) and Tampa Bay finished in the lowest performance–lowest payroll quartiles (4.4), four straight times. Teams in the upper-right portion of the chart enjoyed the best efficiency—the biggest bang for their payroll dollar—while teams in the lower-left portion had the lowest efficiency—poor on-field results coupled with a hefty payroll. Over the four-year period, only the pre–Omar Minaya Mets and the 2006 Cubs made an appearance in the 4.1 box. (The Mets also finished in the third-quartile performance/first-quartile payroll box in 2004.) Another repeat offender in the lower efficiency portion of our grid is the Seattle Mariners, who have had hefty payrolls (second quartile) with worst-quartile wins from 2004 through 2006. Turning to the high-efficiency section of the chart, the Twins, A's, and Marlins had the most appearances over our four-year time period. (See Figure 8.2 for highlights of past four years of performance versus payroll.)

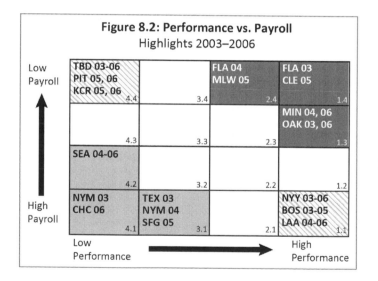

FIGURE 8.2 **Performance versus payroll for 2003–2006.**

PROFILING THE HIGH-EFFICIENCY TEAMS

Are common characteristics shared by the 2005 Indians, 2003 Marlins, and the Twins and A's teams of the past several years? What path did these teams take to be in playoff contention while at least 23 other teams spent more on players' salaries? A key driver of teams in the high-efficiency portion of our grid (1.4 and 1.3) compared to teams like the Yankees, a perennial low-efficiency team (1.1), is the *mix of players by pay grade:* restricted players (up to three years of MLB service), arbitration-eligible players (three to six years), and free agents (more than six years). While the dollar amount of free-agent contracts gets all the media attention, the *amount* a team pays its free agents generally has less impact on payroll than the *number* of free agents on the roster and the *percentage of wins* (WARP) that come from the high-priced end of the pay scale. Restricted players are contractually bound to their teams and are generally compensated at or slightly above the MLB minimum salary, like apprentices who are paying their dues while learning their craft. Once a player exceeds three years of service time, he still remains the exclusive property of his team, but he is eligible to have his salary determined by an impartial arbitrator.[2] After six years of tenure a player is no longer bound to his team, as he is granted his independence and can seek a contract from any interested team, determined by an auction process, with competing teams often bidding up the player's salary to win his services.

To understand the difference in compensation across these pay grades, let's look at MLB-wide data for 2005. Since our goal is to create a blueprint to produce a first-quartile-win team with a third-quartile payroll, it makes sense to evaluate compensation in the context of performance, or marginal wins produced. From the perspective of the team, a player's salary relative to his WARP is a productivity measure—a team's dollar cost per marginal win.[3] Evaluating the performance and pay of more than 500 MLB players, classified by pay grade, allows us to create a *yield curve*—the team's dollar cost per marginal win by player tenure, or pay grade. While it is common knowledge that restricted players are cheaper than arbitration-eligible players and free agents, the yield curve quantifies their pay relative to their performance and allows a team to calculate the dollar impact of shifting the mix. For 2005, on average, the cost per marginal win for restricted players was $167,000, compared to arbitration-eligible players at $1 million and free agents at $2.4 million[4] (see Figure 8.3). The percent mix of MLB players by pay grade is shown in Figure 8.4.

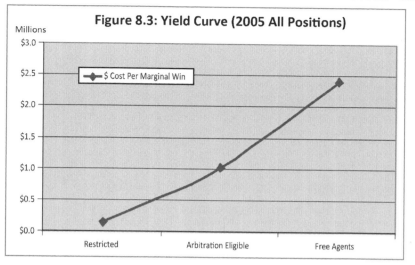

FIGURE 8.3 **Yield curve for all positions.**

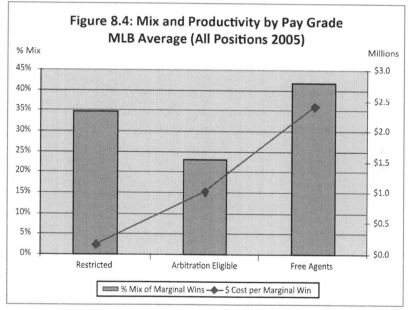

FIGURE 8.4 **Yield curve and mix for all positions.**

To understand the financial power of managing the mix of players by pay grade, we can simply look at the 2006 Florida Marlins, an extreme example of a skewed player mix. The MLB average mix of players on a team's 25-man roster approximately breaks out as follows: nine restricted players, five arbitration-eligible players, and 11 free agents. The Marlins 25-man opening-day roster consisted of 21 restricted players, two arbitration-eligible players, and two free agents. With their mix of inexpensive talent, the Marlins are not only guaranteed a spot in the bottom quartile of team payrolls, but they were *$20 million lower* than the next-lowest team.[5] A way to dig deeper into the team data is to compare both the *productivity* (dollar cost per marginal win, the same calculation that is used in determining the *yield curve*) and *mix of marginal wins* by player classification, to the MLB average. While the Marlins paid a lower than average rate for their free agents, Figure 8.5 tells the real story of how they achieved the lowest over-all payroll in MLB. The Marlins contributed 84% of their marginal wins from the low-cost restricted class of players, compared to a league average of 35%. At the other end of the pay scale, the Marlins had only 5% of their marginal wins from the high-priced free-agent segment, compared to a league average of 42%.

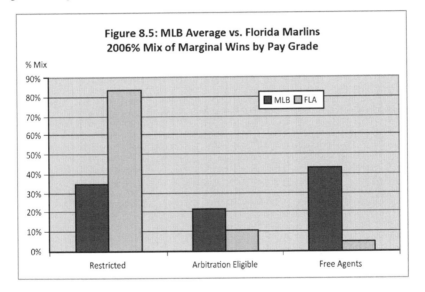

FIGURE 8.5 **Comparison of the Marlins' mix of marginal wins.**

Teams in the upper-right section of Figure 8.2 (the 2005 Indians, the 2004 and 2006 A's, and the 2003 and 2006 Twins) tend to have a high mix of young, inexpensive talent that delivers true Major League–level performance. For example, the 2005 Indians had nine restricted players who played a key role in the team's success, delivering an average of over five marginal wins each. Teams in the lower-right section (e.g., the Yankees, Angels, and Red Sox) tend to have a higher mix of free agents, who, fortunately for those teams, live up to their expectations. For example, the 2004 World Champion Red Sox committed $71 million to six free agents (Damon, Varitek, Ortiz, Martinez, Ramirez, and Schilling), who collectively delivered an impressive 45 marginal wins. The only real disappointment was the $11.5 million, 1.1 WARP Garciaparra, who was traded by mid-season. (Once again the Yankees deviate from the norm of their peer group. They tend to bring in a surplus of free agents, which allows them to overcome failures such as Carl Pavano in 2005 and 2006. They may be the only team that can withstand zero productivity from a $10 million free agent by replacing his roster spot with a more productive high-priced free agent).

Turning to the left side of our grid, those on the top-left (fourth-quartile payroll/fourth-quartile wins) tend to stock up on low-priced graduated minor leaguers, some of whom prove not to be Major League–ready. The 2003 Tampa Bay Devil Rays are a case in point. The last-place team had 22 restricted players, paid at or near the MLB minimum. However, only four of these players were ready to make a significant contribution at the MLB level: Rocco Baldelli (6.8 WARP), Carl Crawford (4.9), Aubrey Huff (7.1), and Victor Zambrano (4.7). The net result was an average of less than 2.0 marginal wins for the large group, translating into 63 total wins and a last-place finish for the young Devil Rays.

Teams in the lower-left section (high payroll/low wins) tend to have a higher mix of free-agent "busts," à la the 2003 Mets' Mo Vaughn, Roberto Alomar, and Jeromy Burnitz. In 2003 these three star players contributed just four marginal wins, while netting over $37 million in collective salary—a cost of more than *$9 million per marginal win*. Figure 8.6 illustrates the characteristics of teams in the various sections of the grid.

Much of the salary differences among teams with comparable winning performances are due to the mix of players by pay grade, rather than poor salary negotiations, or overpaying players within their pay grade. Even if teams with a high mix of free agents and arbitration-eligible players won all its arbitration cases and picked off free agents with good-value contracts, it might not compensate for having too few productive restricted players on the roster. If we compare two teams in the corner boxes on our grid for 2005, it illustrates this point. The Indians finished in the first-quartile wins/fourth-quartile payroll category, with 50% of their marginal wins coming from the low-cost restricted class of players. Conversely, the Red Sox finished in the first-quartile wins/first-quartile payroll category, with 90% of

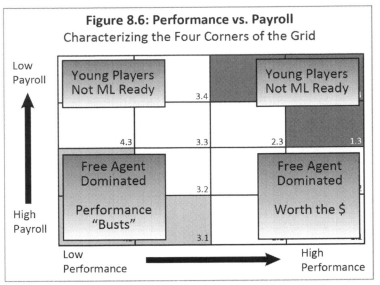

FIGURE 8.6 **Characterizing the four corners of the grid.**

their marginal wins coming from the expensive end of the pay scale—free agents. Boston got superior *productivity* from their free agents, as they paid a lower than average $1.5 million per marginal win. The sole reason the Red Sox were in the high-cost corner of our grid was due to the two times normal *mix* of free-agent players.

The 2005 Indians and the 2005 Yankees further illustrate the point. If we contrast the Indians, a high-efficiency winning team ($41 million payroll), with the Yankees, a low-efficiency winning team ($200 million payroll), we can see the impact of mix on payroll. The three top-performing Indians, Peralta (8.7 WARP), Hafner (7.2), and Victor Martinez (7.1), earned a *total* of $1.3 million, while the Yankees' top three performers, A-Rod (10.9), Jeter (9.8), and Rivera (9.3), earned *over $53 million*. The contrast between the two teams can be summed up by analyzing the distribution of their marginal wins across pay classes. For the Indians, 82% of their marginal wins came from the lower-priced restricted and arbitration-eligible pay classes, while the Yankees got 86% of their marginal wins from high-priced free agents. Figure 8.7 summarizes these statistics.

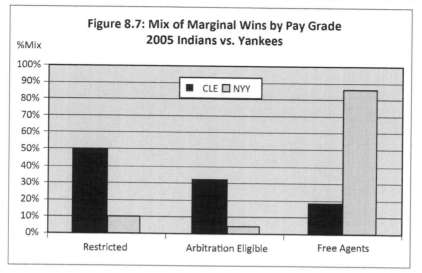

FIGURE 8.7 **Comparison of 2005 Cleveland Indians and 2005 N.Y. Yankees.**

FIRST-QUARTILE WINS/THIRD-QUARTILE PAYROLL: A PLAUSIBLE SCENARIO

Drawing on these insights can help us design a plan to achieve our goal of top-quartile wins with a third-quartile payroll. Under this plausible scenario, a team needs to win approximately 90 games, by generating about 65 marginal wins per year, on a budget of about $65 to 75 million.[6] As a benchmark, let's begin with the average MLB team. The 81 win–81 loss team would have 56 marginal wins. The marginal wins would come from the average mix: 35% restricted players, 23% arbitration-eligible, and 42% free agents. The marginal wins would come at the MLB average of $1.3 million, with a total payroll of about $74 million. By our definition, this average team would be on the dividing line between the second and third quartiles for both wins and payroll. To earn a spot in the first quartile in wins, teams often need to shift their mix in the direction of free-agent players. A four percentage point shift from restricted to free agents (to 31% restricted, 23% arbitration-eligible, 46% free agents) would raise the cost per marginal win to over $1.4 million and raise the total payroll to $92 million, which would likely place the team at the top of the second payroll quartile.

To deliver the same 90 wins (65 marginal wins) with our plausible scenario of first-quartile wins/third-quartile payroll, we can employ three cost-containment and productivity measures.

- Develop a cadre of talented young players who make a major contribution to team performance, similar to the 2005 and 2006 Twins, with Joe Mauer, Justin Morneau, Lew Ford, Jesse Crain, and Juan Rincon. Although the 2005 Twins won only 83 games (second-quartile wins), because they lacked a few pieces of the puzzle, their core of young, inexpensive, highly productive players delivered the goods for the team in 2006, elevating them to 96 wins and the AL Central title.

- Control the mix of free agents. If 50% or more of a team's marginal wins come from free agents, it will be difficult to get sufficient productivity from the other end of the pay scale, restricted players, to balance the total payroll expense. If a team gains 30 or 35 marginal wins from its free agent pool of players, at an average cost of $2.4 million per marginal win, it leaves virtually nothing left to spend on the other segments of the pay scale to buy the additional 30 to 35 wins and still come in at under $75 million in total payroll.

- Pay below market rate for free agents. Given the reduced focus on the free-agent market, as defined by our first two productivity measures, a team should be able to be more selective in their free-agent acquisitions. Whether a team pays an average price, gets a discount, or pays a premium can be influenced by market conditions, not the least of which is whether the Yankees are in or out of the free-agent market for a particular position or player.

By translating these cost and productivity principles into a full 25-man roster using cost per marginal win by pay grade for pitchers and nonpitchers, we can develop a plausible scenario that builds a 90-win team (65 marginal wins) at a payroll of less than $75 million.[7]

A PLAN TO DELIVER THE PLAUSIBLE SCENARIO

To build a template that defines the actions a team needs to take to deliver our target scenario of first-quartile wins/third-quartile payroll, it can be helpful to start at the end result and work backwards. Working backwards from the locker room champagne celebration of our playoff-clinching, 90-win model team, we can retrace their steps to glory. If they followed the template our 65-marginal-win team, they would have garnered 28 marginal wins (43%) from the restricted class of players, 12 marginal wins (19%) from arbitration-eligible players, and 25 marginal wins (38%) from free agents. Based on the league average costs per marginal win, and adding $2 million in costs for nonproductive players such as those on the disabled list, would lead to a payroll of $73.1 million for our 90-win model team. Because our team can afford to be selective in the free-agent market, they can shop for values. Our scenario assumes they garner a 10% discount on prevailing free-agent market rates (see Figure 8.8 for the details of the plausible scenario).

Figure 8.8: The Plausible Scenario
1st Quartile Wins/3rd Quartile Payroll
Mix of 65 Marginal Wins

	Restricted	Arbitration Eligible	Free Agents	Total
Marginal Wins	28	12	25	65
% Mix	43%	19%	38%	100%
$ Cost/ Mrg W	.157	1.030	2.174*	1.063
Total $ Cost	4.4	12.4	54.3	71.1

+ Non-Productive Payroll $ 2.0

Total Payroll $ 73.1

* Blended rate of pitchers and non-pitchers. Dollars in millions

FIGURE 8.8 **The plausible scenario.**

Continuing to work backwards, we can focus on the most financially critical part of the equation—how the team sourced its steady flow of young talent to perpetuate a 28-marginal-win contribution from its restricted class of players. To create our sourcing plan, we will use a plausible scenario that graduates three players per year from the minors to the MLB team. In this scenario, at any point in time, the roster will include nine restricted players: three first-year, three second-year, and three third-year players. Each year, as a group of three players matures into arbitration-eligible players, three new minor league graduates would replace them. (While the real world does not typically function this symmetrically, it is easier to follow the logic with this tidy scenario)

Earlier we discussed the percentage of draft picks, from selected rounds, *reaching* the big leagues. Since that data include players who were one-shot September call-ups, the draft yield estimate is refined to reflect the percentage of players who played at least three continuous years. By recalibrating the draft yield to include only multiyear major leaguers, anticipating an average minor league stay of three and one-half years, and assuming a team has about 50 draft choices annually, the only remaining variable is the marginal win level of our rookies and their progression over their restricted years. Let's assume one rookie per year matures into a long-term big leaguer with higher performance and a long-term trajectory, while his two peers are slower maturing or simply have a lower ceiling, resulting in three-year performance trajectories in Figure 8.9. The plausible scenario generates 6.2 marginal wins from first-year players, 9.6 from second-year players, and 12.2 from third-year players, for a total of 28 marginal wins from nine restricted players—a perfect fit with the mix in our plausible scenario.

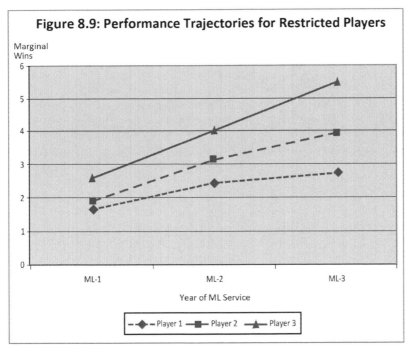

FIGURE 8.9 **A model scenario. Performance trajectories for restricted players.**

A key question is "how far beyond typical MLB team farm system productivity is the plausible scenario?" In the previous chapter we learned that the Twins' and A's histories seemed to prove that this level of productivity is within reach.[8] Also, teams that fall short of developing the needed level of talent from within their farm system can use their forced turnover of their Major League roster to return young prospects. By trading five-year and six-year players for MLB-ready prospects, a team may sacrifice some immediate marginal wins but gain flexibility by resetting their mix toward younger, cheaper players. (See the sidebar, Moneyball and the Oakland A's, which discusses the driving force behind the A's ability to build a winner with a modest payroll.)

Once a GM and the team's farm system director deliver the goal of 28 marginal wins per year from restricted players, the job is not finished. While some will argue that the most challenging piece of the equation is in place, other hurdles exist, namely selectively choosing the right arbitration-eligible players to retain and selecting, as well as managing, the price and productivity of free-agent players. With arbitration-eligible players the development trajectory is a key variable in the decision to retain or trade, and it may even affect the teams' arbitration bid and negotiating strategy. Since the arbitration process generally results in compensation reflecting *actual* performance, not expected performance, a team can benefit if a player is on a steep trajectory, typically in the earlier years of his arbitration eligibility. In a study by Loyola University (Baltimore) professors Burger and Walters, it is estimated that a player's arbitration award increases (relative to the amount of revenue his performance can generate for his team) during each successive year of his arbitration eligibility.[9] Relative to free-agent compensation, a fourth-year player receives 33 to 40%, while a sixth-year player receives 68 to 82% according to this study.[10]

Another important element required to deliver the plausible scenario is being frugal with the dollars per marginal win paid to free agents. Any team is vulnerable to an injury to or a subpar year by a prized free agent, but there are components of the free-agent cost equation that a GM can influence, if not entirely control. Beyond the obvious tactic of negotiating the best possible incentive-laden deal that protects the team on the downside, a GM can also organize and focus his player development system to breed the players at the highest-cost free-agent positions. Our plausible scenario requires a GM to bargain hunt and pay only $2.15 million per marginal win in the free-agent market compared to a MLB average of $2.4 million. One means to this end is to be thrifty on the *rate* paid to the free agent, possibly taking a chance on a high-risk candidate, such as Frank Thomas and the 2006 Oakland A's.

Another possibly more sustainable way to manage free-agent productivity is by managing the *mix of positions within the free-agent category*. At two ends of the free-agent pricing market are second baseman and left-handed starting pitchers. The going rate for second basemen is estimated to be $1.5 million per marginal win, compared to $3.2 per marginal win for lefty starting pitchers.[11] Pity the GM who has no recourse but to delve into the free-agent market for a left-handed starter. An effective way to manage the cost per marginal win of free-agent players is to play at the low end of the free-agent food chain: second basemen, first basemen, and designated hitters. Buying 15 marginal wins at the three lowest value positions, on average costs $27 million in payroll, or $1.8 million per marginal win. If a team needs to staff its pitching rotation from the free-agent market, the same 15 marginal wins are apt to cost $41 million, or $2.7 million per marginal win. If a team can focus its player development resources on pitching and hit the free-agent market for position players, they could conserve precious payroll dollars.

Conserving payroll dollars is not about being cheap and unwilling to spend money in order to make money. It's about eliminating the boom–bust cycle of teams like the Florida Marlins of 1997 and 2003. It's about creating a sustainable business model to give a team the best chance at reaching glory. By simple observation over the past decade, the case can be made that the formula for winning a World Championship seems to be rooted in the frequency of reaching the postseason. Reaching the postseason year after year requires a disciplined plan, such as first-quartile wins/third-quartile payroll, that becomes a blueprint that drives all of the actions and strategies of the organization.

BEYOND TALENT EVALUATION

Is there a road map to building a competitive team at a modest payroll? What strategies can an MLB team employ to raise its chance of successfully sustaining a competitive team year after year? The all too obvious answer may be to corner the market on playing talent. Some will say success begins and ends with superior talent evaluation. If a team can draft and grow talent, they gain the inside track on keeping a lid on their payroll. While the importance of talent evaluation is a key success factor, there is reason to doubt this singular strategy as the "silver bullet" to sustaining an affordable, winning team. Teams have been striving to better themselves at talent evaluation for decades, and while some appear to have a better track record than others (the Braves, Twins, and A's, among others) there are other strategies that can augment the best-in-class performance or compensate for weak performers. Another reason not to rely solely on being the best talent evaluator is that converting talent into performance seems to be a hit or miss proposition, with enormous variability in results. Baseball America, which tracks the results of the amateur draft, concludes that about 65% of first-round choices eventually play in the big leagues.[12] Only 42% of second-round picks reach the majors, declining as each round progresses, with 12% in round five and less than 16% for rounds six through 10 combined.[13] There is no doubt that talent evaluation is a critical stepping stone to consistent success, but the debate will continue as to how much any one team can claim it as their distinct core competency.

Beyond talent evaluation, several strategies can help raise the odds of successfully building a sustainable winning team on a modest budget. These strategies capitalize on the economic framework within baseball today—the dependence on local market revenues for success, the willingness of fans to support a winning team, and the tenure-based pay-grade structure legislated in the CBA. Consistent with the new management model emerging in baseball, these strategies are centered on data analysis and applying some universal financial concepts to player personnel decisions. The following are the four core strategies to efficiently build a sustainable winning team:

- Utilize a framework to measure and project the relative cost of performance in the market for players, by position and pay grade.

- Manage players as investment assets in the same way a money manager would manage a portfolio of investments.

- Be willing to force player turnover to keep the roster young (inexpensive), even in the face of success.

- To build an inventory of the highest-value assets, focus player selection and development resources on pitching, particularly left-handed pitching.

A FRAMEWORK TO MEASURE AND PROJECT PAYROLL COSTS

Even for teams who intuitively apply this approach today, formalizing this set of strategies can serve as an analytical framework to bring greater discipline to their approach to player selection, development, and personnel moves. Any time a player trade or free-agent signing is contemplated, many variables are considered: How does this alter the team's roster mix by pay grade? Does it help the team become younger (in terms of MLB tenure and pay grade)? How does the player's projected productivity—pay relative to marginal wins—compare to the league average for his position and pay grade?

By using this analysis, a team can model various scenarios and better understand the implications of certain moves on not only current payroll, but *future* projected payroll. For example, we can gauge the payroll implications of having two fewer home-grown, restricted pitchers and replacing them with two free-agent pitchers. On average, the difference in replacing two pitchers at $160,000 per marginal win with two pitchers at $2.6 million per marginal win is $11.9 million in additional payroll. Depending on the years of MLB service for the restricted players—whether the player is in his first, second, or third year of MLB service—we can model the salary implications for several years forward.

PLAYERS AS INVESTMENT ASSETS

Analyzing payroll and win scenarios several years into the future forces a team to think in terms of a player's "asset value." A player's asset value is directly related to his expected performance, relative to his cost, the length of his contract, and the going rate to purchase the same marginal wins in the free-agent market. One way to measure a player's asset value is to measure the "spread" between the player's cost per marginal win and the market rate for a free agent's cost per marginal win. As a result, the highest asset values on a team's roster tend to be concentrated in their star rookies, or even their most-talented higher minor league prospects—the players who have the longest "runway" to be paid below market wages. Some will argue that the risk level associated with graduating even a highly touted minor leaguer to the big leagues places him behind an equally talented, Major League–validated rookie in asset value. Any rookie that cracks the starting lineup and can be counted on to deliver five or more marginal wins is arguably among the players with the highest asset values.

Scanning the Rookie of the Year candidate list for 2006, you will find the most valuable assets as we enter the 2007 season. If Prince Fielder, the Brewers first baseman, can sustain his 2006 performance of five marginal wins, as an asset he could be valued as high as $30 million—the current net value his team would otherwise spend to buy his marginal wins on the free-agent market. To buy five wins on the free-agent market for first basemen, a team would expect to pay about $9.7 million per year.[14] Since Fielder has five years remaining (2007–2011) before he is eligible for free agency, he provides the wins for far less money. If he remains a steady five-win contributor, Fielder could earn about $400,000 for each of the next two years, followed by $3.5 million, $5.3 million, and $7.3 million for his three arbitration years. Comparing his projected cost to what a comparable free agent would earn yields a net present value of $29.6 million, the amount of value that will accrue to the team that owns his contract over the next five years (see Figure 8.10).

Figure 8.10: Asset Value of Prince Fielder

	2007	2008	2009	2010	2011
ML Service Year	ML-2	ML-3	ML-4*	ML-5*	ML-6*
Marginal Wins (Projected)	5	5	5	5	5
Cost of Wins on Free Agent Market	$9.7	$9.7	$9.7	$9.7	$9.7
Fielder Projected Compensation	.380	.390	3.5	5.3	7.3
Compensation Discount	9.3	9.3	6.2	4.4	2.4
Net Present Value	$9.3	$8.9	$5.6	$3.8	$2.0

Net Present Value of Fielder as an   "Asset " = $29.6 million

* Arbitration Eligible Years

Figure 8.10 **Prince Fielder's asset value.**

There is one caveat to this calculation. If the team's marginal revenue from the wins Fielder generates is less than the free-agent cost of those wins, then the lower amount should be used as the benchmark for value. For example, let's say the Brewers win-curve says that Fielder's five wins are only worth $6 million in annual revenues to the Brewers, and Fielder's asset value (the NPV of the spread between Fielder's cost and the revenues his wins generate) as a Brewer is $12.7 million. . When the spread between the two valuations—the asset value to his current team versus his asset value to high-revenue, or contending, teams—is large enough, there would be a financial incentive for a trade. Suppose the Mets were looking for a first baseman in the winter of 2007 (instead of one year earlier); Prince Fielder might have been an interesting alternative to Carlos Delgado. They are contracted to pay Delgado $42.5 million from 2007 through 2009.[15] Assuming they are both approximately five-win first baseman, *the Mets would be better off paying up to $40 million to the Brewers, in exchange for Fielder.* Paying Milwaukee $40 million and paying Fielder his restricted and arbitration eligible compensation would be a cheaper way to buy five wins than trading for Delgado.

Cash sales of heralded rookies are nowhere to be found on the baseball landscape. MLB has rules in place that prevent big cash transactions. This may have been born out of owner distrust, dating back to the days when Charles O. Finley tried to sell some of his star players for cash before selling the A's. His purely financial thought process was that his players were worth more individually than as part of the team. Clearly his intentions were not in the best interests of baseball. If MLB could put in place a process whereby the commissioner could ensure that any money from a player sale would be plowed back into baseball operations, teams would have an outlet to monetize talented young players. Permitting asset transfers in exchange for cash would also promote competitive balance. Teams in smaller, economically disadvantaged markets tend to be better at player development, no doubt because they can least afford to take the easy but prohibitively costly route of turning to free agents. Yet MLB's rules limit the value of this competency by preventing teams like the Twins from being the "farm system for MLB." What better way to level the playing field than to have the Twins trade their strength—the output of their prolific player development system—to the Yankees in exchange for their strength—the output of a strong revenue base, namely cash? Before long, the advantages of the high-revenue markets would be mitigated.

There is reason to believe the players' union would also oppose these transactions, which would better allocate playing talent to places where it could deliver the highest value. By creating a mechanism that promotes the efficient allocation of players between teams, some clubs could avert the need to dip into the pricey free-agent market, which the players' union attempts to protect at all costs. A system of allowing players to be reallocated in exchange for cash, substitutes money paid to *teams* (for the purchase of an asset) for money otherwise paid to free-agent *players*. Also, many baseball insiders and fans might think it is heresy to sell off the very player who embodies the franchise's faith and hope to make a run at the playoffs. The public relations risks of such a transaction are filled with peril, but if a team did not have enough complementary players to ensure progress toward the postseason, bringing in cash to invest in other players may be the best way to *strengthen* a franchise.

An example where this approach might make sense for both teams is Kansas City's Mark Teahen as the third base solution for the Cubs (or any high-revenue team in need of a third baseman). Teahen has four years left (2007–2010) prior to eligibility for free agency. Let's assume he remains a five-win third baseman (5.2 WARP in 2006) for the next four years. In Kansas City it is likely that his five wins will be worth $5 million per year or less in incremental revenue to the team, even if the Royals have the good fortune of working their way into the 80- to 85-win range. However, those same five wins on the North Side of Chicago could have substantially more value, upwards of $15 million per year. For the Cubs to satisfy their third base need, they elected to re-sign Aramis Ramirez as a free agent, to a five-year, $75 million deal. Based on his discounted salary as a non–free agent, Teahen's value as an alternative to the Cubs signing of Ramirez is $36.8 million.[16] Paying the Royals anything less than $36.8 million lowers the Cubs' cost of winning compared to dipping into the free-agent market and signing Ramirez. On the other hand, the NPV of his asset value to the Royals is a mere $1 million, because as Branch Rickey once said, "We coulda lost without you." A workable solution for the Cubs third base woes, as well as for the revenue-deprived Royals, might have been a $15 to $20 million cash purchase of Mark Teahen by the Cubs.[17] The Cubs would lower their cost of a marginal win, and the Royals would get cash to invest in scouting and player development, buy a few talented prospects, sign an international free agent or two, and pay a public relations firm to assuage the fans anger and convince them that monetizing Teahen will launch the Royals on a new trajectory for years to come (see Figure 8.11).

Any player's value as an asset is driven by several factors: his expected performance, his compensation relative to the free-agent price for comparable players, the length of time he is under contract, the existence or absence of a "no trade" clause, and his injury history or injury risk. Think of the player's asset value as the price a team might pay to own a player's current contract. On one end of the scale is Hanley Ramirez, a six-plus-marginal-win shortstop with five years left to free agency. On the opposite end of the scale are Yankees like Jason Giambi. Giambi is slated to make $21 million for each of 2007 and 2008, substantially more than it would cost to buy his wins in the free-agent market today. He also has a no trade clause and a poor injury history.

FORCING TURNOVER IN THE FACE OF SUCCESS

Another key element of producing a winning team at a reasonable payroll is the willingness to force turnover of the roster as players mature. In base-

Asset Value of Mark Teahen to the Cubs

	2007	2008	2009	2010
ML Service Year	ML-3	ML-4*	ML-5*	ML-6*
Marginal Wins (Projected)	5	5	5	5
Cost of Wins -- Aramis Ramirez	$13.0**	$14.0	$15.7	$15.8
Teahen Projected Compensation	.380	4.1	6.3	8.6
Compensation Discount	12.6	9.9	9.4	7.2
Net Present Value	$12.6	$9.5	$8.5	$6.2

NPV of Teahen as an "Asset" to Cubs as alternative to Ramirez = $36.8 million

* Arbitration Eligible Years   ** Includes $5 million signing bonus, plus $8 million 2007 salary.

FIGURE 8.11 **Mark Teahen's asset value to the Cubs.**

ball the status quo cannot be maintained, at least not for very long or at the same price. With productive young players as the key to an affordable winning team, even young players eventually become arbitration eligible, sometimes as they are heading into their most productive years. Earlier we stated the requirements to achieve our target of first-quartile wins with a third-quartile payroll: a reasonable goal would be to generate 28 marginal wins from restricted players each year. (For perspective, the 2006 Marlins, winners of 78 games, delivered 30 marginal wins from just *four* of their restricted players—Miguel Cabrera, Dan Uggla, Hanley Ramirez, and Josh Johnson. On the other end of the scale the 95-win 2005 Yankees could muster no more than nine marginal wins from their restricted players, led by rookies Robinson Cano and Chien-Ming Wang.) With the mindset of building a competitive home-grown roster, the organization would focus on maintaining a stream of restricted players who could replace graduates each year. If a player development system is deficient in talent, it is possible to go into the trade market, specifically targeting young players who a team's scouts deem to be MLB-ready. Teams that resist dealing their aging players for young restricted players may be playing it safe, avoiding the risk of a young player not living up to expectations, but they are ensuring that their payrolls will increase. On average, a three-marginal-win player will cost a team $7.2 million in annual salary as a member of the free-agent pay class and about $350,000 as a restricted player. Figure 8.12 shows the salary pattern of a three-marginal-win player over a 10-year career.

AVERAGE SALARY OF A 3 MARGINAL WIN PLAYER BY YEAR OF SERVICE

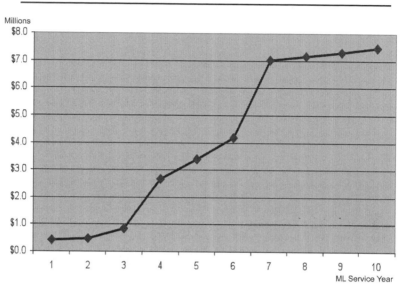

FIGURE 8.12 **Average salary of a three-marginal-win player by year of service.**

Once again we can contrast the 2005 Indians and Yankees to see how they assembled their rosters. Both teams finished in the top win quartile, and while the Yankees had baseball's highest payroll, the Indians managed to deliver their 93 wins with a fourth-quartile payroll. Looking first to the all-important June annual draft as a source of players for the two teams, the 1998 through 2002 drafts are those most likely to provide a restricted player to the 2005 rosters. The Indians produced 14 major leaguers with a career total (through 2005) of 39 marginal wins from those five drafts, while the Yankees' drafts delivered only four marginal wins from 10 Major League players. Surprisingly, only two restricted players (for either team), the Indians' C. C. Sabathia and Jason Davis, are products of their own team's draft. Four other restricted players came to their clubs as undrafted international free agents—the Yankees' Chien-Ming Wang (Taiwan) and Robinson Cano (Dominican Republic) and the Indians' Jhonny Peralta (Dominican Republic) and Victor Martinez (Venezuela).[18] Many of the young players on the 2005 Indians were targeted by GM Mark Shapiro as part of a rebuilding program he initiated after taking over for John Hart in 2001. Shapiro traded soon-to-be free agent Bartolo Colon to Montreal in a deal that netted Grady Sizemore and Cliff Lee. He traded aging Chuck Finley to St. Louis for Coco Crisp and dealt journeyman Russell Branyan to the Reds for Ben Broussard. None of the four players acquired by the Tribe had ever played a Major League game with their former teams.

Many of the Indians' young talents were acquired by trading players who were adequate contributors but beyond their restricted years. These players were swapped for younger, less expensive talent in a conscious effort to improve the team while recasting their payroll on a lower trajectory for several years to come. By contrast, the Yankees often dealt young minor league prospects for more mature, higher-salaried players. Half of the 10 players who reached the Major Leagues from the Yankees' 1998 to 2002 drafts were traded away in exchange for players in the *free-agent* pay class. With a "win now" philosophy and less concern for payroll, the Yankees went in the opposite direction of the Indians by trading future major leaguers for the likes of Sterling Hitchcock, Aaron Boone, Armando Benitez, Jeff Weaver and Randy Johnson.

Is there an optimal time to unload a player? Individual circumstances, such as a team in a rebuilding phase versus a playoff drive, could dictate the ideal time to make a player move. However, short of any specific circumstance, there is reason to conclude that the optimal time to trade a productive player is in the second half of his arbitration-eligible years. During a player's arbitration-eligible years, he still comes at a discount to the free-agent market, particularly if he has progressive improvement, as arbitration is calibrated against previous year's performance, not future expected performance.[19] Once a player is granted free agency (following six years of MLB service), he has no value to his current team, since he is free to negotiate in the open market. As the mid-season trading deadline approaches, a player who is in his fifth or sixth year of MLB service might be an attractive find for a team making a playoff run. It is likely that the acquiring team will be in a short-term mindset and will discount the fact that the player's salary will probably increase as he hits the open market of free agency in a year or so. On the trade market the arbitration-eligible player may be the poor man's last piece of the puzzle for teams who have a more modest win-curve than the highest-revenue teams.

Pitching: Particularly Lefties

Based on free-agent salaries and players' contributions to their teams' marginal wins (the dollar cost per marginal win), pitchers have a higher asset value than position players, and left-handed pitchers are worth an additional premium. This reflects the long-held perception in baseball that left-handed pitchers have greater success against left-handed hitters than right-handed pitchers on right-handed hitters. The option of strategically deploying a left-handed pitcher to potentially help win a ball game is appealing to many teams. Despite the obvious value of lefties, they seem to be in short supply, as only 26% of all starting pitchers are left-handed.[20] Another possible reason for the premium price for left-handers may be inflated expectations of their performance—expecting a three-marginal-win pitcher to be a four-marginal-win pitcher. Whether the primary factor is supply, demand, or both, the net result is that pitchers command a 14% salary premium compared to position players, while left-handers command a 27% premium compared to position players (see Figure 8.13).

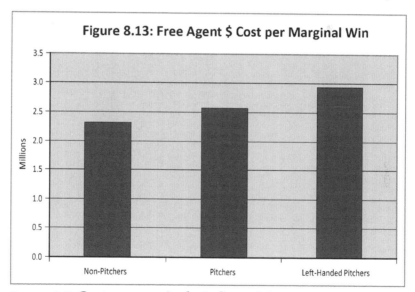

FIGURE 8.13 **Cost per marginal win by position.**

This implies that a three-marginal-win left-handed pitcher (such as the Cubs' Glendon Rusch in 2005) would be capable of fetching 27% more value in the trade market than a position player and 50% more than a first baseman–designated hitter at the same performance level. Another interpretation would be that Andy Pettitte's 9.1 WARP in 2005 is equivalent to an 11.6 WARP performance by a position player, as valued by the free-agent market for left-handed pitching. If a first baseman and left-handed pitcher are considered equal prospects, and the team is on the fence as to which player to draft, the hurler is the better bet, as he is the scarcer, higher-value asset.

Teams that combine superior talent evaluation with some of the principles laid out in this chapter have the inside track in delivering a first-quartile-wins/third-quartile-payroll team. For teams that can execute this approach, there is evidence that significant payroll dollars can be conserved and replaced by fewer development dollars, lowering the marginal cost of winning. The draft record of teams like Minnesota and Oakland show there is potential to generate the yield from a team's farm system to sustain a high-performance, affordable team over the long-term.

Endnotes

1. 2003 to 2006 is the time period used for this analysis, as it represents one Collective Bargaining Agreement (CBA). Comparing how teams perform on these dimensions when revenue sharing and luxury tax rules change adds an unwanted dimension of variation and complexity.

2. The arbitrator is authorized to award either the player's or team's submitted salary offer, rendering their decision based on comparisons of the salaries of player's with similar performance.

3. Since WARP represents wins above replacement level, we use WARP and marginal wins interchangeably.

4. The 2005 performance data are from *Baseball Prospectus.com*'s WARP1 statistic, which is intended to measure wins over what a replacement player would produce. Salary data is from Cot's Baseball Contracts,*http://mlbcontracts.blogspot.com/2005_01_03_mlbcontracts_archive.html*. The data set includes about 20 players from each team who received the most amount of playing time. The data were used to calculate the ratio of free-agent compensation, by position, to arbitration-eligible and restricted players. The sample was then "normalized" by adjusting for the overall 2005 payroll for all teams ($2.2 billion), relative to the marginal wins for all teams (1,701, derived from the implicit .150 winning percentage of a replacement level team compared to the average .500 team). The result is an overall payroll cost per marginal win of $1.3 million for all pay grades of players.

5. Team salary data are from the *USA Today* salary database, *http://asp.usatoday.com/sports/baseball/salaries/totalpayroll.aspx?year=2006*.

6. Since replacement level is defined as a team with 25 wins (.150 winning percentage), 65 marginal wins are required to reach 90 wins. To eliminate the additional complication of salary inflation (or deflation) over time, this analysis is done in 2006 constant dollars. Also, while $72 million in opening day payroll represented the top of the third quartile in 2006, it may be more realistic to consider the ceiling for the quartile to be $75 million to account for injured players on the disabled list and other roster moves.

7. The plausible scenario includes $2 million of nonproductive payroll to cover the expense of players on the disabled list and under-producing players on the roster. To illustrate the impact of nonproductive players, even the 2006 Yankees had 10 players pass through the Bronx (not including the September minor league call-ups when rosters expand) who had either zero or negative WARP, including Craig Wilson, Sal Fasano, Kelly Stinnett, and Bubba Crosby. While these four Yankees performed as true replacement players, only Crosby was paid replacement player wages. Repalcement players are thought to be a widely available commodity, with no significant acquisition costs. Therefore, it is reasonable to expect that their performance would cost at or near the ML minimum salary ($327,000 in 2006).

8. Given the "waste factor" of producing MLB-ready talent at a position, or within a time-frame that is not usable by the ML club, a team may need to target the development of 33 wins per year in order to deliver 28 usable wins.

9. John D. Burger and Stephen J. K. Walters, "Arbitrator Bias and Self-Interest: Lessons from the Baseball Labor Market," *Journal of Labor Research*, Vol. XXVI, No. 2, Spring 2005, pp. 267–280.

10. Ibid., p. 275.

11. This estimate is based on a sample of approximately 225 players who were playing under free-agent contracts for the 2005 season and adjusted to calibrate to an overall free-agent salary to a marginal win ratio of $2.4 million per marginal win.

12. Gary Rausch, "Evolution of the Draft," May 16, 2002, *http://mlb.mlb.com/NASApp/mlb/mlb/news/mlb_news.jsp?ymd=20020516&content_id=26646&vkey=news_mlb&fext=.jsp*.

13. Ibid.

14. Free-agent costs are based on 2005 cost analysis and for the purpose of the player asset value calculation are held constant. If they are allowed to escalate, the player's asset value would be higher.

15. Assuming the mutual option for $12 million is exercised for the 2009 season. Contract details per Cot's Baseball Contracts, *http://mlbcontracts.blogspot.com/2004/12/new-york-mets.html*.

16. Ramirez's 2006 WARP was 5.8, compared to Teahen's of 5.2. For the purpose of this example we'll assuming that Teahen's upside will ultimately place him as the equivalent of Ramirez in win contribution.

17. The Commissioner's Office might object to such a cash transaction, citing that it is not in the best interests of baseball, despite its economic validity.

18. International players are eligible to be signed as free agents and are not subject to the amateur draft.

19. See Note 9.

20. In 2005, 40 of 154 starting pitchers were left-handed.

Moneyball and the Oakland A's

Much has been written about the success formula for the Billy Beane–led Oakland A's. In Michael Lewis' book, *Moneyball*, he cites a strategy of finding players with high OPS (on-base percentage + slugging percentage) as a key to the A's success. These OPS standouts were undervalued by the market, meaning other teams valued them less than their fair value and less than the market valuation for batting average and slugging percentage. Beane took advantage of this market inefficiency after he brought in sabermetric analysts who showed that OPS had a closer link to winning games than did slugging percentage or batting average. Lewis gives credit to Beane for building his team around high OPS players at discounted prices. It's indisputable that Beane's A's enjoyed great success from 2000 to 2004. In 2000 through 2002, Beane delivered first-quartile wins with a fourth-quartile payroll, while in 2003 the A's remained in the top quartile in wins but slipped to the third quartile in payroll. (2004 saw the A's in the second quartile in wins and 16th in overall payroll, a more modest accomplishment when compared to their success of the previous years.)

Studies have shown that Lewis was right about the valuation of high OPS players. In a study by economics professors Jahn K. Hakes and Raymond D. Sauer, "An Economic Evaluation of the Moneyball Hypothesis," the authors validate the lower valuation from 2000 to 2003 but claim the inefficiency was gone by the 2004 season. While the study reassures us that Beane and the A's exploited inefficiency in the way players were compensated and as result enjoyed a discount in their cost of wins, it did not address an important follow-up question. Was this exploitation the key enabler for the A's to deliver three straight years of first-quartile wins at a fourth-quartile payroll level? My analysis indicates it did help, but had far less financial impact than many readers have inferred from *Moneyball*. I contend that the mix of players on the A's roster, by pay grade—restricted, arbitration eligible, and free agents—had far more impact on their ability to deliver top wins/lowest payroll performance.

Focusing on the 2001 season as an example, possibly Beane's crowning accomplishment to date (the second-most wins in MLB, with the second-lowest payroll), we can analyze the composition of the A's roster and get to the core of our question. The roster of the 102-win ball club was heavily skewed to young, captive talent. Of the top 14-win contributors (those with marginal wins of 2.9 or greater, according to Baseball Prospectus' WARP statistics), eight were restricted players

→

not yet eligible for arbitration, four were arbitration eligible, and two were in the free-agent pay grade. The mix of contribution to wins is 62% for the least expensive, restricted, group, 28% for the arbitration-eligible players, and 10% for free agents. In 2000, 90% of the A's marginal wins came at a discount to the market price, since MLB's rules prevent players from shopping their services and achieving a market price through an auction process until they are eligible for free agency.

The group of eight restricted players averaged 5.9 wins each, for a total of *51 marginal wins at a payroll cost of about $2.5 million.* If we take our 2005 estimate of free-agent costs discussed in Chapter 7 and discount it back to 2001, we can estimate the restricted, arbitration-eligible, and free-agent rates per marginal win. If the A's had achieved their 102 wins with the league average mix of 35% restricted, 23% arbitration eligible, and 42% free agents, their payroll would have been in the neighborhood of $104 million. Their payroll of approximately $34 million represented a *savings of $70 million* versus the average mix of players by pay grade. Of the 12 high-impact restricted and arbitration-eligible players on the 2001 A's, seven were originally signed by the A's organization (five drafted in the annual June amateur draft (Giambi, Chavez, Hudson, Mulder, and Zito) and two signed as international free agents (Tejada and Hernandez), while Frank Menechino was acquired through the Rule 5 draft). According to the marginal win statistics from Baseball Prospectus, had the A's not had the services of Mulder (8.7 WARP), Hudson (7.9), and Zito (7.3), and instead had replacement players in their roster spots, they might have been a below .500 team. So while the A's clearly had a keen eye for talent, it may have had much more to do with pitching and less to do with OPS, at least for the 2001 club.

In the first several years of this decade, the A's defined success as winning efficiently—making the playoffs with a low payroll. At the core of the A's formula for success was their ability to draft and develop superstar players, not their ability to find an occasional bargain hitter who was undervalued on the market because his keen batting eye allowed him to take more walks. They clearly schooled their up-and-coming hitters—Giambi, Tejada, and Chavez—on the art of plate discipline, and it contributed to their success. In the end, the cost savings derived from internally growing their talent had far greater financial impact than any inefficiency they exploited in batting statistics. The A's masterfully exploited the ultimate success formula in MLB: draft and develop enough talent to staff your MLB roster internally and reap the discount afforded by captive players as they await their free-agent payday.

PART FOUR

BUILDING THE TEAM BRAND

Deepening the emotional connection between a team and its fans has a direct bearing on the economics of winning for an MLB team. Teams that have a strong brand franchise, like the Chicago Cubs and St. Louis Cardinals, realize a revenue cushion in the form of the deep loyalty of their fans in years when the team is less than competitive. Teams with strong brands are more likely to spend to win, because their revenues sag less in a down year.

In Chapter 9, "A Brand-Building Approach," we discuss the three phases of a team brand, from the first level—building credibility and trust—to the best-in-class third level—creating an emotional bond with fans—and the attributes that determine the strength and level of development of a team's brand. We also discuss how media and communication are changing the geographic boundaries within which teams compete for fans and the ways in which teams segment their fan base in order to grow their brand. The chapter closes with a description of the process teams can use to create an explicit strategy to strengthen fan loyalty and, hence, the value of their brand.

In Chapter 10, "The Value of Fan Loyalty," we review a valuation methodology that ranks each team's brand value. We also discuss the trade-off between building the image of the brand and the more immediate issue of promotional events to fill seats. We end with a profile of the three highest value brands, which have all taken different paths to their financial success, proving there is no one way to build an MLB team brand.

9 | A Brand-Building Approach

Consumer marketing doesn't always get the respect it deserves in the business world. Those who think of the marketing department as the people who generate the attention-grabbing, humorous Superbowl television commercials consider marketers to be the court jesters of the business community, but by any objective measure, marketing excellence—building the image and ultimately the value of brands—is an indispensable function in any company that sells branded products or services. Great marketing can help forge an emotional and personal bond between a consumer and a brand. Brands with strong equity can make an occasional misstep and not lose much favor with a loyal consumer. Brands that lack a connection to consumers are considerably more fragile, and even the smallest miscue can permanently alienate a customer.

With today's uneven financial landscape across Major League Baseball, teams are constantly seeking every chance to generate revenues to help fund a competitive club. An often underexploited opportunity is building the brand equity of the franchise—the value of the loyalty and the passion of a team's fans. The tangible benefits of greater brand loyalty include higher attendance frequency by the otherwise occasional fan, along with higher broadcast ratings. According to a 2002 study on sports fans' involvement, the amount of money and time fans allocate to their favorite team corresponds to their "emotional commitment" to the club.[1] Brand loyalty will also lead to "pricing power"—fans' willingness to quietly absorb ticket price increases or a higher season ticket renewal rate following a down year—leading to greater profitability for the team.[2] It can also translate into a better value for sponsors, leading to a greater retention rate. According to a study of Cubs fans, die-hard fans are not only more loyal to the Cubs, but also more brand loyal to products in general.[3] Teams that build intense fan loyalty have greater value to pass along to their sponsors. The strength of the team as a brand indirectly impacts what happens on the playing field. Building a strong brand means more revenue, which in turn fuels the all-important payroll and player development system. A team with a weak marketing effort is not maximizing the value of the brand and is shortchanging its fans by being less likely to consistently field a competitive team. Deepening the relationship with fans by building a stronger brand clearly has a direct bearing on the economics of winning in baseball.

THE TEAM AS A BRAND

What makes a baseball team a strong brand? Strong brands fill consumers' (fans') needs on both a functional and emotional level. When fans say, "A Sox game is a great place to spend a sunny summer afternoon," they're speaking about a functional need being met. When fans say, "Every time the Dodgers win I love them even more," they're speaking about an emotional need that is being satisfied. For some, the emotional need is linked to winning, but for others it relates to being part of a community—possibly a community of Dodger fans, who "feel the same way I feel about the team." By ranking fans' needs and creating a hierarchy, we can create a simple model of an MLB brand, categorizing its evolution and level of development. The first phase of developing an MLB team brand is establishing *credibility and trust* within the community and the fan base. Phase 2 builds on a foundation of credibility and trust by providing *compelling entertainment value*. Ultimately teams strive for Phase 3, which builds on the first two phases by *creating an emotional bond with fans across generations* (see Figure 9.1). We will discuss each of these phases individually.

PHASE 1: ESTABLISHING CREDIBILITY AND TRUST

While having credibility and trust is not sufficient to build a great brand, it is a necessary first step. Credibility and trust come in many forms, including the connection between the ownership group and the team's fans. Following the 1997 championship season, Florida Marlins owner Wayne Huizenga fractured his credibility with Marlins fans by liquidating the players that brought Southeast Florida their first World Series victory. Ironically just six years later, after diligent GM Dave Dombrowski rebuilt the Marlins into World Champions again, history repeated itself. Marlins owner Jeffrey Loria also sold off his star veteran talent in favor of cheaper, unproven

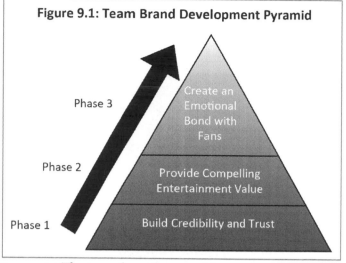

FIGURE 9.1 **The team brand pyramid.**

prospects in an effort to save money at the expense of the quality of the team on the field. These two breaches with Marlins fans place the future of the franchise in great peril, as they chip away at the foundation of any brand relationship, credibility, and trust. In order to gain the trust of fans, team ownership needs to demonstrate a passion for baseball and a commitment to their community.

Credibility and trust go beyond the ownership to the players on the field. If a batter jogs down to first base while grounding into a double play, he's violating the implicit contract he has with fans—to make an effort to play the game to the best of his ability. If this happens one time, the brand isn't necessarily affected, but if management shows a tolerance and acceptance of this type of lack of effort, the brand suffers from a lack of credibility and trust. Another way the players on the field affect a team's credibility is in the composition of the roster. It's important to have several Major League veterans or even a star player on the team. A team that tries to get through a season with a roster filled with fringe players and minor league prospects is testing the patience of its fans and risking its credibility. Even the 56-win Kansas City Royals had proven major leaguers on their 2005 squad. Matt Stairs and Terrence Long, along with their star player Mike Sweeney, complemented a host of youngsters. For all their faults in the 2005 season, the Royals maintained the credibility and trust of their fans by not ridding themselves of Sweeney's $11-million contract. For the 2006 season, the Royals loaded up on mature talent with Reggie Sanders, Doug

Mientkiewicz, Mark Redman, and Mark Grudzielanek, giving hope to the K.C. faithful. While the team ultimately won only 62 games in 2006, ownership cannot be accused of being unwilling to bring in established, quality players.

Also included in the foundation of building a brand is the importance of having reasonable access to your team's broadcasts. A team that televises only 50 games in a season or that delivers radio broadcasts over a low-range FM station violates the credibility and trust with its fans by failing to provide a reasonable opportunity to watch or listen to the team's games. In the context of the proliferation of sports broadcasts today, anything short of a virtual complete schedule of team broadcasts will be a disappointment to fans. During his ownership tenure with the Montreal Expos, Jeffrey Loria went even one step further when he decided to not broadcast—on either local radio or television—any of his team's games, because he was dissatisfied with the financial arrangements of the deals.

Finally, fans have come to expect value for the ticket price and the trek to the ballpark to watch their team play. Beyond a clean ballpark and a courteous staff, they also expect a wide range of food service choices. Over the past 10 years as new ballparks have opened, a hot dog, peanuts, and a Pepsi have given way to gourmet burritos and exotic imported beers. While this is a small part of the customer satisfaction equation, it goes a long way to appeasing the nonfans who attend the game with their friends or spouses, converting their potential objection to attending a game into approval. Fans also include promotional events in their value equation, as they have become conditioned to expect premiums or other giveaway items, viewing them as extra value that helps justify the sometimes steep ticket price. These promotional days often appeal to the young fan who does not have a long history with the team and may not yet be the super-loyal fan that his or her parents have become. In addition to putting a smile on the youngster's face, the giveaway promotion reduces any objections about going to the ball game with Mom and Dad. Even though the premium item may not be targeted at Mom and Dad, it helped them by making it an easy sell to their child. Figure 9.2 outlines the components of the first level of building a brand relationship—credibility and trust.

PHASE 2: COMPELLING ENTERTAINMENT VALUE

The second level of building a brand relationship is to provide *compelling entertainment value.* An important tenet of this level of the brand relationship is the owners' commitment to fielding a competitive team. The Milwaukee Brewers' new owner, Mark Attanasio, shows a passion for the game and a commitment to the community. The follow-up question is, "does the

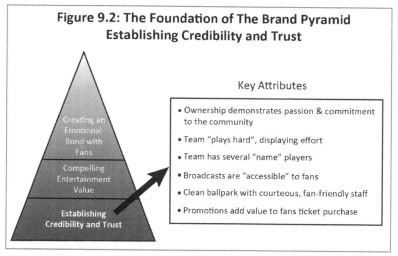

FIGURE 9.2 **Foundation of the brand pyramid.**

owner show a commitment to fielding a competitive team that will ulti-mately contend for a play-off spot?" For the Brewers, the answer appears to be "yes." It's one of the four pledges Attanasio made shortly after taking the reins: build a perennially competitive team, deliver the best fan experi-ence, be a leader in the community, and become a place where people want to work, from players to ballpark attendants and everyone in between. As an indication of his commitment, he has locked up GM Doug Melvin and manager Ned Yost with contract extensions that help provide stability and continuity to the organization. Melvin has gotten excellent mileage from his modest payroll budget, as he meticulously assembled the pieces of a team on the verge of contending with a mix of veterans and young promis-ing talent. Attanasio and Melvin are also turning the Brewers into a team where *players want to stay,* rather than catch the first plane out of town when their contracts expire. When players play hard, act like a team, and genuinely enjoy their environment, fans take notice and begin to buy-in to what the ownership group is trying to accomplish.

Winning helps a team provide compelling entertainment value, but it means more than checking the standings to see the wins and losses. Even teams that are not contenders can still provide compelling entertainment value if their team has the right mix of young promising players and they show *improvement.* While the ultimate measure of the quality of a team is how it ranks compared to the rest of the league or its division, fans also judge a team's quality against its former self. Winning 75, 79, and 84 games in successive years may provide more entertainment value than a team that won 92, 88, and 84 games in successive years, particularly if the second team had aging stars and fans held little hope of an imminent turnaround. Many baseball fans are very astute and often look behind the win–loss totals to the bigger picture of where the team is headed. Much of their view of the entertainment value of the team centers on perceptions and expectations. The 2006 Cincinnati Reds may be a good example of a team that is providing high entertainment value, despite being an 80-win ball club. Improving from 67 to 75 to 80 wins over the past three seasons, the 2006 club combined a blend of young talent, such as Brandon Phillips, with star veterans, such as Ken Griffey, Jr. When a team makes steady year-to-year progress, fans look beyond the 80 wins and recognize the *potential* for a play-off-contending team. The legitimate expectation of improvement, combined with acceptable performance today, creates a sense of optimism and provides high entertainment value

Teams in the second phase of building the brand may not be loaded with big-name marquee players. Often these teams are cultivating the best of their home-grown talent into future marquee players. The Twins are an excellent example of a team that has resisted the high-priced temptation of the free-agent market but still managed to grow their own All Stars, who possess broad fan appeal. First Torii Hunter and Brad Radke, and now Justin Morneau, Johan Santana, and Joe Mauer have emerged as some of the AL's top players, adored by fans and the centerpiece of the Twins' identity.

Beyond a competitive ball game and marquee players, fans also expect a "total entertainment experience" when they make the trip to the ballpark with family in tow. Even though a television viewer may be satisfied with a competitive ball game and knowledgeable announcers, expectations are much higher when the fan is at the ballpark. Viewing the ball game live is intrinsically more entertaining, but the experience may not be sufficient to justify the added cost. According the Team Marketing Reports' (TMR) 2006 Fan Cost Index, the average bill for a family of four to attend a Major League baseball game was over $170.[4] To complement the game, the team needs to provide a thoroughly entertaining experience that goes well beyond a night at the movies, which may cost a family of four about $60, about one-third the cost of the ballgame. Many teams have done an excellent job of making their ballparks family-friendly, by establishing children's play areas, some of which are baseball themed. The teams that focus on creating an event, not just a ball game, ensure that once an inning ends and there is a break in the baseball action, the public address announcer is directing fan attention to some other activity to occupy and entertain them. In the best ballparks, a ball game is a nonstop production for more than three hours on game night. (See Figure 9.3 for the second phase of the brand pyramid.)

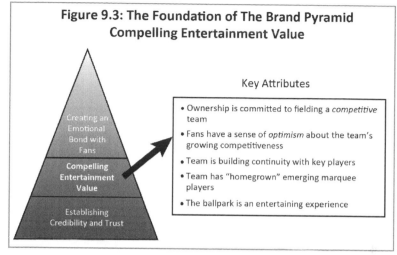

Figure 9.3: The Foundation of The Brand Pyramid Compelling Entertainment Value

Key Attributes

- Ownership is committed to fielding a *competitive* team
- Fans have a sense of *optimism* about the team's growing competitiveness
- Team is building continuity with key players
- Team has "homegrown" emerging marquee players
- The ballpark is an entertaining experience

FIGURE 9.3 **Compelling entertainment value.**

PHASE 3: CREATING AN EMOTIONAL BOND WITH FANS

If credibility and trust are the foundation and compelling entertainment value is the second phase, the third and final phase is tapping into the passion of fans by *creating an emotional bond with fans across generations.* How does a team get to that plateau of being an elite brand in Major League Baseball? One ingredient is ownership and players who are as committed to winning as fans are. In 2006, 29 teams came up short in their quest for a World Championship, but only one owner, George Steinbrenner, publicly declared his team a sad failure. Derek Jeter has often said the only successful season ends with a World Championship. This attitude, backed by a $200-million payroll and a deep run into most postseasons, strengthens the bond between the Yankees and their fans.

Another important element is the make-up of the team's roster. Teams that are loaded with marquee players tend to command a higher profile in the media, which leads to more fan attention. Writers like to write about Derek Jeter, and baseball fans, particularly Yankee fans, will read anything they can get their hands on regarding Jeter. The constant stream of media attention and the pride of having one of the premier players in baseball dressed in pinstripes contributes to the strength of the Yankee brand.

Having a consistently high-performing team also evokes a passion among fans. The St. Louis Cardinals are an organization that has a long-standing, consistent legacy of winning. With nine World Championships, the Cardinals are the second only to the Yankees as the "winningest" franchise in ML history. Their tradition of winning, combined with their present day competitiveness—reaching the postseason in six of the past seven years—breeds a special pride and loyalty among their fan base, which seems to be woven into the fabric of the city's culture. When teams like the Cardinals, Yankees, and even more recently the Red Sox continue to contend for a championship, fans view *themselves* as winners. The identity of a city and its fans often pivots on the fortune of their favorite sports teams, and for many cities, baseball teams are the bellwether of that identity.

Player continuity also contributes to an emotional bond between a team and its fans and is another hallmark of the best MLB team brands. In this era of free agency and transient players, fans are even more appreciative of players who stay in one place and make their home in the community in which they play. Fans tend to identify these players as part of the brand. In the 1960s player continuity may have been measured by the number of 10-year veterans on a team. Today's fans understand the rarity of player continuity and have adjusted their expectations downward accordingly. Fans seem more tolerant of the rent-a-player mentality employed by many teams if the team maintains a solid nucleus of key contributors for four or five years, particularly if they stagger their departures.

Players can further contribute to tapping into fan passion and raising the value of the brand by being accessible. Players who are not only solid on-field performers, but are also likeable or engaging with the media and fans are tremendously valuable brand-builders. The 2004 "Idiot" Red Sox were loaded with players who fit this mold. When Johnny Damon played in Boston, he was a media darling—accessible, highly quotable, and always with a smile on his face. Damon may have been the media centerpiece of the Championship Red Sox, but he had plenty of company, including Curt Schilling, Kevin Millar, and David Ortiz. The accessibility of likeable players puts a face on the team and gives fans more than a logo and a legacy with which to identify. In the future we can expect that a handful of MLB stars will be cultivated as a "personal brand" following the approach of their European soccer counterparts. Englishman and Real Madrid star David Beckham is backed by 19 Entertainment, the marketing machine that brought us *American Idol*. Their branding strategy has been to position Beckham as an icon, rather than just a soccer star.[5] The management team of Manchester United superstar Wayne Rooney hired an image maker to come up with an identity—"Wayne Rooney-Street Striker"—complete with his own logo.[6]

Beyond the performance of the current team and the image of its star players, a team's history and legacy can create an emotional bond with fans. Every team has a history, even the young Tampa Bay Devil Rays, whose biggest highlight to date may be Wade Boggs' 3,000th hit, which came on a home run he hit for the D-Rays at Tropicana Field. The New York Mets have a rich history that is an important element of their marketing and brand-building efforts. After a short beginning as New York's lovable losers, they won the World Series in just their eighth season. They followed with a World Series appearance just four years later, in 1973, and then with their second World Championship in 1986. Tapping into fans' memories of these moments puts smiles on their faces and helps reprise some of the glorious feelings associated with those teams and their success. After all, the point of reminiscing is to recapture even a momentary fraction of our fondest memories from our favorite times. We go to ball games, at least in part, to find the magic moments, which will ultimately become memories we cherish for decades. Reminding Mets fans of the 1986 Championship team by celebrating its 20th anniversary not only sells tickets today but also creates a timeline of connection to a franchise that goes beyond the current players and today's win–loss record. Baseball plays such a prominent role in our society, that for many it serves as a mile-marker for time and the distance traveled during our lives. For a teenage boy who cheered for his 1986 Mets alongside his dad, a team-promoted anniversary celebration will not only evoke memories, but will also encourage him to share his stories with his 12-year old daughter and perhaps even prompt him to take her to a ball game or two this summer, creating more special moments and thereby continuing this cycle.

One of the powerful aspects of celebrating a team's history and legacy is the creation of a memory bridge across generations of fans. By evoking the memories of past teams' highlights, a team activates its best brand-building resources—the family. What better way to emblazon a team in the mind and heart of a young person, than to be told "war stories" by Dad or Grandpa. An insurance salesman might call it a referral, but for a ball club the team is woven into the fabric and culture of the family. Baseball is fortunate to have this marketing vehicle available to them. Not every product or service can engage customers as salespeople. When was the last time you ran into a zealot who tried to convert you to his or her favorite brand of toothpaste? Toothpaste tends to be a very personal item, while baseball tends to be more of a "community good" that lends itself to fans becoming ardent advocates. Teams who focus all of their marketing efforts only on the present and do not create a link to their pasts miss the opportunity to entrench their brands more deeply into the psyches of their fans. The teams with the highest brand value have aggressively drawn on their legacy and connected generations of fans.

Capitalizing on a team's history is one matter; building a tradition is another. Creating appealing rituals and traditions is an important part of a team marketers' role. At the conclusion of every New York Yankees home game, the public address system blares a rendition of a local anthem, "New York, New York." Following a win, the Frank Sinatra version plays, while a loss is followed by Liza Minelli's recording. This ritual is meaningful to Yankees fans. Music is a great way to connect with fans, and playing New York's prideful song reminds fans that New York and the Yankees are an important part of each other's identity. Sometimes music simply entertains, such as playing "Hit the Road Jack" when an opposing team is making a pitching change, but other well-timed music can contribute to the bigger picture of building the equity of the team as a brand.

Another key component of building an enduring emotional bond with fans is for a team to deliver a theme park experience at the ballpark. Sections of the stadium that provide memorable activities for various ages of fans help turn an evening at the ballpark into a family event. The Phanatic Phun Zone at Citizens' Bank Park in Philadelphia could delight any seven-year-old, initiating the process of building a lifelong fan. The Jays Kids' Zone in Rogers Center in Toronto features interactive batting and pitching games along with a concession menu catered to younger tastes. Baseball-related exhibits, such as the team's Monument Park in Yankee Stadium or the All-Star Walk in the Ashburn Alley section of the Phillies new ballpark, connect fans with the team's history and tradition while entertaining them. The Cincinnati Reds have capitalized on their glorious history by creating the Cincinnati Reds Hall of Fame and Museum adjacent to the Great American Ballpark. In the 2006 version of the annual induction ceremony, modeled after the one held in Cooperstown each summer, the Reds paid tribute to former players Tom Browning, Lee May, and Tom Seaver. The ceremony was held during a Reds homestand, shining the media spotlight on many of the other 68 members, who came to town for the celebration, no doubt conjuring up images of the Reds championship teams of the 1970s.

In recent years the emergence of RSN's, such as the Yankees' YES Network and the Red Sox's NESN, have not only provided team ownership another vehicle to monetize fan demand, but also market the brand. Additionally, teams may provide programming beyond game telecasts, which could be another source of revenue that does not exist under the traditional model. This opportunity for additional programming provides more than a revenue stream; it provides an opportunity for teams to create programming focused on marketing the team as a brand to its fans. In today's hi-tech vocabulary this is known as "controlling content," something teams could not do in the more traditional broadcast model.

The Yankees exploit this opportunity with a series it calls *Yankeeography*. These one-hour short films are part highlight footage and part interview and commentary, typically focused on an individual player or era in the Yankees' storied past. From Lou Gehrig to Derek Jeter, Yankee fans can become more intimately acquainted with the heroes of their favorite team, further cementing fans' long-term loyalty. In the past a team simply sold access to its telecasts, but with the YES Network, the Yankees can inundate their insatiable fans with brand-building propaganda that makes them the envy of any marketer. Imagine a Gillette channel on your cable system that could command the undivided attention of consumers for hours at a time? It's not likely to happen in the personal care market, but in professional sports it *is* possible, and one of the greatest brands in the history of sports is leading the way.

Another element of broadcasts that can add to the value of the brand is a high-profile marquee broadcast announcer. Vin Scully of the Dodgers, the classic example of the marquee broadcaster—a soloist who is not accompanied by another commentator—is part of the entertainment. His endearing nature and melodic story-telling do more than entertain; he is part of the brand. When he tells stories about Dodger days gone by, he connects today's fans with the tradition of the Dodgers. More that 50 years as the "voice of the Dodgers" connects Scully with fans born nearly a century apart. While spreading the gospel of "Dodger Blue," Scully is a personal bridge connecting generations and solidifying that emotional bond between the Dodgers and its fans.

Figure 9.4 outlines the attributes of the third level of brand development—creating an emotional bond with fans across generations. While each successive level of the brand pyramid includes components of lower levels, there is a stark contrast between the top and bottom of the brand pyramid (compare Figures 9.2 and 9.4). Every team aspires to reach the third and highest level of brand development, but only a handful of teams can truly claim that they achieved this lofty status.

Figure 9.4: The Top of The Brand Pyramid
Creating an Emotional Bond Across Generations of Fans

Key Attributes

- Fan perception that owners and players want to win as much as the fans
- Team maintains continuity with key players
- Team identity linked with several "likeable, accessible" players
- Team celebrates history/legacy to bridge generations of fans
- Ballpark has feel of baseball theme park
- Enthusiastic employees deliver first-rate customer service
- Regional Broadcast network to augment brand building with team controlled content
- Endearing, familiar broadcasters are part of the entertainment and provide continuity

FIGURE 9.4 **The top of the brand pyramid.**

PENETRATING FRANCHISE BOUNDARIES

Along the path to building a premier brand, teams face numerous challenges. One that has emerged only over the past several years is coping with the blurring of a team's geographic boundaries. Twenty years ago a team truly owned its local market. For fans who wanted to watch baseball, their home team was their only option.[7] Now, for a reasonable price, fans can purchase access to hundreds of telecasts and virtually every radio broadcast from MLBtv, the MLB Extra Innings broadcast package, and XM Satellite Radio for every team in the league. While the Kansas City Royals "own" their local market from an MLB rights perspective, if they were to play .350 winning percentage baseball for too long, the local fans might gravitate to other teams that they could easily follow daily via various broadcast packages. Combine this availability of a team's broadcasts with the speed and accessibility of a team's local media coverage via the Internet, it is easy to imagine how someone could be a Yankee fan from Los Angeles, Chicago, or Atlanta.

What were once hard boundaries are now soft borders penetrable by successful teams and creative, resourceful marketing departments. Teams can either be unnerved by the complexity and threat of deep-pocketed ball clubs invading their marketing turf, or they can view this as an opportunity to sell their brand across the country or even around the globe. By signing Japanese stars, the Mariners and Yankees have established a following in Japan. Fans from the homeland of Ichiro Suzuki and Hideki Matsui also cheer for Seattle and New York, as well as buy hats with their hero's team logo and even watch live telecasts of games, with in-stadium signage in their native language. In addition to being valuable on-field contributors, these players have enhanced the value of the brand by opening up overseas markets to their ball clubs. If that's the opportunity side of our shrinking globe, the threat would be the St. Louis Cardinals branching out to convert neighboring Kansas City Royals fans. As the deeper-pocket Cardinals cross the state and market to western Missouri, the Royals become vulnerable to surrendering formerly loyal fans to their cross-state rivals. Of course, the battle rages every day in markets like New York, Chicago, the San Francisco Bay Area, and Southern California. For many years these have been two-team markets, conditioned to battle their crosstown rivals.

GROWING THE BRAND THROUGH SEGMENTATION

As the evolving geographic landscape forces marketers to broaden their thinking, they are more inclined to consider other forms of "segmenting" the market for baseball. Customer segmentation can be an effective tool to speak more directly to fans in a language that resonates. In contrast to the "one size fits all" mass marketing approach, fans with diverse interests, perceptions, and attitudes are divided into subgroups. These subgroups—demographic, psychographic, or behavioral—allow teams to create a more tailored message and deliver it through targeted media, leading to a bigger bang for the marketing buck. An example of a demographic segment on teams' radar screens is women. The Dodgers launched an initiative in 2005 called Women's Initiative and Network (WIN), designed to develop and expand their female fan base. Inspired by Dodger Vice Chairman Jamie McCourt, the program allows the club to tailor activities such as clinics and fan appreciation days to this high-growth-potential audience. As part of the program, a mini-ticket plan is offered in the form of a two-for-one deal for seven weekday afternoon games.

Women have been a priority for MLB since the commissioner launched an initiative in 1999, based on research that claimed that women named baseball as their favorite sport by a margin of two to one.[8] For baseball, this is a return to its roots in the face of growing competition from other sports and entertainment choices. Females have a long history as baseball fans, possibly buoyed by the Ladies' Day discount promotions of yesteryear. Ladies' Day was first popularized by the 1930 Cubs, which filled Wrigley Field on Friday afternoons by giving free tickets to women. With over-flow crowds exceeding 50,000 preventing paying male customers from at-tending, the club eventually limited the freebies to 17,500 per Friday home game.[9] Ladies' Days evolved from free admission into discounts on regu-lar priced tickets, but were later abandoned by most teams as they sought more full-priced customers to pay the freight of running a big league club.

Women are not the only demographic segment to be targeted by Major League teams. In an effort to connect with their local market demograph-ics, the Tampa Bay Devil Rays have started the Silver Rays, catering to the older population of the Florida Gulf Coast. This Official Seniors Fan Club is tailored to the interests and budgets of the retired set and provides dis-count tickets and special events to this large, important segment of the local population.[10]

These examples only scratch the surface of the segmentation oppor-tunities that face MLB and its teams. Possibly one of the biggest oppor-tunities is building the sport's popularity and appeal to young people by tapping into the passion of older males (40+) who grew up with baseball as "their sport." These loyal fans, many of whom are fathers (or grandfa-thers) of young children, could be targeted with a tailored message and a call to action to share their experience at the ballpark with their children or grandchildren. With the competition from other fast-paced entertain-ment choices, it is no surprise that baseball is losing relevance with young people. One way to renew the fan base is to enlist the loyal, die-hard fans in the cause. Enlisting baseball loyalists as credible spokespersons within their families and social networks can be a powerful way to renew the fan base and pass along some of the history and lore of our national pastime.

With the help of MLBAM, baseball is on the verge of taking segmenta-tion to the next level by categorizing fans by their specific interests, which can be identified and stored by capturing a fan's activity on the MLB.com web site. In an effort to keep fans constantly engaged and connected, ML-BAM likes to send email or text message "alerts" tailored to a fan's interests. Instead of messaging all Yankee fans with the latest news on Alex Rodri-guez, MLBAM's marketing executive prefers to target anyone who has read an A-Rod story or bought A-Rod merchandise on-line.[11] This highly tar-geted approach increases the response rate by talking directly to A-Rod lovers and lowers the nuisance factor for Yankee fans that are indifferent to the imported superstar.

The Team Brand and Sponsors

Developing a strong team brand can be the first step in creating a cycle of attracting high-quality sponsors, which further builds and reinforces the team brand. As marketing becomes more sophisticated, consumer brands are looking for more than awareness and consumer impressions (the number of consumers that see the brand's message and logo). A decade ago, prior to the information and data explosion led by the Internet, consumer brands might have evaluated an MLB sponsorship based on demographic fit, attendance, and viewership. Today the process of wooing sponsors is a bit more complicated, as consumer brands want to be sure there is compatibility between the "values" and images of their brand and the team brand. They also want accountability on the part of the team—a willingness to measure the results of the sponsorship—to ensure that their brand benefits from the team relationship. Keeping pace with sponsors demands, MLB now has access to its fans' detailed spending data. A division of AC Nielsen is the first to capture data combining fans' sports interests with their purchase activity. According to this new data source, MLB fans spend nearly $350 billion per year on consumer packaged goods, with nearly $600 million per year on razors and blades.[12] The same data source also says that 59% of Gillette's Venus Razor purchasers are MLB fans, forming the basis for a potentially long-lasting computer-arranged marriage between Gillette and MLB.[13] Ann Marie Dumais of Nielsen Ventures says, "At a time when media and their audiences are continually fragmenting. Sports sponsorships are becoming an increasingly important marketing tool."[14]

The Brand-Building Process

For any team that wants to accelerate the growth of its brand and move aggressively to the next phase, the process is straightforward:

1. Establish a brand vision.

2. Conduct a brand audit. Gain feedback from key constituents regarding important brand attributes.

3. Identify brand strengths and weaknesses.

4. Determine the opportunity areas on which to focus future brand plans and initiatives.

5. Develop plans and determine their financial impact.

6. Put metrics in place to measure the ongoing process of the brand's development

One critical step in the process is establishing a brand vision that captures the team's aspiration to be an enduring part of family life, a focal point of social activities, and the premier entertainment event in the local market. With that vision in mind, the team would poll season ticket holders, sponsors, hard-core fans, and casual fans to get a read on where the team stands in relation to their vision. Building a brand is a long-term process that demands commitment and resolve. The best way to justify the staying power necessary to sustain investments is to quantify and measure the benefits of achieving the brand vision and building a first class brand. In the next chapter, The Value of Brand Loyalty, we'll discuss a valuation methodology that allows a team to monitor the progress of its efforts and even develop a return on investment for the initiative.

While there is no one way to build a baseball team brand, there are a set of attributes or success factors that define the most efficient path. The wide variation in the development, and ultimately the value, of team brands speaks to the priorities of the ball club. Some teams are so preoccupied with selling tickets to tomorrow night's game that they fail to find the time to invest in an identity that consumers can bond with for years to come. Building this equity in the brand can provide excellent downside protection for a team's finances in years when the team underperforms, and equally important, it can raise the upside stakes during the good times. Developing a best-in-class MLB team brand is like adding another asset to the balance sheet, which contributes to a team's revenue stream and plays a key role in financing a winning team.

Endnotes

1. Michele E. Capella, "Measuring Sports Fans' Involvement: The Fan Behavior Questionnaire," *Southern Business Review*, Spring 2002, p. 35.
2. Soonhwan Lee, Deron G. Grabel, and Cynthia E. Ryder, "A Secret Shopper Project: Reevaluation of Relationship Marketing Efforts," *The Sport Journal*, Vol. 8, No. 2, Spring 2005.
3. Dennis N. Bristow and Richard J. Sebastian, "Holy Cow! Wait 'til Next Year! A Closer Look at the Brand Loyalty of Chicago Cubs Baseball Fans," *The Journal of Consumer Marketing*, Vol. 18, No. 3, 2001, p. 265.
4. Source: TMR, Fan Cost Index for 2006. The MLB average was $171.19 for two adult and two child tickets, four small soft drinks, two small beers, four hot dogs, and two baseball caps; *http://www.teammarketing.com/fci.cfm?page=fci_mlb2006.cfm*.
5. Dan Sabbagh, "Beckham's Image is Still Football's Most Valuable," *London Times*, July 4, 2006, *http://www.timesonline.co.uk/article/0,,5-2254537,00.html*.
6. "Branding Adds Value to Football's Biggest Names," *Design Week*, July 1, 2004, p. 7.
7. Only the Chicago Cubs and Atlanta Braves telecast games on superstations, which were available to many fans across the country.

8. "MLB Announces Commissioner's Initiative on Women in Baseball," *www.mlb.com*, 2000.

9. "35,000 Women Seek 17,500 Free Tickets for the Cubs' Game," *Chicago Tribune*, July 30, 1930, p. 15.

10. "The Silver Rays," from the Devil Rays' web site, *http://tampabay.devilrays.mlb.com/NASApp/mlb/tb/fan_forum/y2006/silverrays.jsp*.

11.   Jeanette Slepian, "Major League Baseball Hits Homerun with Marketing Automation," *http://www.crm2day.com/editorial/50030.php*.

12. "FANLinks Provides New Insights into Buying Behavior of Baseball Fans," From AC Nielsen's web site, *http://us.acnielsen.com/news/20060411.shtml*.

13. Ibid.

14. Ibid.

10 | The Value of Fan Loyalty

How much is fan loyalty worth to an MLB team? To some, loyalty may be no more than an abstract concept, but when marketers think about loyalty to a brand, they see dollar signs. One of the benefits of measuring loyalty is the ability to monitor changes in consumer or fan attitudes and perceptions. Changes in the metric can be read as an approval–disapproval rating of the team by its fans. Tracking the value of the brand should be part of an annual, or at least bi-annual, "check-up" that marketers administer to their brand. A brand valuation can serve as a measuring stick of whether or not a team's brand-building efforts—their marketing programs—are moving the needle in the right direction, as well as being the foundation of calculating a players' marquee value—the financial value of a player's ability to contribute to the emotional connection between the team and its fans.

We can draw on the statistical analysis discussed in earlier chapters to put numbers to the concept. In Chapter 2 we discussed the breakdown of the win–revenue relationship into two components: the *win-curve,* which estimates the change in a team's revenues from 70 to 105 wins, and the *baseline revenues* a team generates at 70 wins or less. While the win-curve captures fan response to the team's on-field performance, baseline revenues are essentially independent of a team's wins and losses. They relate more closely to the size of a team's market, their past marketing efforts, the phase of development of the brand, and ultimately fan loyalty. At any point in time, baseline revenue estimates reflect an annual revenue stream a team can expect from their brand—fans perception of the team and their level of affinity.

Using a team's baseline revenues as a benchmark of brand loyalty, we can create a formula to estimate the dollar value of the brand. When MLB *teams* are sold, the transaction price tends to be in the range of two to three times a team's annual revenues. One method that attempts to isolate the value of the *brand* is to use the same multiple, but to apply it to *baseline revenues*. Using this methodology, Figure 10.1 shows the estimates of brand value in 2006, which are calculated by multiplying 2.5 × each team's local baseline revenues.[1]

Figure 10.1: The Dollar Value of a Team Brand
($ in Millions)

Highest Value		Middle Value		Lowest Value	
Team	$ Value	Team	$ Value	Team	$ Value
NYY	778	PHL	248	DET	183
CHC	542	CWS	247	COL	176
BOS	511	HOU	238	CIN	155
LAD	436	ATL	220	PIT	150
SEA	378	LAA	204	MLW	149
SFG	360	SDP	201	TBD	145
NYM	343	ARZ	199	OAK	137
BAL	293	TOR	198	FLA	135
TEX	259	CLE	189	KCR	109
STL	249			MIN	107

Note: Only 29 teams are ranked as the Washington Nationals are not rated due to their short tenure.

FIGURE 10.1 **Brand value estimates.**

While there may be no "shocker" on the list, one might be mildly surprised to see the Mariners in the fifth position, ahead of the Mets (7) and Giants (6). The Mariners' strength can be attributed to several factors. First, they had strong teams from 1995 to 1997 (two playoff appearances) and even stronger teams from 2000 to 2003, when they averaged 98 wins per season and set the all-time record for regular season wins in 2001. A winning team was a key ingredient in their formula, as it created an intoxicating ballpark experience that made fans want to return for more. A second factor is the marquee talent that called Seattle home during some of the team's strong seasons, including three future first-ballot Hall of Famers—Ken Griffey Jr., Alex Rodriguez, and Randy Johnson. Add to that core the likeable Edgar Martinez, baseball's best-ever designated hitter, and it is no wonder the Mariners became popular. A third factor that enhances the value of the Mariners brand is the team's penetration of the Asian market, particularly Japan, on the coattails of superstar Ichiro Suzuki. Built into the brand value is a revenue stream that capitalizes on the team's appeal both across the Pacific and to local Asian-Americans in the Seattle area. Add to these factors what some call the best ballpark in MLB, and the result is a franchise that knows how to create value. The challenge will be to keep the brand value "bank balance" high while the team rebuilds to be competitive on the field.

An alternative methodology to estimate the value of the brand is to adjust for the size of the market. Those who favor this approach argue that baseline revenues should be broken into two components—brand value and the generic value of the "category." In marketers terms this means that professional baseball, or more specifically MLB itself, *has value independent of the team entity*. For example, if the Texas Rangers vacated Arlington, Texas, and relocated to, say, Portland, Oregon, and a new expansion team, with all new players and a new logo and even potentially a new stadium, were awarded to the Dallas–Fort Worth area, there would still be some level of baseline revenue associated with this "expansion" team. One would expect it to be less than that of the Rangers, since the Rangers have familiar players, a well-known logo, a facility that is synonymous with the team, and a heritage dating back over 35 years. How much less would the baseline revenue be for this unknown entity, the hypothetical Dallas Diamonds? By attributing some portion of the baseline revenue stream to the market itself, based on its size, we can attempt to disaggregate these two components. What we are left with is an estimate of the *brand value* and the *category value*.

To adjust for market size, we will use a market size index from market population data, where the average-size market (100 index) is virtually equal to Detroit. An estimated first $40 million of baseline revenue, for an average-size market, is attributable to the value of "baseball"—the category—and everything beyond that is attributable to the value of the brand. For a team residing in a market with a 200 index, the first $80 million in revenue is attributable to baseball, with the remainder of baseline revenues assigned to brand value, and so on. While the dollar values change for each team's brand, this alternative methodology results in only a few changes in ranking from our first estimate. Figure 10.2 shows the brand value using this alternative methodology.

Figure 10.2: Separating "Category Value"
Brand Value adjusted for Market Size

Highest Value		Middle Value		Lowest Value	
Team	$ Value	Team	$ Value	Team	$ Value
NYY	620	CWS	178	LAA	104
CHC	473	HOU	168	TBD	100
BOS	408	PHL	157	PIT	98
SEA	323	ATL	155	TOR	90
LAD	313	SDP	140	CIN	89
SFG	298	ARZ	138	DET	86
STL	210	COL	137	OAK	84
NYM	185	CLE	130	KCR	82
TEX	181	MLW	116	FLA	77
BAL	180			MIN	63

$ in Millions

Note: Only 29 teams are ranked as the Washington Nationals are not rated due to their short tenure.

FIGURE 10.2 **Brand value versus category value.**

The only ranking change in the top five is that the Mariners and Dodgers switched positions. The Cardinals made a leap from tenth to seventh place. Among the bottom five teams, the Marlins and Royals switched places, and the Tigers slid from 20th to 25th place. Given that the Tigers are in an average-sized market, they significantly under-perform in the area of baseline revenues—the revenues a team are estimated to generate, with a 70-win or less season.

THE IMPACT OF WINNING ON BRAND VALUE

The Tigers and their stellar 2006 season lead us to an important point about baseline revenues and the value of brand loyalty. While we said that baseline revenues are independent of winning, we must acknowledge that over the long-term, baseline revenues and brand value can be affected by a team's on-field performance. In Chapter 2 we discussed the concept of accretion or erosion of baseline revenues that can occur if a team is a chronically winning or losing team over several years. If the Tigers can build on the momentum of 2006 and sustain several consecutive 90-plus–win seasons, they should experience a rise in their baseline revenues and, hence, their brand value. Another way to think of this effect is to visualize the win-curve shifting upward, maintaining its shape and slope but with a higher starting point, or baseline revenues.

What is the magnitude of the gain in baseline revenues and brand value if the Tigers continue to win? The Tigers had estimated baseline revenues of $73 million heading into the 2006 season. This corresponds to the brand value of $183 million (See Figure 10.1). In other words, if the Tigers had won only 70 games in 2006, their *local* revenue would have been about $73 million. Any additional revenue the Tigers earned in 2006 were a direct result of their on-field performance reflected in their 95-win season. Let's say the Tigers win 95 games in 2007 and again in 2008. Our statistical analysis suggests that as the Tigers enter the 2009 season, they can expect an additional $2.2 million in baseline revenues, an increase of 3%. At a brand value of 2.5 times baseline revenues, the implied brand valuation would increase by about $5.5 million, resulting entirely from the fan loyalty and affinity that a consistent 95-win team can breed.[2] On the other end of the spectrum are the Kansas City Royals, whose brand has been eroding by successive 58-, 56-, and 62-win seasons. The Royals are not only a disappointment to their fans, but also a marketer's nightmare. Entering the 2007 season, we would expect baseline revenues to decline by about 4%.

BUILDING THE BRAND VERSUS FILLING THE SEATS

In addition to the role of building fan loyalty by connecting the brand with fans on a deeply emotional level, team marketers face the challenge of luring fans to games with enticing events or promotional giveaways. Ultimately marketers must answer the question of how much of a team's marketing mix—the share of marketing dollars and programs—should be focused on building the image of the team brand, rather than running promotional giveaway days to sell tickets. Together these two, sometimes polar opposites, form the core of a team's marketing efforts. The challenge is in balancing the long-term benefits of a brand-building initiative and the short-term effects of a strong promotional calendar. Every dollar spent on a visor with a team (and sometimes sponsor) logo may be one less dollar spent on building the *image of the brand* in the minds of the fans.

In recent years promo dates have become so frequent that fans come to expect giveaways and handouts to go with their hefty ticket price. For example, the 2006 Orioles' 81-game home schedule included a promotional calendar with 40 promotions at 35 different games. (The O's often combine student nights with fireworks or giveaway items.) The promotions range from price discounts ($5 student night), to giveaway items (e.g., bobble-head dolls), to fan participation activities (e.g., kids run the bases), to celebration events (fireworks or Latino night).

Analyzing attendance and the promotional calendar allows us to estimate the attendance impact of various events for the Orioles' 2006 season. Using a methodology that bears some resemblance to that used in estimating the win-curve, we can create a regression model to explain individual game attendance.[3] By doing so, we can analyze the effect of any individual promotion, or category of promotion, on game attendance. The model suggests that the best way to drive Oriole home attendance is to invite the Yankees into town. With the Yankees as the visiting team, the Orioles average about 16,500 fans more than they draw with the average opponent.[4] The highest impact event on the Orioles' promotional calendar is the bobblehead doll giveaway, worth 7,800 extra fans per game. Other premium giveaway items (e.g., beach towels, blankets, Oriole caps, etc.) generated about 4,200 extra fans, as did the fan participation events. The fireworks nights were responsible for about 2,200 fans, while the student discount nights seemed to have had little impact on attendance. Clearly the promotional calendar plays an important role in the MLB team marketing mix, but it begs for the same type of analytical discipline we applied to estimate a team's win-curve, discussed in previous chapters. Much the same way the forward-thinking ball clubs pursue the value of a win analysis, best-in-class marketing departments use statistical analysis, coupled with fan feedback, to optimize the impact of a busy promotional calendar.

One creative way to address the question of the mix of brand building and promotional events is to merge the two seemingly polar objectives. Developing promotional events that leverage the history and tradition of the team or that feature a marquee player can provide the perception of extra value to fans while advancing the image of the team brand. Examples include creating a series of collectibles focused on either past historic players or championships or current popular players. It is no surprise that the Cleveland Indians had one of their largest crowds of the 2006 season on a chilly Saturday night in April simply because it was Grady Sizemore bobblehead doll giveaway night. This strategy is successful on multiple levels: it is perceived as a high-value premium that has the power to draw people to the ballpark; it helps promote the value of a team's marquee player, merging his positive image with that of the team; and it provides fans with a "collectible" that will adorn their family room for years to come, evoking fond memories of a popular player and a fun night at the ballpark.

COMPARING THE THREE HIGHEST-VALUE BRANDS

The three highest-value team *brands*, the Yankees, Cubs, and Red Sox, are collectively worth between $1.5 and $2 billion. While that does not put them in the same realm as the world's largest consumer brands, we must take into consideration that these are local, single-market brands. While Starbuck's brand may have a value of more than $3 billion, the brand name is ubiquitous in the United States and marketed in 36 countries around the globe.[5] In contrast, each of our three top MLB team brands is marketed primarily in one major metropolitan area, making their brand value all the more impressive. While the previous chapter described a prototypical way to build a team brand, each of our top three has taken a different path to riches.

THE YANKEES

The New York Yankees boast of being the worlds most well-known sports brand. While the claim reeks of American-centricity, since the Manchester United soccer franchise certainly rivals the Yankees, the Yankees are indisputably a formidable brand force. Rating the Bronx Bombers on each of the brand success attributes will give us an understanding of the path the team took to build its brand value. Blessed with the most glorious history of any pro sports team, with the possible exception of the NHL's Montreal Canadiens, the Yankees' brand-building formula has led with their legendary winning history. The product of 26 World Championships in the last 85 years, the Yankees have generations of fans who have passed on their love, support, and enthusiasm for their favorite club to children, grandchildren, and great-grand children. One of the benefits of winning a championship at the rate of one for every three years is the breeding of the previously mentioned brand ambassadors who are passionate and bent on sharing their love of the team with family and friends of all ages. There is also a bandwagon effect. As the team performs with consistency and its popularity grows among core baseball fans, non–baseball fans adopt the team as their favorite and become brand enthusiasts. Being a Yankee fan becomes the popular thing to do in the greater New York area, attracting even more fans. During their past decade of on-field successes, if not before, the Yankees have become intertwined with the very identity of New York.

The Yankees' brand-building formula goes beyond exploiting its storied past. The Yankees also rate very high in several important dimensions of brand development: passion and commitment of the ownership, the ballpark, and the use of a regional broadcast network as a marketing tool. Whether you attribute it to Steinbrenner's ego or to his commitment to excellence, you will not find a baseball owner who wants to win as badly as The Boss. This carries enormous weight with Yankee fans, even those who are irritated by his occasional nitpicking, critical, public remarks. The public may be split over liking versus disliking Steinbrenner, but most respect his devotion and willingness to spend lavishly to field a winning team. When fans dig deeper into the numbers to understand the enormous resource base the Yankees enjoy, they may be less impressed but still grateful.

Historic Yankee Stadium plays heavily into the brand-building formula. In fact, it is not a coincidence that our top three MLB team brands coincide with the three most historic ballparks. Yankee Stadium, Fenway Park, and Wrigley Field have existed for nearly a century and help connect generations of fans. It is easier for fans across generations to relate to the team as a brand if the ballpark provides the continuity. The ballpark has some parallels to a consumer product's packaging on a grocery store shelf. Consumer brands sometimes undergo packaging and graphics changes in an attempt to become more contemporary or relevant or connect with a particular segment of consumers. However, many of the most successful brands maintain a consistent look over the years, evoking trust, stability, and reliability in the minds of their loyal customers. This continuity, for both consumer packaged goods and baseball teams, is an important part of a brand's relationship with its fans. In many cases grandparents or even great-grandparents sat in the same ballpark to watch their beloved Yankees, Red Sox, or Cubs. Those same generations of Pirates fans may have disjointed memories of Forbes Field, Three Rivers Stadium and Heinz Park. The discontinuity of three different ballparks in a 35-year period works against the Pirate brand. However, the experience provided by the convenience and amenities of twenty-first century stadiums helps to build the brand from a different angle.

Because much of the Yankee brand is built on two pillars—winning and tradition—even the mighty Yankee brand has its fragile points. Our analysis shows that few teams' fans are as punishing as Yankee fans if the team fails to play competitive baseball. A 75-win Yankee team is more of a box office disaster than a comparable Cubs or Dodger team, as the expectations of Yankee fans have been conditioned by the club's own propaganda to demand a postseason-worthy ball club. Partly through their own marketing efforts and hype, the Yankees have inadvertently increased their financial penalty for not winning. The ownership of many teams could deliver an 85-win season and look directly into a camera and tell fans they are happy with the progress the team is making, but with the Yankee fan base that argument does not hold water. In Yankeeland, even a 95-win season, with a fast exit from the playoffs in the Division Series, was accompanied by an apology and a pledge to never let it happen again.

The second pillar of the Yankee brand is tradition, much of which is embodied in Yankee Stadium—the House that Ruth Built. The Yankees face an unusual dilemma as they approach the opening of the New Yankee Stadium in 2009. While the motivation is clear—increase the number of luxury suites to capitalize on the large number of high rollers and corporations based in New York—it is not without risk. Normally when a team moves into a new ballpark, it closes down a rundown, undesirable, unpopular ballpark that lacked character in order to impress its fan base with glorious new digs. This will not likely be the case in New York. While the amenities at Yankee Stadium may be lacking, fans are not dissatisfied with it. Yankee Stadium is one of the most storied arenas in all of sports. It fits the brand image of the Yankees like a glove. The team will need to take great pains to bring much of the Yankee heritage forward into the new ballpark, or they will run the risk of tossing out much of their tradition—one of the pillars on which its brand has been built.

THE CUBS

Our analysis suggests the Chicago Cubs are the second-highest-value MLB brand. While the Cubs continue to leverage historic Wrigley Field as the cornerstone of their identity, they don't perform as well against some of the key brand success factors. In the all important "the owner wants to win as badly as the fans" category, the Cubs have filled their faithful with doubt. Cubs fans continually question the commitment level of the Tribune Corporation and their desire to win rather than simply chug along selling 30,000 or more tickets per game nearly regardless of the team's quality. Rather than lacking in desire, the Cubs leadership may just be less resourceful. Because the Cubs play to high-capacity crowds with a sub-.500 team, ownership may be unwilling to pull out all the stops to build a winner. As evidence of fan loyalty and brand strength, the 2006 Cubs played before 3.2 millions fans, or 94% of capacity, despite winning a NL-worst 66 games.[6] This is the most fans drawn by a team winning 66 games or less in baseball history, other than an expansion team in its first or second year. If the Cubs' ownership does not believe they can monetize the incremental demand they would create from fielding a winning club, they may not want to pay the price to try. The Red Sox have shown that a limited-capacity stadium does not limit an imaginative team's ability to generate increased revenue from winning.

The emotional connection the Cubs have built with their fans is built on the combination of a historic and charismatic setting in which to watch a baseball game and the sympathy afforded a perennially losing team. While the Cubs have lost with consistency, they have always seemed to have their share of marquee players: Ernie Banks and Billy Williams, followed by Ron Santo, Ryne Sandberg, Andre Dawson, and more recently, Sammy Sosa. These stars have legitimized the team and differentiated them from other losing clubs, leading fans to conclude that the Cubs plight was more due to bad fortune than bad players and bad management.

The Cubs face a crucial period over the next three to five years as the White Sox, fresh off their 2005 World Series victory and a 90-win season in 2006, mount a campaign to take the Windy City back from the Cubs. It's no secret that the Cubs have "owned" Chicago for decades. The White Sox are beginning to challenge that dominance with a Championship team composed of a likeable, down-to-earth nucleus of players and a colorful, highly quotable manager. In a national poll of fans' favorite Major League teams, from 2004 to 2006 the Cubs have slid from second to fourth, while the White Sox have catapulted from 27th to 11th.[7] If the South Siders create stability and remain competitive, while the Cubs continue to flounder, by the end of this decade Chicago may not be a Cubs town. The fall of the Cubs into second place in the Second City is only a couple of losing seasons away. The winners are Chicago baseball fans, as both teams will be motivated not just to win ballgames, but to win the bigger-stakes battle of being the city's biggest baseball brand and all of the spoils that accompany that title.

THE RED SOX

The Red Sox brand really hit their stride when John Henry and his partners took control of the team and established a more open communication approach, a stark contrast to the tight-lipped Harrington–Duquette regime. Charles Steinberg, the executive vice president and team public relations guru deserves credit for the focus on communicating and reaching out to fans and the media. The Red Sox of the past seven years have leaned on the popularity and accessibility of some high-profile players to provide a personal identity for their team. Over the years Johnny Damon, David Ortiz, Kevin Millar, Curt Schilling, and Pedro Martinez have been the face of the Red Sox. The self proclaimed "idiots," along with rallying cries like

"Cowboy up," gave the team a measure personality not often seen in to-day's image-conscious pro sports scene. Ownership could have obstruct-ed that public view, but instead, in a stroke of marketing genius, chose to let it flourish. Often the team spokesperson is not the star player. Manny Ramirez may be the MVP of the Red Sox on the field, much like Albert Belle was for the 1990s Cleveland Indians, but neither player was the face and image of their team. With the extroverted tendencies of Ortiz, Schil-ling, and company the Red Sox fans and media got to know the team on a personal level, helping connect the ball club to its fans throughout New England and beyond.

Another important aspect of the Red Sox brand is their emergence as the anti-Yankees. There is nothing new about their on-field battle and op-position to the Yankees, which dates back a century or so. However, over the past decade, as the Yankees emerged as a bigger-than-life force in every aspect of the game—payroll, on-field success, revenue—they seemed to ac-complish their success with the brute force of the neighborhood bully. By contrast, the Red Sox seemed to capture the high ground and emerge as the average person's team, with a healthy level of humility and accessibility. The Yankees of "King George" were a far cry from the Red Sox of "the people."

Fenway Park is an important part of the Red Sox brand, in much the same way Wrigley Field is embedded in the Cubs brand. The new owners made a wise choice, one that is entirely consistent with being a team of the people, in deciding to spruce up the vintage ballpark rather than build a new one. Even though a new ballpark, which likely could have been pub-licly funded, would have opened up additional sources of revenue from more luxury suites, the Sox resisted putting their identity at risk. Instead they invested heavily in Fenway to bring some of the amenities to the fans and added a full complement of premium seating to augment their rev-enues. The Green Monster Seats, right-field roof deck, and EMC Club and Pavilion Club and Pavilion Box seats offer a unique vantage point to view a game. They also help inrease the average ticket price to an astronomical $46 per seat.[8] In taking this approach, the team was able to have the best of both worlds—a premium experience for corporations and others who were willing to pay the freight, but accessible, inexpensive tickets at the other end of the spectrum for the average fan.

The Red Sox have built a deep emotional connection to their fans on a solid foundation that began with a string of near-brushes with greatness in the 1960s, 1970s, and 1980s. Until 2004 the Red Sox and Cubs shared the distinction of more than eight decades of futility in their quest for a World Championship. However, unlike the hapless Cubs, who have not been to the World Series in six decades, the Red Sox produced some excellent pennant-winning teams. The miracle team of 1967, known as the "Impossible Dream," and the close brush with history of both the 1975 and 1986 teams give the Red Sox an entirely different profile than the Cubs. We could even throw in the loss to the underdog Cardinals in the 1946 World Series, whose fate seemed to turn on a relay throw from Johnny Pesky that was late, allowing Enos Slaughter to score, catapulting St. Louis to victory. Others will include the 1978 Bucky Dent-ed Sox or the Grady Little 2003 team in the list of near misses. While the Cubs are lovable losers, the Red Sox are the virtual equivalent of the St. Louis Cardinals or the L.A. Dodgers—but a bit more fallible.

The Red Sox made fallibility an endearing quality that formed the underpinning of their emotional connection to their fans. We experience fallibility in everyday life, and while we sometimes expect more from our heroes, we can often better relate to them if they experience the same trials and tribulations as us. For both the Red Sox *and* the average person, some of life's most desirable accomplishments are just beyond our reach. Author John Updike may have said it best in the *Boston Globe* following the 1986 World Series mishap: "All men are mortal, and therefore all men are losers; our profoundest loyalty goes to the fallible."

Endnotes

1. The baseline revenue estimates of each team are the result of the same win-curve regression analysis explained in some detail in the Chapter 2 sidebar, Measuring the Impact of Winning on Revenues.

2. The baseline accretion and erosion effect are not included in the value of a win. In certain cases—the Yankees (accretion) and the Royals (erosion)—the argument can be made to imbed this long-term effect into the win-curve.

3. The dependent variable is attendance for each of 81 home dates. The independent variables include, weekend (versus weekday) games, game-time temperature, various opponent dummy variables, and various groupings of promotional events. The adjusted r-square for the model is .804.

4. The regression equation estimated that three teams other than the Yankees had a positive impact on attendance: Boston (11,978), Washington (9,650), and Philadelphia (6,967).

5. Brand ranking is from Interbrands' 2006 ranking of global brands, *http://www.interbrands.com/surveys.asp*. Starbucks availability in 36 countries (outside the United States) is from their web site, *http://www.starbucks.com/aboutus/CPA-140%20Company%20Factsheet.pdf*.

6. Wrigley Field capacity data are from *ballparks.com*, *http://www.ballparks.com/baseball/index.htm*.

7. Poll from Harris Interactive, "It's All New York: Yankees and Mets—First and Second Favorite Baseball Teams," Harris Poll #54, July 10, 2006.

8. Ticket price data are from TMR, *http://www.teammarketing.com/fci.cfm?page=fci_mlb2006.cfm*.

11 | A New Management Model

A baseball team's success as a business enterprise is tightly linked to its wins and losses. A disciplined, well-run team gets the most productivity from the dollars it spends on its payroll, on its scouting and player development system, and in marketing the team to its fans and sponsors, improving its chances of becoming a winner. On the other side of the equation, a team that consistently challenges for a playoff berth is able to use the fruits of winning to fuel its success as a business. For example, the annual revenue differential for a 90-win Royals team versus a 70-win Royals team is estimated to be about $30 million. If the Royals could produce 90 wins with some regularity, mirroring the track record of another "small market" team, the Oakland A's, the Royals' franchise might be valued $75 million higher than today's valuation.[1] Since winning generates revenue, which improves franchise value, it comes back to having a plan to build a competitive team at an affordable payroll.

A Framework for a Strategic Plan

The formula we discussed in Chapter 1 says a strong scouting and player development system leads to a higher mix of young, low-priced talent on the MLB roster, which allows the team to be a selective "value buyer" in the free-agent market. The net result is a competitive, affordable team, with higher revenues and franchise value and a stronger brand (see Figure 11.1).

This concept is not new. It's the mantra most teams try to follow. Teams operating under the old management model might say, "Tell me something I didn't know." Here's where the new management model takes over.

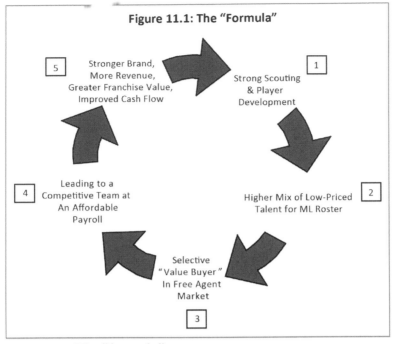

FIGURE 11.1 **The "formula."**

With the tools discussed throughout the previous chapters, the disciplined analytics of the new approach can now put *numbers* with the *concept*. Of course, the devil is in the details. Knowing that a team needs to be better at scouting and player development is about as profound as saying they should "win more often." That advice may fly under the old management model but falls far short of the depth of insight necessary to successfully run a $100 million to $400 million annual revenue business. For example, it would be useful for the Angels to know that an improvement from an 85-win to a 90-win team is likely to generate about $11 million in revenue. If the GM spends more than $11 million to buy five wins, the team will be investment spending; if he spends less, they're likely to generate positive cash flow.

It would also be helpful for the Cubs to know that improving their farm system yield—the number of marginal wins it produces each year for its Major League roster—by 10% frees up an additional $5.5 million per year in salary dollars to spend in the free-agent market to buy more wins at the same payroll level. Understanding the financial impact of a 10% improvement in the farm system's yield gives an organization direction, focus, a goal, and even a budget. If a team knows the financial payoff of an improvement, they know how much they can afford to spend to achieve it. Quantifying the elements of the formula allows a team to move beyond a series of platitudes to create a working tool—a financial model—to build the value of the franchise and sustain a competitive team.

Some will say, "In baseball we can't be that precise. We don't know how a player will perform from one year to the next, so this approach won't work." They're missing the point. No business is precise. The concept of planning is all about creating likely scenarios and understanding how all of the parts—wins, ticket sales, ticket pricing, advertising revenue, fan loyalty, players' salaries, and so on—interconnect to one another. By making assumptions about actions and outcomes, a business can assess the impact and consequences of an important decision. No one can say for sure that a player will generate four marginal wins next year, but it's still useful to know that if he generates only three wins, revenues could suffer by $1.5 million to $2 million.

By integrating the analysis developed throughout this book, we now have the tools for a full strategic plan for an MLB team. We can understand the depth of a team's resource base, the leverage points of its profit and loss statement, and how value is created for the franchise. Since winning is an important part of the value creation equation, the strategic plan also becomes a blueprint for building a winning team. The following steps form the core of a team's strategic plan:

1. Use detailed internal revenue data to create a team-specific win-curve that accounts for a team's nuances, ranging from renewal rates of its season ticket holders to the prospects of additional corporate marketing dollars for a playoff-bound team.

2. Evaluate the division- and league-specific probabilities of reaching the postseason. While some teams strive to win 90 games, Theo Epstein is often quoted as stating the Red Sox' goal is to "win 95 to 100" games in order to stay competitive with the Yankees. For any team, the specific win total that is expected to secure a playoff berth has a great bearing on the value of a win.

3. Audit the farm system to analyze a team's true cost of player development by determining the spending levels relative to the yield. The team would also analyze the track record of scouting and player development to determine if it had a higher competency in developing pitchers versus position players, or geographic strengths and weaknesses. Another component would be an evaluation of the process used to match the highest poten-

tial prospects with the right minor league roster slots to accelerate their development.

4. Create scenarios that estimate players' potential win contributions and review alternative plans to staff the MLB roster over a three- to five-year period. This allows a team to project players that will graduate from their farm system, along with expiring contracts for existing players, so a team can understand its needs and create the optimal, most efficient sourcing plan to fill the spots and improve its competitiveness.

5. Estimate the dollar value of players on the current roster, based on assumptions of their performance level and the team's location on the win-curve. Analyze player value with varying levels of players' performance, incorporating some factor for the chance of injury to better understand the team's risks and downsides.

6. Assess the external market for free agents over the next several years to anticipate the costs and availability of players at key need positions. By combining the costs of internally developed players with the free-agent assessment and the win-curve, a team will be able to determine its marginal revenue and marginal costs of winning.

7. As part of the strategic plan process, the team would also evaluate the phase of development of the team brand, inventorying its core equities and perceptions by its fans.

A strategic planning process will lead to a plan that gives a team a grounding and a set of operating guidelines, particularly useful when the team is faced with an urgent player personnel decision needed to be made in the heat of the moment. The process is about building a three-year or five-year plan to achieve and sustain a 90-plus-win season that is tailored to the economic realities of the team. A side benefit of going through a strategic planning process is that the depth of analysis is more likely to force a team to be more realistic about its current location on the win-curve and its short-term prospects to improve its position.

A key part of the strategic plan is constructing the bridge between a team's on-field performance and its business performance, to show not only their compatibility, but also their synergy. The win-curve quantifies the most direct linkage between winning and business success by quantifying fans' and sponsors' willingness to reach into their wallets at different performance levels, culminating in the value of a win. If the win-curve represents a team's marginal revenue curve, we can make some assumptions about player cost data and ultimately come up with an estimate of the marginal cost of winning—a marginal cost curve.

Marginal Revenue versus Marginal Cost Analyses

The marginal revenue–marginal cost analysis can help a team understand the full financial and economic implications of its player personnel decisions. By integrating the win-curve with the cost of player development and the market rate for free agents, we can create marginal revenue and marginal cost curves for any team. The marginal revenue curve is the most straightforward, as it can be represented by the "value of each win" between 70 and 105. To create the marginal cost curve requires some interpretation, assumptions, and judgment. Let's use the 2007 Yankees as an example, drawing on our win-curve analysis (Chapter 3) and our player cost analysis (Chapter 7). We can begin by assuming that the first wins the Yankees would add to their roster would be their cheapest wins, from internally developed players, at a cost of about $1.5 million per marginal win (from our analysis in Chapter 7). Since the Yankee farm system has been less than prolific, we should assume that we may not get very far along the win-curve by limiting ourselves to internally developed players.

In assessing the Yankees positional needs, the general consensus is that their priorities are to add a right-handed-hitting first baseman, a top of the rotation starting pitcher, and a utility infielder. Let's also assume the Yankees are an 89-win team as they begin the off-season (with the loss of Sheffield for the 2007 lineup and Randy Johnson headed out of town), and the farm system is not capable of graduating a player for any of these positions in 2007. In their quest to stay one step ahead of the Red Sox and the emerging Blue Jays in the tough AL East, the Yankees may be looking to add seven to ten wins. By adding a one-marginal-win utility infielder at an estimated $1.8 million, a three-marginal-win first baseman at $2.5 million per win, and a five-marginal-win starting pitcher at 3.8 million per win, we can establish a version of a marginal cost curve for the 2007 Yankees[2] (see Figure 11.2) .

Another way to look at the same analysis is to zero in on the seven to ten wins the Yankees are seeking to add and plot the cost of developed

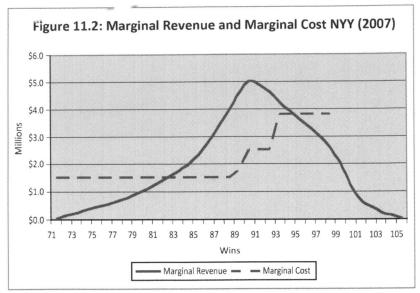

FIGURE 11.2 **Projected 2007 Yankee marginal revenue and marginal cost curves.**

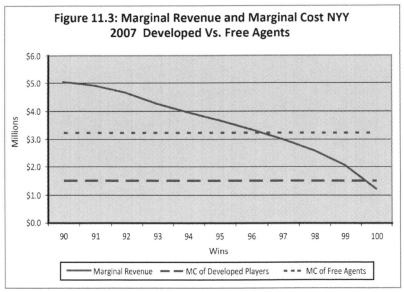

FIGURE 11.3 **Yankee marginal revenue versus the marginal cost of developed players and free agents.**

players, versus the blended cost of the free agents they may be chasing, to fill these voids. When a team is considering multiple simultaneous changes or additions to the MLB roster, it may make sense to look at them as "bundled decisions," measuring their collective, rather than individual impact. These two cost curves are shown along with the marginal revenue curve in Figure 11.3.

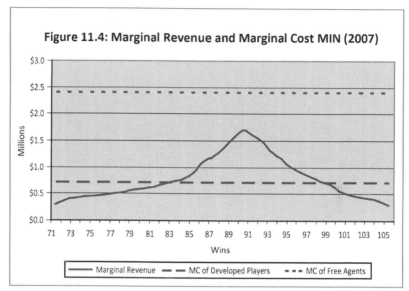

FIGURE 11.4 **Twins marginal revenue and marginal costs.**

In contrast, we can look at a similar analysis of the Minnesota Twins. By comparing the Twins' cost of developed players ($710,000 per marginal win) with, for example, a second-tier free-agent cost of $2.4 million per marginal win, we can see how the team's cost curve relates to its modest marginal revenue curve. Since the highest-value Twins' win is estimated at about $1.7 million, only internally developed players will come in under that low threshold. Any free-agent players will likely be an investment spend by the team. However, the proposed new stadium has the potential to dramatically alter the Twins' win-curve and should provide higher-value wins, allowing them to selectively sign a top-tier free agent without being "upside-down" (see Figure 11.4).

The analysis and insight enabling us to compare marginal revenue with marginal cost can help a team plan the allocation of its resources and better manage the tension between winning and financial returns, an important step along the way to developing a more comprehensive strategic plan for a team.

THE REGIONAL SPORTS NETWORK REVOLUTION

One strategy that has the potential to shift the marginal revenue curve to a higher level is the team-owned RSN. Of the 12 teams linked to an RSN,

Figure 11.5: RSNs and Revenue Opportunity Index*			
Marginal Revenue			
H		CWS CLE HOU STL	NYY SFG BOS SEA NYM CHC
M	COL	LAA ARZ ATL TOR	BAL PHL LAD TEX
L	CIN DET OAK FLA KCR PIT MIL MIN TBD	SDP	
	LOW	MEDIUM	HIGH

*Teams with RSNs are **bold**. Nationals are omitted from chart.   **Baseline Revenue**

FIGURE 11.5 **RSNs and the revenue opportunity index.**

four are among the wealthiest teams (Yankees, Mets, Red Sox, and Cubs), and another four are in the top half of the MLB economic food chain (Orioles, Phillies, White Sox, and Indians). The Royals are the only team among the true have-nots to have an RSN (see Figure 11.5). (As noted earlier, the Royals have announced their intention to exit the RSN business in favor of a contract with Fox Sports Midwest, beginning in 2008.) In a classic case of the rich getting richer, teams endowed with a strong economic base are venturing into the broadcast business to further enhance their economic prowess. It's not an overstatement to say that RSNs are rewriting the economics of MLB teams.

This broadcast arrangement impacts the business of baseball in at least four ways:

- RSNs provide a more direct connection between winning and broadcast revenues. In contrast to the traditional broadcast model, where a team is generally paid a fixed rights fee, regardless of their win–loss record, thereby *disconnecting* broadcast revenues from the team's on-field performance, teams with RSNs get immediate financial feedback. Since ratings, and therefore advertising revenue, rise and fall with on-field performance, team-owned networks participate directly in the revenue stream that winning or losing generates. In a sense, RSNs raise the stakes of winning and losing for an MLB team.

- RSNs are a team marketer's dream, as they provide a unique vehicle for marketing the team and building its brand. Instead of only selling telecasts to an independent network, teams with RSNs can inundate their fans with team-related entertainment and brand-building propaganda, all rolled into one programming schedule. Does the *Yankeeography* of Derek Jeter entertain viewers, or tout his marquee value and build the Yankee brand in the eyes of fans? The answer is "yes" to both questions.

- Until MLB changes the way in which it treats "related party transactions," teams with RSNs may get a break on their revenue-sharing payments. The new CBA is thought to contain provisions that may prevent a team from receiving an artificially low rights fee, reducing their revenue-sharing contribution while they rake in the cash in their RSN. This issue will likely get solved soon, and even if it does not, it ranks among the least important ways in which RSNs are changing the economic face of baseball.

- The most important role the RSN plays is providing an additional vehicle for a team to create financial value, thereby dramatically altering the economics of owning and operating a big league club. RSNs represent an additional separate asset of significant tangible value, while still being intertwined in nearly every way with the team. In the same way companies create value by entering into businesses that have synergies with their core business, teams have branched out into the broadcasting arena. A successful RSN can generate more financial value for a team by turning one of the team's assets—its broadcast rights—into a full-fledged operating business. This strategy creates value because true synergies exist between the team and the RSN and because an MLB teams' broadcast rights are a substantial enough product to form the basis of an entire network. The RSN also creates an additional option for liquidity. A team can build up the RSN, and then sell it, reaping its value, while still owning the team, or vice versa. In many ways, the RSN is a brilliantly conceived brand extension of an MLB franchise.

The ultimate payoff for launching and operating a successful RSN is the creation of an asset that can be of equal or greater value than the team itself. Valued at 10 to 12 times profits, or five times revenue, an RSN could achieve a valuation of several hundred million dollars or more for a mid-market team after just several years of operation. Let's use the St. Louis Cardinals, fresh off their 2006 World Championship, as an example. Cardinals telecasts are currently seen on Fox Sports Net-Midwest (FSN-M), with distribution into about 4.3 million homes, via satellite and cable, in six states.[3] If the Cardinals were to start their own RSN when the current FSN-M agreement expires, by charging cable and satellite operators a modest $1.50 per month, they could generate a potential of $75 million or more in annual fees. In addition, a conservative estimate of the ratings of a 90-win Cardinal team could lead to another $15 million in advertising revenue. A $90-million-annual-revenue RSN owned by the Cardinals has the potential to be valued at about $450 million. As long as the network's operations could cover the current FSN-M rights fee to the Cardinals and turn a normal profit, the Cardinals would have a new asset, which they could factor into their win-curve. Since the RSN's asset value would rise and fall with the team's on-field success, the RSN could add as much as 50% to the value of a win in the sweet spot—the 85- to 95-win range. Over that range a five-win improvement could generate an *additional* $7 million, allowing a team like the Cardinals to justify competing for top-dollar free agents.

WIN-CURVE PLUS

Our example of the hypothetical Cardinals RSN leads us to envision management decisions being made based on more than the revenue variables included in the win-curve described throughout this book. Although some may consider it a more tenuous approach, a team could choose to think in terms of the value of a win being more broadly defined to include not just revenues, but also asset appreciation and other valuation measures.[4] If a team owner wanted to know the full extent of his "value creation opportunity" by improving his team from 85 to 95 wins, he could expand his definition of the win-curve to create a "win-curve plus." This expanded value-of-a-win measure could include the change in asset value of a team's share of their RSN, or other related businesses, as well as the change in franchise value resulting from improving a team from, say, 85 to 95 wins.

The risk of this approach is that one season's win total is not going to completely revamp the valuation of a team. Over the past six seasons, the Kansas City Royals won more than 65 games only once. In 2003 they won 83 games, finishing in third place, only seven games behind the division-winning Twins. The fan excitement and attendance response to their successful season generated an estimated $12 to $15 million in additional local revenue, compared to the surrounding years, when the Royals won between 56 and 65 games. Even if we conservatively assume that the Royals are worth only two times their annual revenue, it's not realistic to assume the franchise value increased $24 million to $30 million in October of 2003 owing to one winning season in the midst of many losing seasons.

In some situations it may be more appropriate for teams to use the win-curve plus concept as a decision-making tool. For a team that has historically been in the middle of the pack, it is reasonable to use the broader metric as they create plans to take the team to the next level of competitiveness. For example, if the Texas Rangers, who averaged 78 wins per year over the past five years (2002–2006), were to put together a three-year plan designed to make them a playoff-contending team, it might be reasonable to use the broader win-curve plus concept to gauge the upside of achieving their goal. Instead of just estimating the revenue change from moving from, say, 78 to 90 wins, they could impute the change in franchise value from having a higher revenue base owing to their improved competitiveness. Likewise, the win-curve plus could include any appreciation in related assets that would benefit from the improved competitiveness of the team, such as Hicks' planned commercial, residential, and retail complex, called Glorypark, in the area immediately around Ameriquest Field.[5]

With the change in the revenue-sharing plan for 2007, increases in ticket prices, and the continued growth of RSNs, selected wins within the sweet spot for teams like the Mets, Yankees, and Cubs, are estimated to be valued as high as $4 million to $5 million or more. When broadening the definition of the value of a win to include the asset appreciation of an RSN, or the appreciation in the value of a franchise or related assets, the win-curve plus values can be even higher.

THE CHESS MATCH

Another change that has affected the way teams operate is the revamped divisional structure that took effect in 1994 and a more subtle change in scheduling, which came about in 2001. Prior to 1994, each MLB team was vying with seven other teams for the best record in their division to qualify for the playoffs. With a balanced schedule, they competed against the other 13 teams nearly equally, by playing 12 or 13 games against each, regardless of their division within the AL or NL. In this format, a team's competitive set was too diffuse for it to operate with any one competitor in mind. Certainly, in the early 1990s teams in the AL had to be aware of the formidable strength of the Blue Jays, but there was little a team could do to directly combat it, given the balanced schedule across the League.

The following year, realignment created six divisions, mostly with five teams each (except for the NL Central with six and AL West with four). Seven years later, in 2001, MLB moved to a less balanced schedule, with teams playing each intra-division rival 18 or 19 times per season, allowing teams to be more competitively focused on specific division opponents. With 46% of a team's games played against just four other teams, teams can study all aspects of their intra-division rivals in the same way chess opponents may study each other's habits.[6] While the on-field chess match between opposing managers has been a staple of the game from day one, the competitive focus also affects the way in which a GM assembles a team's roster. For the 2006 season, the Yankees chose to add left-handed relief specialist Mike Myers to their roster, with the primary intent of neutralizing Yankee-killer, David Ortiz. Of the 132 batters faced by Myers in 2006, 10 were match ups with Ortiz (7.6%), and in more than half of Myers' appearances against the Red Sox he faced *only* Ortiz before heading to the showers.[7] There is good reason to be competitively focused on an intra-division rival with which a team will battle for a playoff berth, particularly in light of the 19 times they meet each season. In the AL Central, while every team attempts to become stronger, they also consider roster moves with an eye on combating the Twins' lefty standouts Santana and Liriano or limiting the damage from White Sox sluggers Konerko, Crede, and Dye—three formidable right-handed hitters.

The competitive focus spills over into other aspects of intra-division rivals' businesses, in much the same way it affects companies that compete head-to-head, such as Pepsi and Coke. As the head of one of Pepsi's divisions, I was once embroiled in a bidding war for the rights to exclusively sell our soda to a prized fast food restaurant account. As the negotiations for this account progressed, it became clear that Coke, the incumbent soft drink, had the inside track on retaining the exclusive rights. Rather than fade peacefully into the night and accept our fate, I strategized as to how we could exploit Coke's apparent "win." I concluded that the next best thing to winning the business was to tie up so much of Coke's funding in this one account that they would be hard pressed to aggressively spend in other areas of the beverage market. So I upped our bid by *several hundred million dollars*, not so that we could *win* the business, but to *lose* the bid at a price that presented a financial hardship to Coke. Of course we ran the risk of "winning" an unprofitable piece of business if Coke refused to up their ante, but after competing head-to-head for years, I understood their mindset and was confident they would top our offer, even if it meant losing money, to retain the business. My bid didn't win the account, but it had a big impact on our main competitor, as it sapped their financial flexibility to spend elsewhere.

This chess match permeates the thoughts of the Yankees and Red Sox, the Angels and A's, the Dodgers, Giants, and Padres, and more and more clubs are thinking this way. In the months preceding the 2006 season, when the Yankees signed Johnny Damon, and the Mets signed Billy Wagner as free agents, both teams not only filled a need at a key position, but they also depleted a head-to-head competitor. In the case of Damon, adding, say, four more wins to the Yankees (versus the alternative of Bernie Williams in center field) might up the Yankees' chances of making the playoffs by about 34%, by taking them from a 90-win to 94-win team. If the signing simultaneously reduced the Red Sox expected performance by two wins, it might add another 10 percentage points to the probability that the Yankees would reach the postseason by weakening their closest, most direct competitor.

While the Red Sox insist they did not bid for Daisuke Matsuzaka in order to block the Yankees from winning his services, in reality, this was an important by-product of their winning bid. By losing out on Matsuzaka, the Yankees will either spend more aggressively in the free-agent market to buy those wins in the form of another pitcher, presumably sapping available dollars from filling another need, or forego a front-line pitcher and lower their expected win total for 2007. The Red Sox's winning bid for the sought-after right-hander was clearly a double victory for Boston.

The free-agent marketplace is a model laboratory for analyzing the competitive dynamics between teams. When a marquee, top-of-the-rotation pitcher hits the free-agent market, teams always need to ask the question, "Which teams are in the market for this player?" If the Yankees and Mets are both in the fray, aside from the player feeling as if he just hit the lottery, teams may need to play their negotiations differently. Although the luxury tax has radically altered the Yankees' math in recent years, the free-agent market price tends to be set by the teams with the highest value wins who perceive themselves to be on the win-curve sweet-spot and who also have a positional need for the player in question. Free-agent shortstops will probably continue to be relatively undervalued because of the Yankees' (Jeter) and Mets' (Reyes) absence from the shortstop free-agent fray. It's often healthy to view a potential decision through the lens of a competitor, as well as your own, as it can help a team formulate a winning strategy.

THE FUTURE

As we look ahead to the next 10 to 20 years, Major League Baseball's future may be brighter than it has ever been. A leading indicator of baseball's financial prospects is the public posturing and length of time necessary to secure a labor agreement between MLB and the MLBPA. Considering that last year's negotiations were entirely stealthy and the agreement was reached well ahead of the deadline, it is fair to say that the insiders believe there is plenty of money to go around and satisfy all parties. The World Baseball Classic helped to further connect Major League Baseball to Latin America and Asia, where the game's popularity rivals its stature in the United States. Importing Japanese, Korean, and Taiwanese stars has helped MLB tap into the Asian market and grow revenues by marketing the game abroad. Just because the League as a whole is destined to grow total revenues, the growth is not without its issues.

COMPETITIVE BALANCE AND REVENUE SHARING

While much of this book discusses analytical tools and insights some teams use to manage their business, the implications of these analyses are broader. In particular, the win-curve analysis shines a bright light on the issue of competitive balance. Much of the debate about competitive balance tends to center on the debate about who wins and loses from year to year. Those who think all is well make their case around the fresh mix of teams in the postseason each year, coupled with the fact that in recent years, World Championships have come from wild card teams or an 83-win Cardinal team. I'm in the camp that believes competitive balance has far less to do with wins and losses and more to do with a team's economic resource base, based on its win-curve and other economic realities associated with its local market. There will always be factors that interrupt the linkage between winning and a team's economic resource base, such as poor talent evaluation, a reluctance to invest in player development, and even luck. Despite factors that make the link less than perfect, over the long-term the most important factor determining the level of competitive balance in MLB is likely to be the disparity in the economic resource base across teams.

In analyzing a team's resource base, we have looked at factors such as the size of a team's market; the number of corporations based in the market (a good proxy for corporate sponsors and suite holder opportunities); the age, debt, and ownership structure of the stadium; and the strength of the team's brand. One important conclusion from that analysis is that market size alone falls far short of explaining the degree to which a team has an economic advantage or disadvantage.[8] A shortcut alternative to examining each of these factors is to define a team's economic resource base through a simple combination of a team's baseline revenue (the revenue for a 70-win, noncompetitive season) and the marginal revenue from wins(the win-curve). By rating each team in a three-by-three grid on both dimensions—the level of their baseline revenue and the amount of marginal revenue they generate when they win—we can separate the haves from the have-nots. Figure 11.5 classifies six teams as those with the highest economic resource base (Yankees, Mets, Red Sox, Cubs, Giants, and Mariners) and nine teams in the low-low category (Reds, Tigers, A's, Marlins, Royals, Pirates, Twins, Brewers, and Devil Rays).

To get a snapshot of the difference between the haves and the have-nots, we can refer back to the analysis in Chapter 1, where we compared the economics of the hypothetical 95-win seasons for the Yankees and the Royals. If we think of a team's affordable payroll as the spread between its revenues and costs in a given year, MLB's local market-driven business model means some teams can afford to spend $100 million more than other teams without running a deficit. This confirms that competitive balance issues are serious and the revenue-sharing provisions included in both the 2002 CBA and the early interpretations of the newly ratified 2006 CBA fall short as a remedy. For starters, the 2002 CBA categorizes teams based on *actual revenues* rather than their economic resource base, that is, their *revenue opportunity*. Why should an inept, but high-resource-base team, that generates low revenue *receive* dollars from the revenue-sharing pool? By using actual revenue as a measuring stick, the revenue-sharing system commingles opportunity and performance, with the latter carrying the most weight. The second design flaw with the revenue-sharing provision is the *marginal tax* on revenues, which requires each team to contribute a portion of every revenue growth dollar into a revenue-sharing pool. Rather than reducing the incentive for a team to grow its revenue base, it would be better to tax teams a *fixed amount* based on their revenue opportunity.

If revenue sharing is truly a mechanism to improve competitive balance, the best design principles would be focused on narrowing the team-to-team gap of the financial gains from winning. The ideal revenue-sharing system would reduce the baseline revenue of the haves while increasing both the baseline revenue and the marginal revenue from winning of the have-nots. The first step would be to transfer *fixed dollars* from the haves to have-nots, which would effectively shift baseline dollars—the dollars a team generates independent of winning. Furthermore, the system could be dramatically enhanced if a "kicker" was added for the on-field performance of any team in the have-not category. For example, the system could consist of a fixed revenue sharing payment of, say, $20 million to the Pittsburgh Pirates, but also include a variable payment based on their wins—another $10 million if they achieved a .500 winning percentage, an additional $7.5 million for each five-win increment above 81 wins, and so on. This approach would change the slope of the Pirates' (and other teams with a low economic resource base) win-curve, adding $1.5 million to the value of a win, after some minimum threshold and up to some cap (e.g., 90 wins).

This would cause the Pirates to recalculate their participation in the free-agent market. Under the current revenue sharing plan, the Pirates' estimated win-curve shows that they stand to make about $5.8 million in incremental revenue if they can move from an 83- to an 88-win team. The Pirates are not likely to find a free agent who is a five-win player, such as Johnny Damon, for $5.8 million. For the same five-win improvement, their intra-division rivals, the Cubs, stand to gain an estimated $14.6 million in incremental revenue. By eliminating the marginal tax and adding the win kicker, the value of the same five wins to the Pirates would be $15.6 million, compared to $20.5 for the Cubs. (Figure 11.6 shows the five-win value of the alternative revenue-sharing plan compared to the current plan.) Under this plan the commissioner's office and the teams that paid money into the pool would have less concern over how the recipients spent their revenue-sharing dollars. In this ideal "pay for performance" system teams would have every incentive to field a winning team—so much so that it might create a different problem for the well-endowed clubs: a more formidable on-field competitor.

Figure 11.6: Revenue Sharing could shift the win-curve

Value of 5 wins - 83 to 88 wins ($in Millions)

	Current System of Revenue-Sharing	Alternative System Of Revenue-Sharing*
Cubs	$15.6	$20.5
Pirates	$ 5.8	$15.6
CHC-PIT Gap in $ Value of Wins	$ 9.8	$ 4.9

*Alternative plan would include a "win Kicker" of $1.5 million per win above 81 wins, for teams with a low economic resource base.

FIGURE 11.6 **An alternative revenue-sharing framework that could shift the win-curve.**

The ultimate test of a revenue-sharing plan's ability to improve competitive balance is whether it narrows the gap between the haves and the have-nots on the important dimension of the marginal revenue from wins. One metric that can determine if the gap is narrowed is the standard deviation, for all teams, of the marginal revenue from wins. By comparing the current revenue-sharing plan to no revenue sharing, our analysis indicates that there is virtually no change in the standard deviation. However, a revenue-sharing plan that eliminates the marginal tax in favor of a fixed payment tax and includes "win incentives" such as those outlined above can reduce the standard deviation of teams' gains from winning by as much as 25%.

Despite having little effect on competitive balance, the current revenue-sharing plan will have a significant impact on players' salaries for 2007 and beyond. Any time there is a tax on marginal revenue, two things happen: there is less incentive to grow revenue, as part of the gain gets paid into the revenue-sharing pool, and a player's dollar value is reduced. Since wins generate dollars, but *fewer dollars when there is a marginal tax*, the value of the player producing those wins goes down. With the new 2006 CBA, baseball may need to brace itself for some possibly unintended consequences, primarily the impact on player's salaries. What some take for lunacy in the recent off-season free-agent market may simply be the reflection of the new reduced marginal tax rates contained in the new CBA.

Under the previous CBA (2002 through 2006), teams were assessed a marginal tax on revenues ranging from an estimated 39% to 47%. Under the new agreement, the tax rate is virtually the same for all teams, at approximately 31%. A team that formerly was taxed at 47% and got to keep only 53% of its revenue growth will now be taxed at 31%, keeping 69% of its revenue growth. The reduced tax will increase the value of a win for these teams by 30% (16 percentage points on a base of 53%). This means that for the same location on a team's win-curve, a five-win player has increased in value by 30%, because he now generates 30% more net revenue for his team. For the past several years, Manny Ramirez's contract, paying him in the vicinity of $20 million per year, was viewed by many to be prohibitively expensive. The change in the revenue-sharing tax suddenly places him nearer to the market rate for the remaining two years of his agreement. If he can maintain his lofty offensive performance and stay healthy, it is quite possible that his team will exercise his reported $20 million per year club option for 2009 and 2010—an event that seemed unthinkable just one year ago.[9] The new revenue-sharing tax should lead to free-agent compensation levels that will have fans and executives scratching their heads. Left-handed starting pitchers could be breaking into the $4 million per marginal win territory, with power-hitting outfielders receiving commensurate salary gains.[10]

THE CHALLENGES AHEAD

The game has flourished under the leadership of Comissioner Bud Selig, with his single biggest stroke of genius being the addition of the wild card to the playoff format. Even if it creates only an illusion of competitive balance by producing a league-wide race for an at-large bid to the postseason, it has generated tremendous excitement in many cities in September, a month that is traditionally weak, save for a few teams. He has also presided over MLB in an era that saw the renewal of baseball's physical infrastructure, although it is not without its controversies. The stadium dialogue seems to quickly degenerate into a "he said-she said" by "greedy owners" and "ungrateful municipalities" about who gets the most benefit from a new ballpark and consequently, the appropriate mix of public versus private funding. The two sides seem to argue so vehemently out of self-interest, citing the results of previous parks, selectively choosing the data that fits their points of view, that they neglect to get at the key issue. "Do stadiums enhance the local economy?" may be the wrong question. The right question is *"Under what conditions can stadiums enhance the local economy?"*

Many stadiums may not be an economic boon to cities or neighborhoods, but they *can* be. For example, many would say that the Cubs are the lifeblood of the Wrigleyville neighborhood in Chicago. Two key variables that determine a stadium's contribution to the local economy are the number of day games the team plays and the way the ballpark is configured within the urban setting. While most teams play two-thirds of their games at night, leaving a short pre-game and post-game timeframe for local businesses to capitalize on the crowd, the Cubs play nearly two-thirds of their games in the daytime. With day games ending near the dinner hour, local businesses may have three or four times as many hours of business with which to capture financial gain from the ball game crowd. Also, ballparks that disrupt the urban grid, sending it into a mad scramble, can do more harm than good to the local economy, while those that neatly fit, like Wrigley and Fenway, can help local retailers build their businesses. Instead of resorting to a yes–no posture on publicly funded stadiums, public officials would better serve local citizens, fans, and teams by studying the issue and declaring the *conditions under which they would entertain public funding*. For publicly funded projects, officials should have every right to mandate the conditions that would contribute to the economic development of the area, leaving team owners in a position to receive the funding only if certain win–win conditions are met. If ticket revenue and broadcast revenue are expected to decline somewhat with an increase in the number of day games, the team would simply factor the reduction into their decision regarding a public funding proposal.

With the stadium issue largely behind him, since 80% of all MLB teams will likely have a "new" stadium by the end of this decade, renewing baseball's fan base could be the commissioner's biggest challenge of the next decade. Fans who became forever attached to the game during the 1950s, 1960s, and 1970s are aging. To many of them—the die-hard fans—baseball can do no wrong. Steroid scandals, astronomical players' salaries, and work stoppages may make them cringe, but not forsake their loyalty to baseball. As these fans age, baseball needs to replenish them with younger fans who can pass the game on to their children and grandchildren and continue the cycle of baseball's growth in popularity. MLB needs to convert the financial heyday they are experiencing into a renewal of the youth market, by working tirelessly to find ways to connect with young fans—to gain their attention and then deepen that connection emotionally. It will require new marketing vehicles that are in step with today's youth. Gone is the culture of the pick-up ballgame at the school yard, merging kids' favorite activity with their favorite sport. The internet, video games, and malls have altered the adoption model—marketing-speak for how young people become acquainted with and build an affinity for a product or service. In the end, we can only hope that MLB can convert their new economic heyday into rebuilding the fan base for tomorrow.

On a team level, the new management model is more important now than ever before. While the prospects for local revenue growth remain strong in many markets, the surge in national, central fund revenues is even more impressive, with the influx of dollars from new richer network television deals and the continued ascent of MLBAM. The influx of Asian players also bodes well for revenue growth from the contracts like the MLB broadcast package in Japan. The six-year, $275 million deal that runs through 2009 will undoubtedly increase substantially when it's renewed, with the likes of Matsuzaka and his countrymen joining MLB in record numbers. As MLB's cash payments to all teams increase, some economically disadvantaged teams may spend more on player development and payroll, but the increased cash does not alter their investment equation. Low-marginal-revenue teams that decide to increase their payroll may still find it difficult to justify the financial return from spending in the free-agent market, making player development the better, albeit longer-term, alternative. Throwing money at the farm system isn't necessarily the answer, though, unless the productivity is high enough to justify the investment.

Using analytical tools to make investment decisions will be even more critical in the next five years than it has been in the past. Even the heretofore economically disadvantaged teams have the potential to use the larger, evenly distributed national dollars as something of an equalizer compared to their well-off counterparts. Some may think that using analytical tools to guide where and how a team spends its money is more important when cash is scarce than when teams are flush with central fund money. Actually, a team's spending decisions (scouting and player development, free-agent signings, brand building investments, etc.) will become even more important as teams make *more spending decisions* and *deploy more capital*. One thing is for certain: more teams will be making their move, as there is no shortage of financial resources. A lot of dollars are changing hands around the diamond.

Endnotes

1. A $75-million increase in franchise value is derived from a $30 million revenue differential, multiplied by 2.5, a typical revenue multiple for franchise valuations.

2. These cost estimates for free-agent players begin with the work discussed in Chapter 7 but incorporate an estimate of the impact of the new revenue-sharing tax rates on free-agent compensation.

3. "Helitech Scores Naming Rights to Fox Sports' Booth," *St. Louis Business Journal,* March 29, 2006.

4. The revenue impact of RSNs is already included in the broadcast revenue component of the win-curve, but the asset value and its potential appreciation is not included. Also, the win-curve does not include the change in the value of the franchise that may result from the team's revenue increases or declines.

5. Glorypark is being developed in conjunction with Steiner + Associates, *http://www. ci.arlington.tx.us/news/2006/archive_0506_12.html.*

6. AL West teams play intra-division rivals 19 or 20 times, while the NL Central teams play 16 or 17 games against their in-division counterparts.

7. Ortiz was two for nine against Myers in 2006, with one walk. His first two plate appearances were a three-run HR and a single. He then proceeded to be retired by Myers the next seven times they met, with the final plate appearance resulting in a walk. Data from *MLB. com.*

8. My presentation entitled "Restoring Competitive Balance to Baseball" was presented at the SABR Convention in Toronto in August 2005 and is available through the Society for American Baseball Research (SABR).

9. Ramirez's contract details are from Cots Baseball contracts, *http://mlbcontracts.blogspot. com/2004/12/boston-red-sox.html.*

10. The $4 million per marginal win salary level refers to estimates that are based on *Baseball Prospectus.com*'s WARP as the marginal win measure. Estimates using WSAB as the marginal win measure will be higher.

Index

Locators followed by f indicate figures.

About the Author

Vince Gennaro has been a consultant to Major League Baseball teams since 2006 and is President of the Society for American Baseball Research (SABR). He also appears regularly on MLB Network's studio shows including Clubhouse Confidential, a television show featuring leading edge baseball analytics. Vince also founded the Diamond Dollars Case Competition series, which brings students and sports executives together in a forum that encourages students to apply their skills to solve real sports business problems. In addition, he teaches in the Graduate Sports Management programs at Columbia University and Manhattanville College. This follows a successful business career, which is highlighted by a 20-year career at PepsiCo, and ownership of a pro sports franchise.

At PepsiCo, Vince was President of Pepsi's Fountain Beverage Division, the general manager of a billion dollar bottling business, and led the world's leading snack brand, Doritos. An entrepreneurial startup endeavor early in Vince's career complements his success with a blue chip Fortune 50 company. At the age of 27, he raised capital, led the purchase of a franchise in the Women's Pro Basketball League—the forerunner of today's WNBA—and served as its President and General Manager.

Vince's innovative work in baseball analytics—ranging from player evaluation and the development of new metrics, to placing a dollar value on players—has been the subject of articles in *The Wall Street Journal, The New York Times,* and *CNN Money.* He has also written for Yahoo! Sports and contributed to *The Wall Street Journal.* He is a frequent guest commentator in the media on sports business topics, appearing on the YES Network, CNBC and Bloomberg TV, WFAN radio in NYC, and many other broadcast outlets.

Vince serves on the Advisory Board of The Perfect Game Foundation. He holds an MBA from the University of Chicago.

Made in the USA
Lexington, KY
30 November 2014